Inside the room it is even darker. It is like walking in ink. Blind, she feels her way through the half familiar landmarks of beds and bookshelves. And then there is the wall. She presses against it, trying to stifle the breaths that tear at her throat. Her heart thuds. Blood from the wound is sticky, and at her touch there is a white leap of pain that lightens the darkness.

She hears the footsteps now, drawing closer. Along the corridor doors are opened, one at a time, until there is only hers left. The smell of petrol is sweet and heavy in its threat. She hugs her stomach, feeling the small pulse of new life inside, curled and vulnerable. The footsteps stop. A whisper of the door opening. Her name.

Some moments burn in the mind for ever.

Where There's Smoke

Simon Beckett

CORONET BOOKS
Hodder & Stoughton

First published in Great Britain in 1997
by Hodder and Stoughton
First published in paperback in 1998
by Hodder and Stoughton
A division of Hodder Headline PLC

A Coronet Paperback

10 9 8 7 6 5 4 3 2

British Library Cataloguing in Publication Data

Beckett, Simon
Where there's smoke
1. Artificial insemination, Human – Fiction 2. Thrillers
I. Title
823.9'14 [F]

ISBN 0 340 68593 X

Typeset by Hewer Text Composition Services, Edinburgh
Printed and bound in Great Britain by
Clays Ltd, St Ives plc

Hodder and Stoughton
A division of Hodder Headline PLC
338 Euston Road
London NW1 3BH

For Hilary

ACKNOWLEDGEMENTS

Thanks to Dr Sheila Cooke and the team at the University of Sheffield's Department of Obstetrics and Gynaecology, Jessop Hospital; Dr Gwilym Hayes, Consultant Forensic Psychiatrist at Wathwood Hospital Regional Secure Unit; and Judy Winter, Head of Student Services at the University of Derby.

The article on pages 234–239 refers to two works which are: Faulk, M (1988) *Basic Forensic Psychiatry*, London, Blackwell Scientific Publications; and Jackson, H F (1994) *Assessment of Fire-setters* in *The Assessment of Criminal Behaviours of Clients in Secure Settings*, Eds McMurran M, Hodge J.

PROLOGUE

Some moments burn in the mind for ever.

The landing is dark. Light comes from a window at the far end, enough to run by. Breath comes hard. From the stairs sound heavy footfalls of pursuit. The landing ends in a last doorway. There is no more running, only the need to hide.

Inside the room it is even darker. It is like walking in ink. Blind, she feels her way through the half-familiar landmarks of beds and bookshelves. And then there is the wall. She presses against it, trying to stifle the breaths that tear at her throat. Her heart thuds. Blood from the wound is sticky, and at her touch there is a white leap of pain that lightens the darkness.

She hears the footsteps now, drawing closer. Along the corridor doors are opened, one at a time, until there is only hers left. The smell of petrol is sweet and heavy in its threat. She hugs her stomach, feeling the small pulse of new life inside, curled and vulnerable. The footsteps stop. A whisper of the door opening. Her name.

'Kate.'

The light is turned on.

Some moments burn in the mind for ever.

CHAPTER 1

The warehouse had been burning all night. Smoke roiled into the sky, a darker cloud in an overcast morning. The bonfire smell of it thickened the air, giving the spring day a premature flavour of autumn.

The rush-hour faces outside King's Cross were turned to the dark column as Kate came up the steps from the Underground. The smoke rose above the rooftops in front of her, then the buildings closed in and blocked it from view.

Kate barely noticed. A tension headache was creeping up her neck. She had just started chewing an aspirin, grimacing at the bitter tang, when she turned a corner and found the fire dead ahead.

She halted, startled to find it so close, but carried on when she saw the street wasn't cut off. The roar and crackle of the blaze grew as she approached. Set back from the road, the warehouse was surrounded by a confusion of uniforms and yellow helmets, white cars and red engines. Hoses snaked across the ground, flinging streamers of water into the smoke. The flames licked out in random snatches of colour, indifferent to them.

A hot breath of wind brushed her face, dusting it with ashes. She turned away, eyes stinging, and realised with surprise that she had slowed to a standstill. Irritated with herself for gawking, she walked on, skirting the small crowd that had gathered by the police cordon.

The warehouse was left behind. By the time she reached the Georgian terrace, several streets away, Kate had forgotten it. Most of the buildings in the terrace were run down, but one, cleanly painted, stood out like a raised hand in a classroom. Embossed in gold letters on its downstairs window were the words, 'Powell PR & Marketing'.

Kate went in. Three desks were fitted into the small office, angled to face each other. Standing behind one of them, a tall West Indian man with a shaved head was pouring water into a coffee filter. He gave her a grin.

'Morning, Kate.'

'Hi, Clive.'

The filter machine hissed and gurgled. He tipped the last of the water into it and set down the jug. 'Well. The big day.'

His voice had a faint Geordie lilt. Kate went to one of the two big filing cabinets and slid out a drawer. 'Don't remind me.'

'Nervous?'

'Let's say I'll be glad to find out one way or the other.'

The coffee filter had subsided to low hisses. Clive poured two cups and handed her one. He had worked for her almost since she had started the agency, nearly three years earlier, and if ever she made anyone a partner, it would be him.

'Did you pass the fire on your way in?'

'Mm.' Kate was flicking through the folders inside the cabinet.

2

WHERE THERE'S SMOKE

'Been burning half the night, apparently. Bad about the kid, wasn't it?'

She looked at him. 'What kid?'

'The baby. A group of squatters were living there. They all got out, except for the baby. It said on the news the mother got burned trying to go back for it. Two months old.'

Kate put down her coffee cup. She was aware of the stink of smoke still clinging to her, and looked down to see tiny flecks of grey ash dotting her clothes. She remembered its feathery touch on her face, the tickle as she had breathed it in. She felt the sting of it again.

She closed the filing cabinet without taking anything out. 'I'll be upstairs.'

Her office was on the first floor. Kate closed the door and batted the grey specks from her navy blue skirt and jacket. She knew she wouldn't feel comfortable in the suit again until she'd had it cleaned. Hanging her jacket behind the door, she went to the room's single window. Her reflection showed faintly in the glass as she looked out. Beyond it, the smoke was a spreading stain on the sky, against which her dark hair was invisible. Only her face was clear; a pale oval hanging in space.

She turned away and went to her desk. Downstairs, she could hear voices as the others arrived. The front office was too small for Clive and the two girls, but the only other spare room needed redecorating and a new ceiling before anyone could work in it. It wouldn't be cheap. Kate sighed and reached for a file. As she opened it there was a tap on her door.

'Come in.'

A girl entered, carrying a Cellophane-wrapped bunch of

red roses. Her plump face was openly curious as she handed them to Kate. 'These have just been delivered.'

A small envelope was tucked into the stems. Kate opened it and slid out the plain white card. A short note was written on it in swooping, forward-slanting script. She read it, then replaced the card in the envelope. She handed the roses back to the girl. 'Thanks, Caroline. Take these outside and give them to the first old lady you see, will you?'

The girl's eyes widened. 'What shall I say?'

'Anything. Just say they're with our compliments.' Kate gave a tight smile. 'And the nearer to ninety she is, the better.'

She stopped smiling as soon as the door closed. She took out the card and read it again. 'Commiserations in advance. Love, Paul.'

Carefully, Kate tore it in half, then in half again before throwing it into her waste bin. Her entire body had tensed. She forced herself to relax.

She turned to the file again, but the sudden beep of her telephone stopped her. She picked it up.

'Yes?'

It was Clive. 'Paul Sutherland from CNB Marketing's on the line.' His tone was neutral. 'Do you want me to tell him you're busy?'

Kate hesitated. 'No, it's okay. I'll take it.'

There was a series of clicks. She closed her eyes, briefly. A second later she heard the familiar voice.

'Hi, Kate. Thought I'd ring and see if you'd got the flowers.'

'Yes. A little bit premature, though, I think.' She was pleased to hear her voice was steady.

4

'Oh, come on. You don't seriously think you're still in with a chance, do you?'

'Let's just wait and see what happens, shall we?'

She heard him sigh. 'Kate, Kate, Kate. You *know* what's going to happen. You've done well to get this far, but don't kid yourself.'

'Is that all you wanted to say? Because if it is, I've got work to do.'

There was a chuckle. 'Now don't be like that. I'm just giving you some friendly advice, that's all. For old times' sake.'

Kate clenched her jaw.

'Kate? You still there?'

'You've not changed, Paul. You always were a prick.' She regretted the words immediately. The amused laugh came down the line again, this time unmistakably pleased with itself.

'And didn't you just love it? But I can see I'm wasting my time trying to talk sense to you. Poor little Kate's got to do things her way, even if it means getting her fingers burned. Just try not to be too disappointed.'

The line went dead. Her knuckles were white as she banged down the receiver.

The bastard.

Kate fumbled in her bag, came up with a disposable lighter and a battered packet of Camels. Her hand shook as she put one in her mouth. She flicked a flame from the lighter and held it close to the cigarette without lighting it. The taste of stale tobacco was cold on her tongue when she inhaled. The flame quivered, but did not quite touch the cigarette.

She held it there and counted to ten, then to ten again.

The second time it was easier. Grimacing, she clicked off the lighter and dropped the unlit cigarette into the bin. The packet and lighter went back in her bag. She put a sugar-free mint into her mouth to take away the taste.

The shakes had gone, but her headache was back, fingering its way across her scalp. Kate wished she'd not tied her hair back so tightly that morning. She kneaded her temples, gently. *Is it worth it?*

When the invitation to tender for the Parker Trust account had landed on her desk six weeks earlier, she had gone into the pitch without any real expectation. The Trust specialised in the low-profile handling of investments for wealthy clients, funding just enough Worthy Causes (the words had been capitalised in their brief) to qualify as a charity. She had been surprised that they had even heard of Powell PR, let alone were prepared to consider them for a long-term, expensive campaign.

Then, amazingly, she had been short-listed. The shock of that still hadn't worn off when she discovered who the other short-listed company was, and who she would be pitching against.

From then on, the pitch had ballooned until it filled her entire horizon. Clive joked that she might as well install a bed at the office, to save going home at all. You're not happy unless you're working, he'd said. She had smiled, but behind it had been a dark stirring of panic. *Happy?* That night at the gym she had strained until her muscles screamed, trying to burn off her restlessness like calories.

Now the waiting had concertina-ed into the final hours. Redwood, the chairman of the board of trustees, had told her he would let her know the Trust's decision before noon.

Winning would mean financial security, perhaps eventually bigger premises. It would establish the agency's reputation, opening the way to bigger and better accounts.

Kate didn't let herself consider what losing would be like.

She found she was clicking her ball-point pen aimlessly in and out. She stopped, put it down, and determinedly reached for the file she had opened earlier. She began to read it and make notes, haltingly at first, then more fluidly. But every few minutes her eyes would stray to the clock on the wall.

The morning passed slowly. Each time a call came through she stiffened, expecting it to be from the Trust. None were. At five to twelve she gave up even the pretence of trying to work. She sat in the silence of her office, looking at the clock and waiting for the phone to ring. The second hand crept round the dial, bringing the noon deadline closer. She watched as it converged with the other two. The three formed a single, vertical finger, poised for a moment, and then the second hand ticked indifferently into its downward sweep.

Kate felt the anticipation leak out of her. In its wake was a heavy residue of disappointment. The Parker Trust were almost obsessively punctual. If she'd won the pitch she would have heard by now. She didn't move as the fact of failure sank in, no longer a possibility but a reality to be faced. Abruptly, she shook herself. *So you didn't get it. It's only a pitch. There'll be others.*

She sat straighter in her chair, doggedly re-opened the file she'd been working on.

The phone beeped.

Kate started. It beeped again. She picked it up. 'Yes?'

Caroline answered. 'It's Mr Redwood from the Parker Trust.'

Even though she knew what he was going to say, Kate felt her heart bump. She cleared her throat. 'Put him through.'

There seemed to be more clicks than usual as the transfer was made. The line hummed, hollowly. 'Miss Powell?'

'Good afternoon, Mr Redwood.' She allowed a faint emphasis to creep into the 'afternoon'.

'I apologise for the tardiness of the call. I realise you would have been expecting to hear sooner.'

The voice gave an accurate picture of the man. Scottish. Thin, dry and humourless. Clive had called him anal, and Kate hadn't been able to argue.

'Yes,' she said, simply.

'Yes, I'm sorry about that.' He didn't sound it. Kate felt a flash of antagonism. 'It's our policy to inform the unsuccessful tender first,' he went on, 'to put them out of their misery, as it were, and it took a little longer than we anticipated.'

It took a moment for the implication to register. Suddenly confused, Kate floundered. 'I'm sorry . . . You've spoken to CNB?'

She heard Redwood give an exasperated sigh. 'Perhaps I'd better start again. I'm pleased to tell you that your tender has been successful. The board of trustees has decided to invite your agency to handle our campaign.'

Kate felt an almost out-of-body detachment. Outside, a siren Dopplered in and out of existence.

'Miss Powell? Is there a problem?'

8

'No! No, I . . .' She made an effort. 'I'm delighted. Thank you.'

'Again, I apologise for the delay.' His voice became tinged with disapproval. 'I'm afraid CNB were reluctant to accept our decision. The person we were dealing with became quite . . . insistent.' Redwood brought himself up short. 'Well. Congratulations, Miss Powell. We look forward to working with your agency.'

Kate said something, she wasn't sure what. They agreed to meet later in the week. He rang off. She listened to the purr of the dialling tone before setting the receiver back in its cradle. From downstairs she could hear the drone of a photocopier, the peal of someone's laughter. She stared blankly out of the window. For a moment she thought the patch of darkness outside was a raincloud. Then she remembered.

After a while she got up to tell the others.

The bus stopped outside the shops near her flat in Fulham. As Kate stepped off, it occurred to her, belatedly, that she could probably afford to get a taxi from the tube station now. Old habits died hard. She went into the Asian supermarket and bought a pint of milk and a packet of rice. After a moment of indecision she added a bottle of white Rioja to the wire basket.

There was a chill in the air as Kate left the shop, a reminder that spring had yet to reach further than the calendar. A drizzle had started, and she began walking faster, hoping to get home before it grew heavy enough to merit an umbrella. She almost trod on the child's mitten lying at the edge of a puddle. It formed a vivid splash of red against the dirty brown pavement, and couldn't have been there long because it still looked new and clean.

Kate picked it up, glancing up and down the street for the pram or buggy it must have dropped from. No one was in sight, so she cast around for a wall or window-ledge to put it on. There was nowhere, except back on the muddy pavement. Reluctant simply to discard it, she looked at the forlorn little object in her hand. The mitten was no bigger than her palm, and suddenly the memory of the warehouse fire came back to her. Kate felt her throat constrict, and before she knew what she was doing she had tucked the mitten into her pocket and walked on.

The drizzle had stopped by the time she reached her flat. The wrought-iron gate in front of the Victorian terraced house was open, as it always was since the hinges had dropped and wedged it against the path. The tiny garden, no bigger than a large rug, had been flagged over by a previous occupant, but a gap had been left in the centre for a thorny huddle of rose bushes. They needed pruning, Kate noticed absently. She went into the small open porch and unlocked the front door.

Envelopes were splashed on the black and white tiles in the cramped hallway. She bent and picked them up, shuffling through for those addressed to her. There were only two; one a bill, the other a bank statement. The rest was junk mail. She divided it up and put half on her ground-floor neighbour's coconut-fibre welcome mat. As she straightened, the door opened and the old lady who lived there beamed out at her.

'I thought I heard someone.'

Kate mustered a smile. 'Hello, Miss Willoughby, how are you?'

Her heart sank as the woman emerged further, leaning heavily on her walking stick. The dark green woollen dress was immaculately pressed, as usual, and the blue-grey wig sat incongruously on top of the wizened face, like a hat.

'Very well, thank you.' She looked down at the circulars on her mat. 'Are they for me?'

Kate picked them up again and handed them to her, resigned to seeing the routine through. 'Nothing exciting, I don't think.'

As far as she could tell, Miss Willoughby never received any letters. But she always came out to check when Kate arrived home. Kate knew she was only using the post as an excuse, and usually didn't mind chatting to her for a few minutes. That evening, though, it was an unwelcome effort.

Miss Willoughby peered through her gold-rimmed spectacles at the fliers and special offers, and for a moment Kate thought she might escape easily. She started drifting towards her door, but then the old lady looked up again.

'No, nothing there for me. Still, you never know, do you?'

Kate forced a smile of agreement as Miss Willoughby leaned both hands on her walking stick, a sure sign that she was settling herself for a lengthy conversation. But before she could say anything else, a grey shape emerged with a clatter through the cat flap in the front door.

The tom cat miaowed and rubbed around Kate's legs, then darted towards the old lady's doorway.

'No, you don't, Dougal,' Kate said, grabbing it. The cat, a big tabby, squirmed to be put down. 'I'd better take him in. If he gets in your flat we'll never get him out,' she said, seizing the opportunity.

Miss Willoughby's smile never wavered. 'Oh, that's all right. But I won't keep you. I expect you'll both be hungry.'

With a final goodnight, she went back inside as Kate unlocked her own door. There was a cat flap in that as well, but Dougal saw no reason to use it when Kate was there to let him in. She closed the door behind her before letting the cat jump down. His miaows receded towards the kitchen as he ran up the carpeted stairs. Kate followed more slowly, feeling churlish now for dodging the old lady. Sighing, she took off her jacket, wrinkling her nose at the lingering smell of smoke. She put it on a coat-hanger, ready to take to the cleaners, and it was only when she saw the bulge in one pocket that she remembered the mitten.

The irrationality of the impulse that had made her keep it disturbed her. Decisively, she took it out and went to the bin in the kitchen. The lid sprang open when she stamped on the foot pedal, releasing a faint, sweet smell of rot. Kate looked at the hash of egg shells and vegetable peelings, holding the mitten poised above them. But she was no more able to throw it away now than before. She took her foot from the pedal, letting the lid slap down, and went back into her bedroom. Pulling open a drawer, she thrust the mitten far into the back under a pile of clean towels, then pushed the drawer firmly shut.

Kate went back into the hall, untying her hair with a little sigh of relief. The message light was flashing on the answerphone. She played back the tape, but whoever it had been had hung up without speaking.

Barefoot, she went into the lounge. Like the rest of the flat, its walls were plain white, partly because she preferred

12

the simplicity of such a colour scheme, and partly because the house faced away from the sun and was quite dark. Even now, when it was still light outside, the white walls did little to lift the gloomy twilight.

Kate switched on a table lamp. The furniture in the room was clean-lined and modern, except for an old pine seaman's trunk that served as a coffee table. On the wall was an abstract oil she'd bought from an exhibition, the only splash of colour on the otherwise blank backdrop. The flat was much cosier in winter, when the long nights came and she could draw the curtains and fill the corners with artificial light. Now, though, dark as the flat was, there was something not quite right about having a lamp on when it was still daylight outside.

She turned it off again and switched on the TV instead. Idly, she flicked through the channels. There was nothing on that interested her, but it illuminated the room a little, and the sound of voices gave the flat a less empty feel.

There was a miaow as the cat wrapped himself around her legs, butting his head against her ankles.

'You hungry, Dougal?' She picked him up. He was big, even for a tom, with close-set eyes that gave him a stupid, perpetually surprised expression. He had come with the flat, an extra that hadn't been mentioned by the estate agent when she'd bought it. The middle-aged couple who'd lived there before hadn't bothered to take their pet with them when they'd left. Kate hadn't wanted a cat, but Dougal had been either too stupid or too determined to accept that.

He wriggled free and jumped onto the floor, miaowing.

'All right, I know it's dinner-time.' Kate went into the kitchen and took a tin of cat food from the wall cupboard.

The cat jumped up onto the work surface and tried to eat the meat as she was forking it into the dish. She pushed him back down. 'Just wait, gutbucket.'

Kate set the dish on the floor and watched as the cat began to gulp at the food. She considered getting something to eat herself. She opened the fridge, stared inside, then closed it again. A bray of false laughter came from the lounge. Kate went back in. A sitcom was on the TV, noisy and colourful. She switched it off. The hysterical images disappeared as the screen went blank, the laughter abruptly severed.

Silence crowded into the room. It seemed darker than ever, but she made no move to turn on the lamp. From the kitchen she heard the faint sound of the cat's dish softly scraping on the kitchen floor.

What's wrong with me?

Winning the Parker Trust account was the biggest coup of her career. She should have been euphoric. Instead she felt nothing. There was no satisfaction, no sense of having achieved anything. Nothing, after all, had changed. She looked around the darkening lounge. *Is this it? Is this all there's going to be?*

The sound of the cat-flap slapping shut came from the hallway. Dougal had eaten his fill and gone out again. She was alone. All at once the darkness, the quiet was oppressive. She turned on the lamp and quickly set the CD playing without caring what was in it.

The sound of Tom Jones belting out 'It's Not Unusual' filled the room. Kate went into the hallway and picked up the phone. She had made no arrangements to go out that evening, knowing that if she had lost the pitch she wouldn't want to. Now, though, the thought of staying in by herself appalled her. The phone rang only twice at the other end before a woman's voice answered.

'Hello?'

'Hi, Lucy, it's Kate.'

'Oh, Kate, hi! Hang on.' There was a hollow *clunk* as the receiver went down. Kate heard Lucy raising her voice in the background. There was a childish objection that she overruled, then she was back. 'Sorry about that. Slight disagreement over which programme we want to watch.'

'Who won?'

'I did. I told her she could either watch *EastEnders* with me or go to bed. So she's suddenly an *EastEnders* fan. Anyway, how did it go?'

'We got it.'

'Oh, Kate, that's *fantastic*! You must be over the moon!'

'Well, I don't think it's really sunk in yet.'

'It will! So you're off out celebrating tonight, then?'

Kate transferred the receiver to her other ear so she could hear better over the noise from the CD. 'Er, no. Look, I wondered if you fancied going out somewhere? My treat, so long as Jack doesn't mind babysitting.'

'Tonight? Oh, Kate, I can't! Jack's not going to be in till later.'

Kate kept the disappointment from her voice. 'It doesn't matter. It was pretty short notice.'

'I *know*, but we've not been out together for *ages*! Tell you what, why don't you come over? Bring a couple of bottles of wine, and with a bit of luck we can be pissed by the time Jack gets home.'

Kate felt her spirits lift. 'Are you sure?'

'Of course. So long as you don't mind playing aunty again if the kids aren't in bed.'

Kate smiled at the thought of Lucy's children. 'I'd love to.' She told Lucy she'd be over in an hour and hung up, her melancholy gone. She was busy again, with somewhere to go and something to do. She would laugh and play with Emily and Angus, get a little drunk with Lucy, and kick herself out of any self-indulgent blues. She did a hip-twitching dance as Tom went into overdrive.

She phoned for a cab, then poured herself a glass of wine from the fridge. 'Cheers,' she toasted herself. She took the glass into the bathroom and put it on the edge of the bath while she undressed. She studied herself briefly in the mirror as she waited for the water to run hot, wishing as usual that she was tall and elegant instead of small and trim. But, on a high now, she didn't let it worry her.

She showered quickly, humming as the stinging water sluiced away the day's events. She had dried herself and was just beginning to dress when the doorbell rang. The cab was early. *Damn.* Kate hesitated, debating whether to throw on more clothes before going to answer it. A second, longer ring decided her. Pulling on a towelling robe, she ran downstairs.

The blurred silhouette of a man was visible through the coloured diamonds of the stained-glass panel. Kate unlocked the door and opened it a crack.

'Sorry, you're too—' she began, and stopped.

Paul was standing in the porch. He grinned at her. 'Too what?'

The sight of him froze her. She tried to kick-start herself over the shock.

'What are you doing here?'

'I've come to offer my congratulations.'

He lifted up the bottle of champagne he was gripping by the neck. Kate could smell the beer on his breath, sour and mingled with a waft of cigarette. There was something about his smile that she didn't like. She kept hold of the door, barring him.

'I'm going out.'

His grin broadened as he slid his gaze down her body. She resisted the impulse to clutch the robe tighter. 'The taxi'll be here any minute. I've got to finish getting dressed.'

He moved his eyes from her breasts. 'Don't mind me. Won't be anything I've not seen before, will it?'

He stepped forward as she began to protest, and she instinctively moved away from him. That was all the space he needed to wedge his shoulders in the doorway, levering the door open against her pressure. He forced her back another pace, and then he was inside.

'Paul!' she began, but he brushed past her.

'Come on, Kate, I thought you were in a hurry?'

He went heavily up the stairs, bumping off the wall as he stumbled against it. Kate stood in the small hallway as his footsteps clumped into the lounge. *Don't go up, leave him, don't go up!* a small voice shrilled. But she didn't know what else she could do. Closing the front door, but not the one to her flat at the bottom of the stairs, she ran after him.

Paul was sprawled on the sofa, arms spread across its back. His face was flushed. He hadn't changed much since the last time she had seen him. His dark-blond hair was a little longer, and she noticed the slight tightness of shirt against gut. But the condescending arrogance with which he greeted the world was still the same.

He smirked at her. 'Nice place you've got here.'

'How did you find out where I live?'

'If you wanted to keep it a secret, you should go ex-directory. And I'd change the message on your answerphone, if I were you. You sound really bored on it.'

Kate stood by the doorway. 'I want you to leave.'

'Aren't you even going to offer me a drink?' He waggled the champagne. 'No?' He let the bottle drop onto the sofa. 'So much for congratulations.'

'Why've you come, Paul?'

A look of uncertainty touched his face, as though he didn't know himself. Then it was gone. 'To see you. What's the matter – too good to talk to me now?'

'There's nothing to say. And I've told you, I'm going out.'

'Where?'

'To Lucy's.' The reflex to tell him came before she could stop it. She hated herself for the automatic surrender.

The unpleasant smile was back on Paul's mouth. 'So you're still seeing that cow?'

'She isn't a cow, and who I see isn't any of your business anyway.'

His smile died. 'I'd forgotten how fucking smug you are.'

Kate didn't say anything.

'Oh, spare me the injured look!' Paul regarded her sourly. 'Christ, you haven't changed, have you? St Kate, still acting as if butter wouldn't melt in your mouth.'

He sat forward, suddenly. 'Come on, don't pretend you're

18

not enjoying this! You did it! You beat me! You can crow about it, I don't mind.'

'I just want you to go.'

'What, just like that?' He looked at her with mock surprise. 'This is your big chance! You finally gave that bastard Paul Sutherland his comeuppance! Don't you want to rub my face in it?'

Kate felt the old guilt working. Beating him hadn't given her the lift she'd expected, but she couldn't deny it had been an incentive. The strength of her desire to apologise, to say he was right, maddened her. 'What makes you think you're important enough for me to be bothered?'

He grinned, pleased to have provoked her. 'Because I know you. I know what you're like. Christ, I should do, I lived with you long enough.' The thin veneer over his anger was beginning to crack. 'God, look at you. Miss Superior. You think you're it, don't you? Well, you're not. You're nothing. If not for me you'd still be peddling shitty little accounts!'

'That's not how I remember it.'

'No? Who gave you your first fucking break, then?'

The retort came before she could stop it. 'And that wasn't all you gave me, was it?'

He stared at her. 'What's that supposed to mean?'

Kate looked away. 'Look, Paul, this is pointless. I'm sorry you're disappointed, but—'

'Disappointed? Why the fuck should I be disappointed? Just because some conniving bitch screws me out of an account I've been working my balls off for?'

'I didn't screw you out of anything.'

'No? Who did you screw, then? Was it the whole board, or just Redwood?'

She held open the door. 'I want you to go. Now.'

He laughed, but there was no humour in it. 'Come on, Kate, you can tell me. Did he touch your spot like I used to?'

'Get out! Now!'

He was up off the sofa before she could move. He grabbed her around the throat with one hand. The other pressed against her chin, forcing her head back.

'*Don't fucking tell me what to do!*'

Kate felt his spittle fleck her face. His breath was thick with alcohol. She tried to prise his hands from her, but he was too strong. His face worked.

'You *bitch*! You think you're so fucking clever, don't you?'

He jammed her back against the door. The handle dug painfully into her spine. Then she saw the expression in his eyes alter, and suddenly she knew what was going to happen next. As though the thought had prompted the action, he dropped one of his hands and wrenched aside the bathrobe, ignoring her struggles as he grabbed her breast. He dug his fingers into her.

'Paul – *No!*'

The hand on her throat choked her, stopping her from screaming. His leg went between hers, forcing them apart, pinning her. There was no space to kick or knee him. She tore at his wrist. Tiny points of light began to spark her vision. She felt his hand at her waist, yanking at the belt that still held the robe closed. *No! God, no!*

Abruptly, she stopped struggling. Feeling the lack of resistance, Paul looked up. She forced herself to smile at him over his hand.

'Bedroom . . .' she croaked.

For a moment he didn't move, and she thought he was too far gone to listen to her. Then a grin touched his mouth. He stepped back, and as the pressure on her throat relaxed and his leg slid from between hers, she shot her knee up at his groin and pushed out as hard as she could.

It was too soon. Her knee skidded off his thigh, and even as he reeled away, he was already grabbing for her again. She lunged through the doorway, feeling him close behind her as she stumbled down the hall. He caught hold of her bathrobe as she reached the top of the stairs, checking her, dragging her back in an unequal tug of war. She could see the door standing open at the bottom, and in desperation spun round and wrenched the robe from his fingers.

She pitched back against the wall as it ripped free, her teeth snapping together painfully. Paul toppled the opposite way, into the open stairwell. He caromed off the banister and tumbled untidily to the bottom, crashing into the door and knocking it back against the wall before sprawling onto the black and white tiles of the entrance hall.

Breathless, Kate ran down after him. His eyes were screwed shut, mouth frozen in a pained 'O' as she stepped over his legs and opened the front door. Dazed, he didn't resist as she tucked her hands under his arms and began dragging him backwards. He was heavy, but there wasn't far to go. It was only when his hips bumped down off the porch that he seemed to realise what was happening.

'Whoa—' he said, stiffening, and Kate let him drop. His head cracked onto the concrete path, but even as the '*Ow!*' was forced from him, she was already running back inside. She banged the front door shut and leaned against it, panting. Her back and shoulders ached from the effort.

For a few seconds there was silence outside, then she heard him grunt and curse as he scraped to his feet.

'Fuck!' Another groan. 'Bitch!'

She heard him take a step towards the porch. 'If you're still there when I get upstairs, I'm calling the police!' she shouted. She turned to find Miss Willoughby standing in the doorway behind her. Below the wig the old lady's face was shocked.

'Is everything all right?'

Kate saw her bathrobe was flapping open. She pulled it around her, trying to compose herself. 'Yes. I'm sorry, it's . . .' An explanation defeated her. 'Everything's fine.'

With Miss Willoughby staring after her, she hurried upstairs into the lounge. Keeping to the side of the window, she edged forward until she could look down onto the path. Paul was standing by the gate, rubbing the back of his head and glaring into the porch. He glanced up at the window. Kate jerked back, but he gave no sign of having seen her. Finally, with a last black look, he turned and walked slowly away.

Kate watched until she could no longer see him in the dusk. Then she sagged. Her legs felt weak, and it was all she could do to make it to a chair before they gave way. She shook as she wrapped the bathrobe tight across her chest and hugged herself.

The sudden clamour of the doorbell made her jump. *God! Now what?* Cautiously, she went back to the window and peered out. Whoever it was, they were out of sight on the porch. She hesitated, then crept back downstairs. The doorbell rang again when she was half-way down, almost making her miss a step. Mouth dry, she unlocked the door at the bottom. In the fading light, the figure framed in the stained-glass panel was even more indistinct than before.

Her voice cracked a little as she asked. 'Who is it?'

'Cab for Powell.'

The voice was Cockney, nothing like Paul's, and she rested her head against the wall. She almost told the driver she had changed her mind: the urge to lock herself inside and crawl into bed was overwhelming.

'Give me ten minutes,' she called instead, and ran back upstairs to get dressed.

CHAPTER 2

The little girl was losing the fight to stay awake. Her eyelids drooped, flicked open, then drooped again. This time they stayed shut. Kate waited until she was sure Emily was asleep before softly closing the book and standing up. Disturbed by the slight shift of the mattress, the little girl turned on her side and burrowed under the sheets until only a tuft of pale hair was visible.

Kate quietly slid the book onto the shelf. In the other bed Emily's brother, younger by almost two years, lay on his back, sturdy arms and legs thrown out with eighteen-month-old abandon. Angus had kicked off most of the covers. Kate pulled them over him again. She turned down the dimmer switch on the wall until the light from the Mickey Mouse lamp faded to a dull glow.

The sound of the two children's breathing was a soft sibilance in the half-light. Kate had been absurdly flattered when they had both wanted her to take them to bed, Angus first, then his sister half an hour later. A wave of affection constricted her throat as she looked at the two of them sleeping. Gently, she closed the bedroom door and made her way downstairs.

The house was a decaying, detached villa in Finchley, with high moulded ceilings, a mahogany-banistered staircase, and

25

a small walled garden that Lucy called 'the jungle'. The ceilings were flaking and the banister cracked, but it was better than the cramped and cold apartment where Lucy and Jack had lived before. The house had been left to them several years earlier by an aunt, and they still didn't seem to have unpacked properly. Toys, papers and clothes were scattered on chairs, on the floor and over the backs of radiators. It was the sort of house Kate wished she'd been brought up in. She stepped over a red tricycle lying on its side at the bottom of the stairs and squeezed round a pile of boxes stacked untidily against the wall. Jack ran his desk-top publishing business from the converted cellar, and the over-spill from it cluttered the entire house.

Lucy was putting more coal onto the fire as Kate went into the lounge. It tumbled out of the scuttle with a clatter, covering the flames completely. A damp smell came from it. Lucy set down the scuttle and wiped her hands on a rag. Her eyes were a vivid, almost violet blue as she looked up at Kate.

'She get off okay?'

'Out like a light.'

'You should come more often. They're always on their best behaviour when you're here.'

Kate smiled and sat on the floor. The coal had smothered the heat from the fire, but already smoke was beginning to rise like steam from the black chunks. The lounge was big and draughty, and Lucy and Jack kept a fire going on all but the hottest nights. Kate curled her legs under her and leaned back against the settee. In front of her, the coffee table was littered with the wreckage of a Chinese takeaway, fried rice and noodles congealing in foil containers. A half-empty bottle of white wine stood among them.

Lucy pushed a blonde curl out of her eyes and sat down on the floor near Kate. She picked out a cold prawn. 'I knew I should have cleared this lot away,' she said, chewing. 'I'll have put on half a stone by tomorrow.'

'You could always come to the gym with me.'

'No, thanks. If God had meant women to be slim he wouldn't have invented chocolate.' She popped another prawn into her mouth. 'Anyway, look what happened the last time I went to a gym. I met Jack.'

Kate poured them both more wine, then settled back against the old leather settee. She felt drowsy and comfortable. She had known Lucy for seven years, but it seemed much longer. Lucy had been a receptionist at the agency where Kate had been given her first PR job, and where Paul Sutherland had been marketing director. Her pneumatic figure and tendency towards tight clothes had turned men's heads, but two children and a sweet tooth had changed all that. If she minded the trade, though, she didn't show it. Sometimes Kate envied her.

Lucy sucked her fingers. 'So you're adamant you're not going to the police about Paul?'

'I don't think there's much point. It'd only be his word against mine.' Kate reached for her wine glass. 'Besides, nothing really happened in the end.'

'It would have if you hadn't stopped him. And how do you know he won't try it again?'

'I'll be more careful. I don't think he will, though. He was just drunk and worked up about the losing the pitch.

I can't see even Paul being stupid enough to make a big thing of it.'

Lucy gave a laugh. 'I can.'

Kate accepted this without comment. Lucy had tried to warn her off Paul Sutherland from the start. She hadn't listened.

'So what happens now you've won the pitch?' Lucy asked. 'Are you going to back off and take things a little easier?'

'I wish. Now's when the hard work really starts.'

Lucy selected another prawn. 'So delegate. You're always saying how good Clive is.'

'He is, but I can't dump everything on him.'

'So you'll try and do it all yourself, until you have a—' Lucy broke off. 'Well, until you drop,' she finished.

The first flames licked through the coal as the fire began to burn in earnest. Kate watched them. 'I enjoy working,' she said.

'That doesn't mean you can't have a social life as well.'

'I've got one.'

Lucy snorted. 'Going to the gym's hardly what I'd call being a party animal.'

Kate rubbed her neck. Probing tendrils of another headache announced their presence. 'Don't go on about it.'

'I'm sorry, Kate, but I can't just sit back and watch you work yourself into a frazzle.' The firelight gave Lucy's blonde hair a reddish tint. 'I know running a business isn't easy – God knows, Jack puts enough hours into it. But you need some sort of existence outside work.'

Without warning, Kate's vision blurred. The fire dissolved into sparkling prisms. She turned away, blinking her eyes clear.

'Kate? What's wrong?'

'Nothing. I'm all right.'

Lucy tore off a piece of kitchen roll and handed it to her. 'No, you're not. You've been in an odd mood all night.' She waited until Kate had blown her nose. 'Is it what happened with Paul?'

'No, I'm just being a silly cow, that's all.'

Lucy just looked at her.

'I don't *know* what's wrong,' Kate blurted. 'I should be ecstatic, but I just feel . . .' She tossed the wad of kitchen roll onto the fire. It held its shape for a moment, then disappeared in a spurt of flame. 'I don't know how I feel.'

The flame died down, leaving a grey curl of ash. A thin tail of smoke wavered up from it. Kate looked away, unconsciously brushing at her sleeve.

Lucy was watching her. 'You need a holiday.'

'I don't have time.'

'Then make time. I know starting your own agency was the best thing you could have done after the mess with Paul, I'm not disputing that. But it's not healthy to carry on burying yourself in it. If you were enjoying yourself I wouldn't mind, but you're obviously not.'

'I'm just feeling a bit low, that's all.'

'Oh, come on, Kate, that's bollocks, and you know it.' Lucy sighed and set down her glass on the coffee table. 'Look, I don't want to go on about it. But you can't let one bad experience sour you for life. It's time you put it behind you.'

'I have put it behind me.'

'No, you haven't. Before you started seeing Paul you used to be going out all the time, but since then you've just cut yourself off from everybody.'

Kate shrugged. 'People lose touch.'

'Only if you let them. How many people did you bother to tell when you moved into your flat? I bet most of them don't even know where you live any more.' Lucy waited for her to deny it. Kate didn't. 'And you haven't so much as been out for a drink with another man since you split up with Paul, and that's been more than three years, now.'

'I haven't met anyone I want to go out with.'

'You haven't tried. I've seen you when we're out together. You've got this aura around you that says, "Don't touch."'

'What do you want me to do? Fall flat on my back for every man I meet?'

'No, but you don't have to turn into a nun, either. Come on, be honest. Can you seriously tell me you don't miss sex?'

Kate avoided looking at her. 'I don't think about it much.'

'That's not a straight answer.'

'All right, then, no, I don't particularly miss it. Okay?'

'Then there's something wrong with you.' Lucy began to take a drink, then lowered her glass as another argument occurred to her. 'I know some women are perfectly happy putting their career before everything, but I just don't think you're one of them. And, let's face it, you're not getting any younger.'

'Thanks.'

'Well, you're not. You're thirty-four next year. You might like to think you're Superwoman, but your biological clock's running the same as everyone else's. Don't you think it's about time you started thinking about having a family, and—'

'Oh, come *on*!' Kate's wine sloshed as she banged down the glass.

'Hear me out—'

'I don't have to, I know what you're going to say! I should get married, settle down, cook tea! Sorry, but I don't think so. You might be happy being a housewife, but there's more to my life than that!'

She was surprised herself by the heat in her voice. Lucy looked at her for a moment, then wrapped her arms around her legs and gazed at the fire. 'Perhaps there is. But I'm not the one who's been in tears, am I?'

The flames popped and crackled in the silence.

'Sorry,' Kate said. 'I didn't mean that.'

'It's all right.' Lucy turned to her again. 'I meant what *I* said. And you can scream and shout all you like about not wanting a relationship, and not wanting to settle down. But I've seen how you are with Angus and Emily, so don't try to tell me you don't want children, because I won't believe you.'

Kate tried to produce a denial, but none came. Lucy nodded, as if this confirmed her point, but before she could say anything else they heard the front door being unlocked.

'Sounds like the reading finished early,' Lucy said, cocking her head. She leaned forward quickly and put her hand on Kate's knee. 'All I'm saying is, ask yourself what you really want. And then do something about it.'

She fixed Kate with a firm look, then sat back as footsteps approached down the hallway. Kate reached for another piece of kitchen roll.

'Are my eyes red?'

Lucy stretched, twisting her hands from side to side above her head. 'No, and it wouldn't matter if they were,' she said, through a yawn. 'When Jack's had a couple of pints he wouldn't notice if you were starkers.'

The lounge door opened and a heavily built man bustled in, grinning. His wiry, black hair was thicker on his forearms than it was on his head. He bent and kissed Lucy.

'All right, luv? Hi, Kate.'

Kate smiled at him. He examined the cold contents of the foil containers, absently rubbing his slight paunch, then sank down into the high-winged leather armchair behind Lucy. Lucy leaned back against his legs.

'Good meeting?'

'Not bad. Gavin's got a new collection of poetry he's thinking of putting out, and Sally's got an idea for a new distribution system . . .'

Kate stopped listening. Although being with Jack and Lucy was like putting on a comfortable pair of slippers, she knew she would leave soon. The thought of going back to the barrenness of her empty flat depressed her, but sometimes she couldn't help feeling like an outsider, a spare setting at an already complete table.

She stared back into the fire as Lucy and Jack's voices lapped around her. A piece of coal made a snapping noise. The flames danced and quivered, always on the verge of shapes that she could never quite recognise.

That night Kate dreamed she was in a railway station. It was vast. People hurried past, ignoring her. She knew her train was about to leave, without knowing where it went from. In front of her was a huge timetable, but the words on it were somehow indecipherable. Gripped by a terrible urgency, she began forcing her way through the crowds, but as she did, she became aware that she had lost something. Even in the dream she didn't know what it was, only that she couldn't go on without it. She tried to retrace her steps, pushing back against the mass of people, but she was in another place now, further away than ever. The urgency became panic. She ran blindly through the station, filled with an awful need to find what she had lost, knowing that time was running out. And all the while everyone around her walked with assured intent, and the Tannoy blared out in a foreign language.

The dream left her with a vague sense of unrest next morning. As she drank her orange juice and waited for the toast to pop, she had the feeling that this wasn't the first time she'd had it, only the first she could remember.

Kate decided she wouldn't mention it to Lucy. She would only read too much into it.

CHAPTER 3

Later, she was to wonder what would have happened if she hadn't seen the magazine. Redwood had been on the phone again, making yet more amendments to the campaign. Two weeks after winning the pitch, he was still calling her most days, and when he finally rang off Kate put down the receiver with a feeling of weariness. She opened the Trust's file, stared at it for a moment, then tossed it down on her desk and sat back.

Sod it.

She went down to the basement kitchen, deciding to have tea instead of coffee for a change. The kettle was half full. Kate switched it on and dropped a teabag into a mug as she waited for it to boil. On the work surface nearby was a copy of *Cosmopolitan*. Idly, she picked it up. The glossy cover offered the usual mix of celebrity interviews and sex. One of the captions declared, 'Men: Who Needs 'Em?'. Underneath, in smaller letters, it added, 'Donor Insemination: The Shape of Things to Come?' Kate ran her eye over the other captions. Then back. She flicked through the pages.

She began to read.

Behind her, the kettle gouted steam before turning itself off. Kate didn't look up. She stood with her hip resting against the work surface, motionless except for when she turned a page. Only her eyes moved, running over the words in a waking REM. At one point she flipped back to reread a passage on a previous page. She lingered over it, then resumed where she had left off. She was turning to the next page when the door opened.

Kate jerked her head up. Josefina paused in the doorway. The Spanish girl had an empty coffee jug in her hand. She gave Kate a nervous smile.

'I did not mean to frighten you.'

'No, I was . . . I was just making a cup of tea.' Flustered, Kate turned to the kettle and saw it had already switched itself off. She clicked it on again. The girl went to the sink. Kate saw her glance at the magazine, and hurriedly closed it.

'Sorry, is this yours?'

Josefina brushed a heavy hank of hair from her eyes. 'It's all right. You can read it, if you like.'

'No, I've finished with it, thanks.'

Kate put the magazine back on the work-surface as Josefina began to fill the coffee jug from the tap. There was nothing knowing about the way the Spanish girl had smiled, Kate told herself. Why should there be? She'd only been reading a women's glossy, for God's sake. There was nothing wrong with that. So why was she blushing?

The kettle boiled. Kate busied herself pouring boiling water onto her teabag.

On her way home, she stopped off and bought a copy of the magazine from a newsstand.

Lucy was already at the café when Kate arrived. It was lunch-time, and most of the tables were already full, but

Lucy had managed to claim one on the pavement under the red awning. As Kate approached, she was flirting with a waiter, a pair of sunglasses pushed back on her head to hold her hair from her eyes. The waiter grinned as he went back inside.

Kate pulled back the white plastic chair from the table and sat down. It was warm from the sun.

'Not interrupting anything, am I?'

Lucy gave an easy shrug. 'Don't begrudge me my little pleasures. I've got to pick the kids up from the crêche in just over an hour.'

They opened the menus. Kate ordered a Greek salad without really looking. Lucy ordered moussaka, giving the waiter another smile as she thanked him. He took the menus with a flourish. She watched him walk away.

'Have you ever noticed how Greek men have lovely bums?' She turned back to Kate with a sigh. 'Anyway, this is a surprise. I thought I'd never see you now you've got the new account. How's it going?'

'Don't ask.'

Lucy didn't any more. She was more interested in the argument she and Jack were having over buying new hardware for his business. Kate fuelled her monologue with the occasional nod and smile, hearing none of it. Further down the street, a group of workmen were digging up the road. A traffic warden stopped by a car, wrote down its registration number. A few feet from him, a tramp rummaged in a waste bin. Kate watched them without seeing. She looked back at Lucy and tried to pay attention. She found herself twirling and untwirling her napkin around her finger, and made herself stop.

The waiter returned and set their food on the table. Kate picked at the oil-drenched salad and white cubes of feta without appetite. She realised Lucy was looking at her, expectantly.

'Sorry?'

'I said, how's the salad? These aubergines are gorgeous! I've got a recipe for moussaka from a magazine, but it doesn't taste anything like this!'

The opportunity made Kate's heart race.

'I was reading a magazine article the other day.' Her tone was studiedly casual. 'About artificial insemination.'

'Oh, yes?' Lucy didn't so much as glance up.

'Yes, it's . . . you know . . . surprising how many women have it.'

Lucy was engrossed in a mouthful of moussaka. 'Jack's cousin did. Her husband was impotent. Some sort of hideous accident, or something, so the only way they could have kids was thingy. Artificial whatever.'

Kate forgot her nervousness. 'Did they use his sperm or a donor's?'

'Oh, Kate, *please*, not while I'm eating!' Lucy pulled a face. 'Anyway, I don't know all the details. They emigrated.'

She bent over her food again, then stopped. She gave Kate a sharp look.

'How come you're so interested?'

Kate made a show of forking up more of her salad. 'I'm not. It's just . . . you know, an interesting subject.'

She was acutely aware that Lucy was still not eating. There was a silence. Kate kept her attention on her food. Then Lucy spoke.

'You're *not*!'

'Not what?'

'Thinking about having it!'

Kate tried an incredulous laugh. 'Me? Oh, come on!'

'You *are*, aren't you!'

'No! Of course not!' She tried to look Lucy in the eye, but couldn't. 'Not seriously. I was just, you know . . . Look, will you stop staring at me like that?'

'I'm sorry, Kate, but what do you expect?' Lucy set down her knife and fork, the moussaka forgotten. 'Well, this is one for the diary, isn't it? What's brought this on? Not what I said the other night, surely?'

Kate felt relief that the subject was finally broached. 'Only partly. But when I thought about it, you were right. It *is* time I decided what I want.'

'I didn't mean you'd got to rush out and do something straight away, though.' Lucy was looking at her with disbelief. 'And certainly nothing like *this*!'

'I know you didn't, but when I saw that article, it just *gelled*. I mean, I *do* want children. I even tried talking about it once to Paul, for all the good that did. Then, after we broke up, there didn't seem any point in even thinking about it.' She leaned forwards, warming to her argument. 'Because I'm single, and want to stay that way, I've just assumed that having a baby isn't an option. But why shouldn't it be? You know, it isn't as if—'

Kate broke off as a shadow fell across the table. She looked up. The tramp she'd seen earlier was standing in front of them. His hair and beard were wild and matted, his clothes rags. He stank. He held out his hand in supplication, but didn't look at either her or Lucy. His eyes stared at a point above them, remaining fixed on it even though his head was constantly moving from side to side in a syncopated twitch.

'*Jesus loves you. Jesus loves you. Jesus loves you.*'

The words were delivered in a flat mumble. Before Kate could react the waiter came rushing out of the café, began hustling the man away. The tramp slowly moved off, his mantra and twitch uninterrupted. Shaking his head, the waiter watched him go.

'They should be locked up,' he said, giving them a grin as he went back inside.

The people at the other tables returned to their food. The incident seemed to be ignored by common consent. Lucy turned back to Kate. Her forehead was tucked into a frown.

'You're not serious, are you?'

Kate felt her enthusiasm begin to dampen. 'I've not actually decided anything, if that's what you mean. I wanted to see what you thought I should do.'

Lucy sat back. 'Lord, Kate, I can't believe you even have to ask! Don't get me wrong, I've nothing against artificial insemination in itself. For a couple who can't have kids, like Jack's cousin, I suppose it's a godsend. But not for a single woman.'

'You think it's a bad idea, then?' Disappointment uncoiled in Kate's stomach.

'Of course I do! I mean, raising kids is hard enough when there's two of you. It must be a nightmare for a single parent! Any woman who'd voluntarily get herself into that mess wants her head looking at. And what about the agency? You've only just got that big account you've been chasing for ages. They'll be really pleased if you spring maternity leave on them!'

WHERE THERE'S SMOKE

Kate noticed that the woman at the next table was sitting perfectly still, her head cocked in their direction. She lowered her voice.

'It wouldn't be for nearly a year yet. And I wouldn't need that much time off. I could work from home. Besides, I thought you said I should have a life outside the agency? What happened to deciding what I want and then doing something about it?'

'Yes, but within *reason*! All right, if you want a baby I can understand that. But don't you think this is leaping to extremes? What's wrong with trying the normal way first? You know, husband first, baby second?'

Kate glanced at the woman at the other table, who had now edged her seat nearer. She leaned closer to Lucy. 'Because I don't *want* a husband. And I'm certainly not going to get involved with someone just so I can have their baby. I've been on my own since I was nineteen. I *like* being independent. Why should this be any different?'

'Because it *is* different.'

'Why is it? Just because I don't have a partner doesn't necessarily mean I can't still have a baby. I can afford it. I'm not some naïve teenager. So why shouldn't I?'

'Come on, Kate, you know as well as I do! If you'd got yourself knocked up accidentally, that'd be one thing, but you're talking about letting yourself be . . . be *impregnated* by a complete stranger! These clinics don't even tell you who's sperm they're using, do they?'

'No, but they're careful.'

'I should hope they are, but it still doesn't alter the fact that you wouldn't know who the father was, would you?'

That was something that Kate wasn't entirely happy

about herself. But she wasn't going to admit as much to Lucy.

'Hundreds of women have it done,' she said, dodging the issue.

'Yes, but as a last resort, not from choice! That's just asking for trouble!'

Suddenly Lucy turned to the woman at the next table. 'Perhaps you could give us your opinion, since you seem so interested. How do you prefer your sperm, hot or cold?'

The woman reddened and quickly turned away. Lucy looked back at Kate with a hard smile.

'What was I saying?'

Kate had covered her eyes with her hand. She tried not to laugh. 'Telling me it's asking for trouble.'

'Yes.' Lucy looked at her plate, as though she'd just remembered it. 'Well, what else can I say? I can't believe you're even *considering* it. I'm sorry, but you wanted my opinion and that's it.'

Kate said nothing. She sat with her chin resting on her hand, prodding with her fork at the salad.

Lucy sighed. 'Obviously that's not what you wanted to hear.'

'I just wanted your opinion, that's all.'

Lucy's eyes were very blue as she looked across at her. 'I don't know why. You're going to please yourself anyway.' She looked down at her plate, torn between further censure and the cooling moussaka. She sighed again.

'If you're really set on the idea, then I don't suppose it can hurt just to talk to someone. They'll probably tell you the same as me, but at least you'll have got it out of your system.' Lucy spread her hands. 'There. Is that what you wanted me to say?'

Kate grinned, but Lucy hadn't finished.

'I just hope you don't do something you'll regret, that's all,' she said. Then, before Kate could respond, she turned to where the waiter was wiping down another table. She beamed at him and held out her plate.

'You couldn't be a love and pop this back in the microwave for two minutes, could you?'

They walked to the tube station. The café was on a side road near Oxford Circus, a convenient mid-way point for both of them. Lucy was chatting about something, but Kate barely listened. She felt that even her fingertips were tingling with excitement. Now that she'd told Lucy it was as though a burden she'd been carrying around had been shucked off and left behind.

Lucy was still talking as they started down the steps to the Underground. Suddenly she gripped Kate's arm.

'Oh, shit.'

Kate looked up. Her excitement curdled and died.

Paul Sutherland was walking up the steps towards them. A second later, he saw them and it seemed to Kate that a flicker of unease crossed his face before his customary arrogance replaced it. She faltered, but Lucy forced her to keep moving.

'Come on. Too late for that.'

He stopped directly in front of them, blocking their path. Kate ignored the irate looks from the other people who had to jostle past. Her mouth was dry.

'Hello, Paul,' Lucy said, brightly. 'Assaulted anyone else lately?'

He gave her a cold look. 'You've put on weight.'

'That's what having two children does for you. What's your excuse? Still taking lunch from a bottle, are we?'

His cheek muscles worked, but he didn't respond. He looked at Kate.

'You ruined my shirt and nearly cracked my head open. I hope you're satisfied.'

The impulse to apologise almost won through. She felt herself wavering, on the brink of reverting to a former self. Then her anger kicked in.

'What did you expect?'

'I didn't expect you to get hysterical, that's for sure.' His tone was scathing and familiar. 'You need to see a shrink.'

Kate felt gagged with fury. Lucy spoke for her. 'One of you does, but it isn't her. And I think you'll find attempted rape's more a police matter, anyway.'

Heads turned as people streamed past. Paul gave Lucy a murderous look. 'You stay out of this.'

Kate had regained control of herself. 'There's nothing for her to stay out of. You're not worth bothering with.'

She took another step down, so they were almost touching. She stared at him.

'Are you going to move?'

There was a moment of stasis. Then he broke his gaze from hers and moved to one side. Kate brushed past without giving him another glance. She held herself tense as she walked, feeling him staring after her. Lucy followed a step or two behind. The sunlight was cut off as they entered the cool of the subway tunnel. Paul's shout reverberated after them.

'*Fucking bitch!*'

Kate carried on walking, her eyes fixed straight ahead. The shouts pursued her, bouncing off the hard walls.

'*You think you're so fucking clever, don't you? Well, ask your friend who she used to shag. Go on, you smug bitch! Ask her!*'

The shouts became indistinct as they went further into the station. Kate was conscious of Lucy beside her, but didn't look at her. Neither spoke. She walked through the crowded foyer and stopped by an out-of-order ticket machine. A few feet away the turnstiles rattled and clacked as people pushed through. Lucy cleared her throat.

'Look, Kate . . .'

'Is it true?'

Lucy hesitated, then nodded. The rigidity that had supported Kate so far ebbed out of her.

'Why didn't you *tell* me?'

Lucy's face was uncharacteristically distressed. 'Because it was *ages* before you started seeing him. I didn't even *know* you then. I hadn't even met Jack. It wasn't anything serious.'

'So why keep quiet about it?'

'What else could I do? I couldn't say anything once you'd started seeing him, could I? You'd have thought I was just being catty!'

'But why didn't you tell me *afterwards*?'

'What, in the state you were in when you split up? How could I?'

'Lucy, that was three years ago! Why haven't you said anything before now?'

Lucy shrugged, helplessly. 'There didn't seem much *point*.

And the longer I left it, the harder it got. I always *meant* to, Kate, honest! I just . . . well, I never seemed to get around to it.' Her forehead creased in consternation. 'Sorry.'

Kate turned away. Coming on top of her earlier excitement, the revelation had left her drained. But, as the initial shock wore off, she realised that if Lucy had confessed to having had a relationship with Paul – to having *fucked* him – it would have ended their friendship. Even up to a year ago, perhaps less, Kate knew she probably couldn't have coped with it. So how could she blame Lucy for keeping quiet? More to the point, if it had been before Kate even met him, what business of hers was it anyway? Suddenly, it all seemed too long ago, involving people she could barely remember.

Lucy was watching her, anxiously. Kate gave her a tired smile.

'Don't look so grim. I'm not going to excommunicate you.'

Lucy was still unconvinced. 'You're not cross?'

'No, I'm not cross.'

Relief lightened Lucy's face. 'Oh, thank God for that! I thought, God, if that bastard's gone and stirred things up after all this time, I'll kill him!' Sudden doubt presented itself. 'He hasn't, has he? You really mean it?'

'Of course I mean it.'

As she spoke, Kate wondered if that was true. There was no jealousy or resentment, but a kernel of disappointment had begun to form. Lucy's contempt for Paul had always been a reassuring constant. Now it seemed unreliable. Abruptly, Kate wanted to be alone.

'Look, you'd better go,' she said. 'You'll be late for the kids.'

Lucy gave her a hug. 'I'll ring you.'

Kate watched her disappear into the crowd, then went through the turnstile and made her way to the Victoria line. She stood on the escalator, letting it carry her at its own speed instead of walking down as she usually did. *Lucy and Paul.* Even the words didn't seem right together.

A movement caught her eye. A bearded man was coming up the opposite escalator, carrying a baby in a papoose on his back. The baby was goggling across at the people on her side, and Kate smiled as it spotted her. She turned her head to watch it go past, and a sudden thought took the smile from her face.

She could have had a child by Paul.

The thought made her go cold. She reached the bottom of the escalator and stepped off. Around her, people were rushing for the platform where a train had pulled in, but Kate barely noticed. She walked slowly, lost in the narrowness of her escape. If, *if*, she decided to have a baby, she would make damn sure it had a better father than that, even if he was only a father *in absentia*. Faceless donor or not, before she committed herself she would want to be sure he wasn't another Paul. Or someone even worse.

She shuddered to think of it. She'd made a bad mistake once.

This time she would be more careful.

CHAPTER 4

When she was six, there had been a suburban cinema not far from her home. It had been run-down and struggling even then, on a downslide that would end with it becoming first a bingo hall, then a supermarket, and finally a car park. But for Kate, who had never been to any other cinema, the chewing-gum-patterned carpet and threadbare seats didn't matter. They were part of the darkened atmosphere, along with the rustle of crisp bags and the cigarette smoke that meandered in the flickering beam of light overhead. The images on the screen were a window to another world, and once lost in that technicolour glamour, the shabby theatre, school, and even home itself became insubstantial as ghosts.

Her visits to the old cinema were rare, but all the more treasured because of that. When she found out that *Jungle Book* was being shown again, it became her mission in life to see it. The film wasn't new, but that hardly mattered to Kate, who had missed it the first time around. Her mother told her they would go to see it 'soon', a typically vague assurance that she was already coming to interpret as 'never', unless she pushed. Which she did, until finally her mother agreed to take her on a Saturday morning.

First, though, there came the ritual of Weekend Shopping.

Kate's mother had insisted that the best cuts of meat for her father's tea, and for Sunday lunch the next day (another ritual, equally sacred), would have gone by the time the film was over. So Kate had trailed around after her, agonising over each minute spent in the butcher's and greengrocer's as her mother intently considered each item before she either bought it or moved on to another.

By the time they arrived at the cinema the feature had already started, and Kate's mother refused to pay for something they wouldn't see all of. The ticket clerk suggested coming back for the later showing, but her mother was already drifting out, the attempt made, duty done.

They had gone home, where her mother had continued with the business of fretting over her father's tea. Kate watched as she chopped vegetables and carefully cut off every scrap of fat from the meat, so that her husband wouldn't have to face that chore himself when he ate it. Kate had waited until her mother was completely engrossed, and then quietly set off for the bus stop.

The ticket clerk, a florid woman with badly permed hair, had recognised her when she slid the money she had taken from her piggy bank through the hole in the glass screen.

'Let you come on your own, has she?' the woman asked, mouth tightening in disapproval.

Kate let her silence answer. The woman pushed her ticket through the slot.

'Don't deserve kids, some people,' Kate heard her mutter, as she went inside.

It was early evening when she arrived back home. Her parents were furious. Looking back, Kate supposed they must have been worried, but that didn't come through at the time. Only the anger. Her father had hit her and sent her to bed without anything to eat. Her mother, bewildered at her daughter's wilfulness, followed his example, as she always did. 'Your father's tea was ruined! Ruined! You *bad* girl!' she had hissed before closing the bedroom door.

Kate cried herself to sleep, hungry and with her father's handprint livid on the skin of her leg.

But she had still seen the film.

As she had grown older, the incident had passed into family lore, diluted and joked about, but never forgotten. 'Just took herself off, without a word to anyone,' her mother would say at family gatherings. 'Typical Kate. Even then she was always a stubborn little thing. Determined to do what she wanted.'

And, accepting the polite laughter, Kate would look at her mother and still see the perplexity in her eyes behind the social smile.

She wondered what her parents would say if they had been alive to see what she was doing now. She told the taxi driver to stop as soon as she saw the gas tank she'd been given as a landmark. She knew it was irrational, but she didn't want him to know where she was going. The driver, a middle-aged Indian man, spoke to her over his shoulder through the glass partition as she handed him the fare.

'Do you want a receipt?'

It was her suit, Kate thought, that and the leather briefcase, marking her as a businesswoman. She had worn them as camouflage, she saw now, a pretence that her visit was official, not personal.

'No, thanks.' She wanted only to be away from the taxi, with its musty odour of cigarettes and worn leather. She climbed out quickly onto the pavement, delaying over putting away her wallet and smoothing her skirt until the taxi pulled away with a rattle of blue exhaust. The fumes trailed in the still, warm air, dissipating slowly.

Squinting in the harsh sunlight, Kate looked around to get her bearings. The street was deserted. Nearby a newsagent's shop stood with a curtain of multi-coloured plastic strips hanging in its open doorway, swaying slightly. Further along was a garage, wooden doors pulled back to reveal a shadowed interior. The tinny echo of a radio came from inside, but there was no other sign of life.

The sun bore down on her shoulders. Its dry heat was hot on the back of her neck, contradicting the spring chill in the air. She could feel it pressing against her through the lightweight jacket as she began walking. The empty street made her feel as self-conscious as if she were on display.

The clinic was on the opposite side of the road to the gas tank. It was set slightly back from the pavement, with spaces for car parking in front. Flat-roofed and brick, it was as unprepossessing as a warehouse.

Kate felt a flutter of nerves as she approached. A single step led to glass-panelled double doors. On the wall at one side of them was a small white plastic sign. In plain black lettering it said, 'Department of Obstetrics and Gynaecology'.

What am I doing? The question jumped out at her with sudden clarity. She looked around, guiltily. But no one was watching. The street was still empty. The doors creaked as Kate pushed them open and went inside.

They swung shut behind her with a squeal. She stood in a small foyer. The floor was tiled with yellow vinyl squares, scuffed and pock-marked but clean. The place had the bottled-up smell of any public building. A sign saying 'Reception' pointed down a corridor. Kate hesitated a moment before following it.

The door to the reception office was slightly ajar. She knocked lightly on it and pushed it open. The two women in the room turned to look at her. One was middle-aged and sat behind a desk. The other was younger, and stood holding a folder.

'I'm . . . I have an appointment,' Kate said.

The younger woman smiled. 'Kate Powell, is it?' Without waiting for a reply she strode forward, her hand outstretched. Kate took it. 'I'm Maureen Turner. We spoke on the phone.'

Her manner was relaxed and friendly and, with a sudden inversion, the building no longer seemed quite so dingy and alien. Kate smiled back, relieved.

The woman spoke to the older one. 'We'll be in the end interview room, Peggy. Can you arrange for two teas to be sent in?' She turned to Kate again.

'Is tea all right? The coffee filter's on the blink, I'm afraid.'

'Tea's fine,' Kate answered, realising as she said it that she didn't really want anything. But the other woman was already walking out.

'It's just down here.'

Kate fell in step beside her. Their footsteps clicked on the tiled floor, slightly out of synchronisation. The woman opened a door at the far end, holding it open for Kate to precede her. Inside, it was hot and airless. Several low plastic armchairs were set around a wooden coffee table. It looked like a teachers' staff room, Kate thought.

The woman went to the big window and began wrestling to open it. 'I think we'll let some fresh air in before we start,' she said, straining against the window catch. 'Sit down, make yourself comfortable.'

Feeling anything but, Kate chose the nearest chair. Air leaked out of the plastic cushion in a slow hiss as she settled into it.

The window came open with a jerk, and the woman brushed her hands as she turned away from it.

'There. That's better.'

She sat down herself and gave Kate another smile. 'You found us without too much difficulty, then?'

'Yes, fine. I got a taxi from the tube station.'

'Probably wise. I'm not the best when it comes to directions.'

Kate smiled politely. She knew the small-talk was intended to put her at ease, but it was having the opposite effect. She felt her edginess returning.

The woman set her file on the low table between them. 'Are we the first clinic you've approached?'

'Yes, I got your number from my GP.' Kate hoped her nerves didn't show.

'So you haven't had any counselling on donor insemination before?'

'Uh, no, no I haven't.'

'Fine, that's no problem. Now—'

There was a rap on the door. It opened immediately and the older woman Kate had seen earlier came in, carrying a tray. There was a pause while she set it down and left. Kate fought the urge to fidget, answering yes to milk, no to sugar as the tea was poured and stirred. A cup and saucer was passed across. Kate took it and sipped, tasting nothing but heat and a faint sourness of milk. She put it down again.

The woman took a sip from her own cup before placing it on the table.

'To start with, as you know, I'm a counsellor, not a doctor, and this is just an introductory session. All that's going to happen today is that I'll tell you a little about donor insemination itself, and the legal aspects that are involved. Then, if you're still keen, we'll take a couple of blood samples for routine tests. But I'll come to that later. If you have any questions, or if there's anything you feel unsure about, feel free to stop me and ask.'

Kate nodded, not trusting her voice. She reached for her cup again, to give her hands something to do.

'Right, now, I gather you're unpartnered?' the counsellor continued.

'Is that a problem?' Kate set down the teacup without drinking.

'No, not at all. I know not all clinics will treat unpartnered women, but we try not to discriminate. However . . .' Kate stiffened as her expression became more sober '. . . we are required by the HFEA – that's the Human Fertilisation and Embryology Authority, the regulatory body – to take into account the welfare of the child. So later I'd like to talk about how you see yourself dealing with issues like combining work with raising a child, and the pros and cons of telling your child how it was conceived. Is that all right?'

Kate said it was. The words 'your child' rang in her head, so that she had to concentrate on responding.

'The insemination procedure itself is quite straightforward,' the counsellor went on. 'The sperm's kept frozen in straws, like a tiny drinking straw, until we need it. Then we use one of these . . .' she picked up a slender metal tube, which reminded Kate of a blunt-ended knitting needle, from the coffee table '. . . to introduce the sperm into the cervix.'

She smiled. 'We leave it to thaw out for a few minutes first. But that's basically all there is to it. It doesn't hurt, you don't need an anaesthetic, and there's no more risk of miscarriage than with a normal pregnancy. You don't even have to get undressed, except for your pants and tights. And you can carry on as normal afterwards just as you would after ordinary intercourse.'

Kate sat forward to examine the tube. Her nervousness was forgotten now. 'How do you know when to do it?'

'Obviously, it has to coincide with your ovulation cycle, which you'll be responsible for timing yourself. We'll double check ourselves when you come in for your treatment, to make sure the egg's about to be released. If it was, and we were satisfied everything was okay, we'd go ahead.'

'How many, uh, treatments does it usually take?'

'It varies. Some women become pregnant in the first cycle, but we can go up to nine. Other clinics might do more, but we take the view that if it hasn't worked by then, it probably isn't going to. And at three hundred pounds per cycle it wouldn't be fair to carry on indefinitely.'

She gave Kate an apologetic look. 'I should point out that as a single woman you won't be eligible for any help with costs from the NHS. You are aware of that, aren't you?'

Kate said she was. She hadn't expected any help anyway.

'In that case I'll move on to the donors themselves,' the counsellor said, and Kate felt some of her earlier nervousness return. 'To begin with, we screen every one for relevant medical and family history, and test them for HIV, hepatitis, and other sexually transmitted diseases. Then the sperm is frozen and stored for a minimum of six months, until a second HIV test has been carried out, to reduce the risk of infection.'

Kate had been listening intently. 'Are the donors all anonymous?'

'If you mean as far as you would be concerned, then yes. But of course their identity's known to the clinic.'

'But there's no way I could find out who it was? If I wanted to, I mean,' Kate persisted. She had gathered as much from the magazine article, but she wanted to be sure.

'Absolutely none. We're forbidden by law to reveal who they are.'

'But what if there's a mistake, or something goes wrong?'

The counsellor was clearly used to such anxieties. 'If we had any doubts about a donor, we wouldn't use them. That's why we check with their GP and carry out all the tests beforehand. But we have to protect their interests as well. It'd hardly be fair if they had to worry about the Child Support Agency knocking on their door in ten years' time. We can't disclose their identity any more than we can disclose yours. And I'm sure the last thing you'd want would be for some stranger to turn up and announce that he's the father of your child and wants visiting rights.'

'Has that ever happened?' Kate asked, alarmed.

'Not so far as I'm aware. But that's the whole point of the donors remaining anonymous, so that problems like that don't occur.'

Kate accepted that, but she still hesitated before asking the next question. 'How much would I know about the father?'

'It's better to think of them purely as the donor, not the father,' the counsellor corrected her, with a smile. 'We're allowed to divulge certain non-identifying information, such as their hair and eye colour, occupation and interests. But any more than that would risk infringing the donor's anonymity.'

'So who decides which donor to use? It isn't just a random selection, is it?'

'Oh, no! We only use donors from the same ethnic group as the recipient, and we try to get as close a match as possible as far as body type and colouring. Even blood group, if we can. We can't guarantee a perfect match, but we do our best.'

Despite the reassurance, Kate felt her unease growing. 'Supposing I didn't want the same physical type as me? Can I specify what sort of donor I want?'

'Well, we try to co-operate with your preferences within reason, but there are limitations. For one thing we only have a limited donor panel to choose from, so if we have to change the donor during treatment it might not be possible to find exactly the same physical type again.'

'You mean you might use more than one donor?' That was something the magazine article hadn't mentioned.

'We'd try not to, but sometimes it's unavoidable. If, for example, we ran out of samples by the donor we'd been using.' The counsellor's face grew concerned. 'You look as though you have a problem with that.'

Kate struggled against the growing tide of disillusionment. 'It's just that . . . well, I know the donor has to remain anonymous, but I thought I'd have more say in who it was. Or at least be told more about them. What sort of person they are. I didn't realise I'd have to let someone else decide for me.'

'I'm afraid we can't let people pick and choose to that extent,' the counsellor said. She sounded genuinely sympathetic. 'It isn't the same as a dating agency. There are strict guidelines we have to follow.'

Kate couldn't bring herself to look at the other woman. 'It still seems like I'd have to take an awful lot on faith, that's all.'

'We do vet the donors very carefully.'

'I know, it isn't that.' She shrugged, embarrassed. 'I just can't imagine having a child by someone I know so little about.'

The admission made her feel stupid and naïve, but she recognised the truth of it. She knew now that she could never accept having a child if she couldn't choose the father herself. She felt her face beginning to burn.

'I'm sorry,' she said. 'I've wasted your time.'

'Not at all. That's what these sessions are for. It's a big decision, and you need to be sure before you make it.'

'I suppose it's the same at every clinic?' Kate asked, without much hope.

'More or less. You certainly wouldn't be able to find out more information about the donors, wherever you went. Unless you go abroad, perhaps. The law might be different somewhere like America. I daresay you can even choose the donor's IQ and shoe size over there.'

Kate forced a smile. Even assuming that that was true, she couldn't afford either the time or the money to go to another country for treatment. She prepared to leave. But before she could, the counsellor, who had been watching her worriedly, seemed to reach a decision.

'Of course,' she said, carefully, 'some women don't bother with clinics at all.'

Her expression was guarded as she looked across at Kate.

'It isn't something I'd recommend, obviously. But you find that some lesbian couples, for instance, carry out DI on themselves because a lot of clinics refuse to treat them. They ask a male friend to be the donor.' She paused to let that sink in. 'It really isn't all that difficult when you think about it. All you need is a paper cup and a plastic syringe.'

Kate knew why the counsellor was telling her this, but she was too taken aback to say anything.

'I'm not suggesting anyone should try it, you understand,' the counsellor added quickly, seeing her expression. 'It would mean using fresh sperm, so there wouldn't be any of the legal or medical safeguards there'd be at a clinic. I just thought I'd mention it as a matter of interest.'

'Yes, but I don't think . . .'

'No, no, of course. I probably shouldn't have said anything.'

She clearly wished she hadn't. There was a silence. The counsellor sighed.

'Well, perhaps you'd like to have another think about what you want to do,' she said.

Depression settled on Kate as she waited at the tube station. When the train arrived, she sat in a window seat and stared out into the blackness of the tunnel. Her reflection in the glass would wink out when the train came to the sudden brightness of a platform, only to return again when the platform was left behind. At one stop, a sullen-looking young woman got on with a fractious baby. Kate watched as she hissed a warning to the child, giving it a quick shake, which did nothing but make it cry harder. After that, the young woman ignored it, staring into space as if the squalling infant on her knee wasn't there.

Kate looked away.

She came out of King's Cross into the weak afternoon sun and made her way to the agency. The burned-out warehouse was still standing, although the lower-floor windows had been boarded up. Its blackened roof timbers stood out against the blue sky like steepled fingers, and a faint scent of charred wood lingered around it. Kate had almost grown used to the blackened shell, but now she walked past quickly, like a child hurrying by a graveyard.

She threw herself into her work as best she could for the rest of the day, succeeding in holding back the disappointment for a little while, at least. But it was still there waiting for her. With a sense of dread she heard the others preparing to go home, and knew it couldn't be avoided for much longer. She was still trying to, even so, when Clive came up to her office.

'We're going for a quick drink,' he said. 'Do you fancy coming?'

'Oh . . . thanks, but I think I'll skip it for tonight.'

Clive nodded, but didn't go out. 'Look, don't mind me asking, but are you all right?'

'Fine. Why?'

'You just seem a bit preoccupied lately.'

The impulse to tell him almost won out. 'It's probably trying to guess what quibble Redwood's going to come up with next,' she said, lightly. 'Thanks for asking, but I'm fine, really.'

He looked at her for a second or two, then accepted it. 'Okay. See you tomorrow.'

Kate said goodnight. Clive went back downstairs, and a little while later the front door slammed. In its aftermath, the office sank into the hollow quiet of an empty building. She tried to continue working, but found herself listening to the stillness until it seemed to be soaking into her. She cleared her desk and went home.

The sun was setting when Kate arrived at her flat. As she went down the path, she took her keys quietly from her bag, hoping to get in for once without being intercepted by Miss Willoughby. But as she reached out to unlock the front door, it swung open of its own accord.

Cautiously Kate pushed it open the rest of the way. The door to her flat was still closed and unmarked, she saw with relief, and afterwards she would recall with guilt that her first concern had been a selfish one. Then she saw that the old lady's door was ajar.

'Miss Willoughby?' Warily, she stepped into the entrance hall and knocked on the half-open door. 'Hello?'

Silence greeted her. Kate gave the door a gentle nudge. The flat's hallway yawned in front of her. At the far end a doorway led into what looked like the lounge. A noise was coming from it, a low murmuring, indistinct but constant.

'Miss Willoughby? Are you there?'

There was no answer. Kate stood uncertainly, not sure whether to close the front door or not, torn between wanting a quick means of escape and not wanting anyone else to walk in. Finally, she shut it. Then she went into the old lady's flat.

WHERE THERE'S SMOKE

A fusty smell of boiled vegetables and camphor, a distillation of old age, closed around her. Kate slowly made her way down the hallway towards the lounge. She stopped just before she reached it, suddenly struck by the absurdity of what she was doing, wondering if she shouldn't simply run upstairs and call the police. But the silence of the place mocked that as cowardice. She stepped forward and pushed open the lounge door.

The noise she had heard came from the television, playing a quiz show at low volume in one corner. Light from it flickered over the dark Edwardian furniture, and over the parlour palms, aspidistras and rubber plants that filled the room. Their profusion was so great that it took Kate a moment to see that the drawers on the old bureau were pulled out. The cupboard doors of a sideboard were also open, their contents strewn untidily on the floor.

'Miss Willoughby?'

There was a low moan. Kate turned to where it came from and saw a pair of thin, stockinged legs sticking out from behind the drop-leaf table.

She ran over to them.

The old lady was lying on her back. Her head was turned sideways, and her forehead and cheeks were smeared with blood that looked like black oil in the dim room. One eye was swollen shut. The wig she always wore had slipped off, exposing a bony scalp covered with thin strands of white hair. She looked like a baby bird fallen from the nest.

The eye that wasn't swollen flickered open as Kate crouched beside her. She muttered something indistinct.

'Don't try to talk,' Kate told her, frightened that the effort would cause the ragged breathing to slow and stop. She looked wildly around, both for a telephone and to make sure that no one was behind her. But there was neither. She hesitated a moment longer. Then, as the eye slid shut and the voice slurred into silence, she turned and ran upstairs.

CHAPTER 5

The running machine whirred at a higher pitch as Kate stabbed her finger on the touchpad to increase its speed. The rubber belt of the treadmill whipped away from under her feet, almost throwing her off it. She picked up her pace, arms and legs pumping, chest heaving as she went into the final sprint.

Of all the equipment in the gym, Kate liked this the best. There was something faintly absurd about running as fast as you could without actually getting anywhere, like a hamster on a wheel. It was exercise reduced to its most basic, most pointless form, yet she still found it satisfying. Its repetitive nature relaxed her, loosened the kinks in her mind.

In the early post-Paul days, she had tried different types of meditative techniques, from simple deep-breathing to yoga. She had abandoned them all, finding the effort of sitting still too taxing. But pounding away the miles on the treadmill, Kate found she could pass whole chunks of time either thinking about nothing at all, or concentrating on a particular problem while her body exercised itself.

It didn't help now, though. There seemed too many strands, all plucking her in different directions at once. She had slept badly after finding the old lady the night before. The hospital had told her that morning that, as well as suffering from severe shock, Miss Willoughby had a broken hip, broken wrist and concussion. From what the police could gather, two youths, one white, one black, had knocked on her door claiming that one had been taken ill. Once inside, they had punched her and then ransacked every drawer in the flat. Probably looking for money for drugs, the police had said.

Kate hammered away on the treadmill, trying to burn away some of her anger and disgust. Her emotional landscape was clouded enough as it was after the visit to the clinic. She was still unable to reconcile herself to the idea of becoming pregnant by someone she knew virtually nothing about. She had tried telling herself that there was no option, that if she was serious about having a child she would be happy to abide by the clinic's rules, and the clinic's choice.

But she couldn't accept that, either.

The running machine beeped as the programmed time elapsed. She stabbed at the touchpad again, reducing the speed until she was running at a gentle jog. She continued for a few more minutes at that pace, then gradually slowed the treadmill to a stop and stepped off. Her breathing was deep and heavy, but not laboured. She went to the water cooler and drank two paper cupfuls before going into the changing room and stripping off her sweat-soaked leotard. The shower jets peppered her face as she held it up to the spray. She waited until it stung, then turned off the stream and went into the wooden box of the sauna.

The dry heat wrapped itself over her like a hot towel. The scorched air, spicy with the smell of baked pine, pricked the inside of her nose when she breathed. Another woman was sitting on the lower of the three benches, sweat running off her. She offered Kate a smile as she closed the door and stepped up to the highest bench. Kate returned it and spread her towel on the hot slats before she sat down.

The heat bore into her. She settled back, gingerly letting her shoulders touch the hot wooden panelling. Almost immediately she could feel the water from the shower dry on her skin, and be replaced with perspiration. Through the wall, she could feel the pulse of a distant generator. Other than that, the sauna was dark and silent, separate from the world outside. She closed her eyes and let herself drift.

'Best part of it, this, isn't it?'

Kate opened her eyes and gave the woman an acknowledging smile, but said nothing. She wasn't in the mood for conversation. The woman, though, apparently was.

'Do you mind if I put some water on the stones?'

Kate opened her eyes again. 'No, go ahead.'

The woman rose from the bench and went to the wooden bucket by the brazier. She took the ladle from it and poured water on the hot grey rocks. Steam gushed from them with a hiss, and Kate felt a wave of heat hit her. The woman sat down again on the lower bench. She was about Kate's age but heavily built, with large, low-hanging breasts and a loose, flabby stomach. When she leaned back, Kate saw the red striations of stretch marks running across her belly.

'Two more minutes and I think I'm done,' the woman said, amiably. She puffed out her cheeks and wiped a strand of damp hair from her forehead. 'You feel as if you've sweated about a stone off just from sitting here, don't you?'

'I wish,' Kate said. The woman glanced at her and cocked an eyebrow.

'You don't look as though you need to.' She patted her

stomach. The flesh of it wobbled like suet. 'It's when you get one of these that you've got to worry. I was expecting to snap back into shape after I'd given birth.' She grinned. 'Fat chance.'

'What did you have? A girl or boy?' Kate's disinclination to talk had vanished. She tried to keep her eyes on the woman's face, but the flaccid stomach held a morbid fascination for her.

'Both. Twins, six months old, now. We'd got it all planned, we were going to wait until we were thirty and then just have one.' She chuckled. 'So much for planning. And to add insult to injury I've got this as a reminder.'

She nodded down at the folds of flesh. 'They call it an apron, would you believe? The doctors have told me I can have plastic surgery, but I thought I'd try and work it off first. I feel like telling everybody, "I'm not really fat! This isn't my fault!"' She laughed again. 'Well, I suppose it is. Serves me right for having kids in the first place. I just wish they'd warned me I could end up looking like this. I might have had second thoughts.'

'Do you think you would? Really?' Kate asked. She felt a twinge of unease, not so much from the idea of her own body changing, as the thought of regret afterwards.

The woman wiped sweat from her forehead. 'No, not really. You know what you're getting into, don't you? But if I were you I'd make the most of a flat stomach while you've got it. It's never the same afterwards, I don't care what anyone says.'

She stopped and suddenly regarded Kate. 'Don't tell me you *have* got kids?'

Kate was glad her face was already flushed from the heat. 'No. Not yet.'

The woman laughed again. 'Thank goodness for that. I'd have thought life really *was* unfair then!'

She stood up. Her stomach hung in front of her like a deflated beachball.

'Well, that's enough for me. 'Bye.'

Kate smiled as the woman left the sauna. Cool air swirled briefly against her as the door was opened and shut, then the heat closed in again. She looked down at her own stomach, taut and unlined, and tried to imagine it flabby and loose.

She closed her eyes again and tried to relax, but the post-exercise mood was broken. When another woman entered the sauna, Kate went out to shower and dress.

The hospital was only two tube stops away from the gym. She went through the automatic doors into the clinical atmosphere of overheated air and disinfectant with a familiar sense of apprehension. First her father, then her mother had died in hospital. Her father had lingered in a coma for weeks after being knocked down, and after that her mother had sunk into a gradual fade that ended less than a year later in the same intensive care unit, as her reluctant heart finally gave up. Since then, the long corridors and harshly lit waiting rooms of any hospital seemed to Kate like a separate world, a surprise cul-de-sac from normal life where death and bad news waited. As she went into the lift, it occurred to her that maternity hospitals were an exception. The thought cheered her, briefly, before the lift doors closed.

The ward was long, with a central aisle running between parallel rows of beds, like a barracks. Walking down it, Kate almost went past Miss Willoughby without recognising her. One side of the old lady's face was a livid bruise, with stitches cutting across her forehead and cheek. The eye that had been swollen shut the night before was now the size and colour of a Victoria plum, startlingly vivid against the pale flesh and white wisps of hair. Her wig had been left behind when they had loaded her into the ambulance the night before, and without it she looked shrunken and robbed of identity.

Kate stared at her from the bottom of the bed, shocked despite having told herself what to expect. The old lady was asleep, and Kate felt an urge to turn round and leave. But as she was wrestling with the temptation, Miss Willoughby stirred, and her single good eye slid open.

Kate forced herself to sound cheerful. 'Hello, there!'

The old lady looked at her without recognition. Then a slow smile lit up her face. 'You shouldn't have bothered to come.'

Her voice was slow and drowsy with painkillers. She made a feeble attempt to push herself up on her pillows, but it amounted to little.

Kate held out the bunch of flowers she had brought. 'I hope you like carnations.' As she said it she saw that the old lady couldn't take them with her wrist strapped up. 'I'll put them in water.'

There were several empty vases by a sink at the end of the ward. Kate arranged the flowers in one and took them back to Miss Willoughby's bed. A burst of laughter came from the bed opposite, where a group of half a dozen or so visitors were clustered around an elderly woman. She was sitting propped up by pillows, surrounded with cards and flowers. Kate set down the vase on Miss Willoughby's bedside cabinet. There was nothing else on it except for a water jug and glass.

'So, how are you?' she asked, aware that question was inane, but unable to think of anything else to say.

'Not too bad.' It was an effort for the old lady to keep her eye open. Her mouth worked as if she was thirsty. 'They've pinned my hip, so that's all right. My eye hurts a little, though.'

Kate looked at the swollen flesh of her face. It made the back of her legs creep. 'Can you remember what happened?'

A slow frown crossed the old lady's face. 'I can remember two young men coming to the door. Boys. They were very polite. One of them felt ill . . . He wanted a drink of water, so I let them in. I started to ask if they wanted tea, but . . . I think one of them must have pushed me . . .'

Kate couldn't bring herself to say anything. Miss Willoughby moved her head slightly from side to side in a tired shake.

'I can't understand it . . . I used to teach, but it wasn't like this . . . I'd got nothing for them to steal. Why do this for a few pounds?'

'I didn't know you were a teacher,' Kate said quickly, seeing her growing upset. The old woman's frown faded as older memories replaced the more recent one.

'I taught for nearly forty years. At the same school. Girls.'

Her eye slipped shut, and Kate thought she'd fallen asleep. But a moment later she spoke again. 'You wonder where it goes to, the time.'

She did doze for a while then. Another burst of laughter

came from the group opposite. Kate looked over at the sprawl of generations, from the elderly woman in the bed to a toddler a girl was helping to balance on the foot of it. A middle-aged woman saw Kate looking over and smiled. Kate smiled back and looked away.

She quietly pushed back her chair and stood up, but Miss Willoughby's eye twitched open again.

'I'd better get off,' Kate said, feeling as if she had been caught out. But the old lady only nodded.

'Thank you for coming.' Her voice was more drowsy than ever. 'Lovely to see you.'

Kate felt a prick of conscience. 'I'll come again. Is there anything you'd like bringing? Or anyone you want me to phone? To tell them where you are?'

'No. No one, thank you.' A worried expression crossed her face. 'My plants, though . . . They're due for watering . . .'

'Don't worry. I'll look after them.'

The old lady looked relieved. 'I think the key's in there . . .' Her unbandaged hand jerked towards the cabinet. Kate opened it and found a key ring on top of Miss Willoughby's clothes.

'I'll come again soon,' she said, but the old lady gave no sign of having heard. Kate made her way out. At the entrance to the ward she looked back. The visitors surrounding the other bed were also getting ready to leave, slipping on coats in a torrent of goodnights. The elderly woman kissed them all in turn. A few feet away, Miss Willoughby lay alone. The solitary vase of carnations on the bare cabinet looked as stark as an exclamation mark.

Kate went down the corridor to the lifts.

CHAPTER 6

A s soon as she saw Lucy Kate could tell that something was wrong. They had arranged to meet at lunchtime in the park, where they could have a sandwich from the snack bar while Angus played. But as she approached the bench where Lucy sat, she could see that her face was flushed behind her sunglasses, her blonde hair even more unkempt than usual. Emily was at nursery school, and Angus sat alone on the grass in front of his mother, bleary-eyed and snuffling in the aftermath of recent tears as he half-heartedly played with a toy fire engine.

The child looked at Kate through wet lashes, unsmilingly, as she greeted him and sat beside Lucy on the bench. She had been almost bursting with her own news, but now she pushed it forcibly into the background.

'What's been going on?' she asked.

Lucy gave a terse shake of her head. Through the dark screen of the sunglasses, her eyes were all but obscured.

'Don't ask. He's feeling sorry for himself because he's had a slap.'

Angus regarded his mother tearfully. Kate looked with surprise from the red handprint on his chubby leg to Lucy. Lucy's reprimands were usually no more than stern words, and even they were rare.

73

'What did he do?' she asked. 'Murder somebody?'

It was meant to lighten the situation, but Lucy's mouth tightened as she glared at her son. 'Practically. We were by the pond and this little girl came up to him, just wanting to play, so he hit her on the head with his fire engine.'

Kate's mouth twitched, but it was obvious that Lucy wasn't in a laughing mood. 'He didn't hurt her, did he?'

'Of course he hurt her!' Lucy leaned towards him, raising her voice. 'You made her head bleed, didn't you? You bad boy!'

Angus began to cry again, covering his eyes with pudgy hands.

'Oh, Lucy . . .' Kate said.

'Don't feel sorry for him! Bullies don't deserve it!' The last was addressed to her son again. Still sobbing, he clambered to his feet and tottered towards them, arms outstretched.

'No, I don't want you,' Lucy said, as he approached her. 'I don't have anything to do with bullies.'

With a heartbroken wail, the little boy turned and buried his head on Kate's legs. She could feel him quivering with the force of his sobs, and knowing Lucy wouldn't like it but unable to help herself, she reached down and picked him up. His small body was heavy and solid, radiating heat. He settled against her, burying his face against her neck. It felt hot and wet.

'Come on, Lucy,' she said, over his head. 'Don't you think you're going a bit over the top?'

Lucy didn't say anything for a moment, then some of the tension seemed to ebb from her. 'Okay. Give him here.'

Sensing his mother's change in mood, Angus turned to her, holding out his arms. Lucy heaved him from Kate and set him on her knee. Kate felt a momentary sense of loss as the child was taken from her. She watched the little boy snuggle against his mother.

'Are you sorry now?' Lucy asked, but the bite had left her voice. 'You're not going to be a bully again, are you?'

Angus shook his head, hiccuping as his sobs began to subside. Lucy smoothed his damp hair off his forehead and gave Kate a rueful smile.

'You've got snot on your shoulder.'

Kate wiped it off with a tissue. She could still feel the weight of the child's body against her, like ghost pains after an amputation.

'So what's really the matter?' she asked.

Light sparked off Lucy's sunglasses, hiding her eyes. 'One of Jack's clients has just gone bust. Owing us ten thousand.' She broke off, looking out over the park. 'We can't afford to lose that sort of money. And Jack's just upgraded all his hardware for the business.' She gave a shake of her head, still not looking at Kate. 'I don't know what we're going to do. We might have to sell the house.'

'Oh, Lucy, no!'

Lucy shrugged. 'It might not come to that. Jack's gone to see the bank today. But if they turn sludgy . . .' She didn't bother to finish.

Kate quickly ran through her own financial situation. 'I might be able to lend you something. Not ten thousand, but it might help tide you over. So you can keep the house.' She knew how much Lucy and Jack loved their home. If they had to sell, they would never have anywhere like it again.

Lucy smiled, bleakly. 'Thanks, Kate. I appreciate it,

but ... well, let's see what the bank says, shall we?' She took a deep breath. 'You can imagine that I wasn't in the best of moods to start with, though. And when this little monster ...' she gave Angus a squeeze '... turned into Hannibal Lecter, it just capped things off nicely.'

She gave a grin. 'Anyway, so much for my traumas. How's your neighbour?'

'About the same.' Kate had visited Miss Willoughby again, but the old lady didn't seem to have improved.

'Have the police caught the sods who did it?'

'Not yet. She hasn't been able to give very good descriptions, so unless they catch them doing something else it isn't very hopeful.'

Lucy shook her head. 'God, doesn't it make you seethe, though? They want birching! An old woman in her eighties, and on her own too! What a way to end up.'

Kate was silent. She thought about the old lady's flat, bare of family mementoes. The only photographs on display were formal, framed ones of a school, fading pictures of Miss Willoughby with other people's children, all long since grown-up. She wondered if any of them ever remembered their old teacher. Loneliness was the smell of cooked cabbage and old age.

'I've found a clinic,' she said.

Lucy looked startled at the change in tack. 'What?'

'I've found a clinic. To carry out the donor insemination.'

'I thought you'd given up on that idea?'

'No. I just didn't like the thought of an anonymous donor. But I phoned the HFEA, and they said that although clinics have to keep their own donors' identity confidential, there are some that'll let you use a "known donor" instead. Someone that you know, that you've picked yourself.'

'Like who?' Lucy sounded appalled.

'I don't know yet.' It was enough for the moment that she knew it was possible.

'For God's sake, Kate, I thought the whole idea was that you didn't *want* the father involved!'

'I still don't, but that doesn't mean I don't care who he is.'

'Yes, but the point is he'll know who *you* are as well, won't he? I thought an anonymous donor was bad enough, but at least then you don't have to worry about what he's going to do afterwards! Supposing he changes his mind and decides it's his baby as much as yours? You're leaving yourself open for all *sorts* of problems!'

'Not if I'm careful who I choose. And he'll only have the same standing as an ordinary donor. He won't be recognised as the legal father, so he won't have any rights to custody or anything. I'll just have to make sure that's clear from the start.'

Lucy bit off whatever she had been going to say. 'So have you actually found a clinic that'll do it?'

'There's one in Birmingham—'

'Birmingham!'

'I know it's a long way, but they seem pretty good.' That wasn't the only reason. Kate had phoned a good portion of the clinics listed in the HFEA's brochure – including the one she had already been to – before eventually finding one that was prepared both to treat a single woman and use a known donor.

Lucy was tight-lipped with silent criticism. 'So what do you do now?'

'I've made an appointment to see the counsellor. I suppose I'll take it from there.'

Angus had begun to fidget. Lucy slid him off her knee. Sniffling, he tottered back to his fire engine. 'Don't you think this is all getting a bit out of hand?'

'Why? You said yourself there was no harm in talking to somebody about it.'

'Yes, but you've already done that.' Lucy watched Angus sit down heavily on the grass and pick up the red plastic toy. 'This isn't just talking any more, is it? You're acting like you're planning to actually go ahead with it.'

'You mean you thought I wasn't serious.' Kate heard the acerbic note creep into her voice.

'No, but . . .' Lucy stopped.

'What?'

'It doesn't matter.'

'Yes, it does. What?'

Lucy sighed, as though she found the entire subject tiresome. 'Well, I just know what you're like. If you get your mind set on anything, you're like a dog with a bone. You won't let go, and I can see this turning into something like that. Another "project" you've got to see through. And I think you're making a big mistake.'

Kate could feel the blood rushing to her cheeks. 'And that's all it is, is it? Another project?'

Lucy wore the expression of someone who wanted to talk about something else, but wasn't prepared to let go of their point. 'No, I'm not saying that's *all* it is, but—'

'Yes, you are!' Kate could feel the last strings of her temper slipping through her fingers. 'You act like this is just some sort of – of *whim* you can talk me out of!'

A flush had begun to creep up Lucy's neck to her cheeks, which were still red from earlier. 'Look, Kate, it's your life. If you're serious about wanting a baby like this, then I'm not stopping you. But I still think you're digging a hole for yourself, and you're not going to get me to change my mind, so you might as well stop whingeing on about it.'

The words hung in the air between them. The silence grew, broken by distant laughter in the park and the sound of Angus pulling the fire engine's ladder up, then down.

'I'd better go,' Kate said.

Lucy gave a terse nod. Neither of them mentioned the lunch they were supposed to be having. Kate walked away without looking back.

Her anger barely diminished during the tube ride back to the agency. Even there the conversation still left her raw enough to snap at Caroline for failing to find a file quickly enough. She went upstairs to her office. It was stuffy and close, so she opened a window and turned on the fan before sitting down to work.

The breeze from the fan stroked her face as she called up the Parker Trust file. But the concentration wouldn't come. She found herself either staring out of the window or doodling on her notepad while the laptop's curser blinked, waiting. When the phone rang, she answered it, irritatedly.

It was Lucy. 'Sorry,' she said. 'I shouldn't have had a go at you.'

Kate's sense of umbrage lingered a moment longer, then collapsed. 'It's okay. I was a bit touchy myself.'

'Fancy coming round for dinner some time this week? We

can have a proper talk then. And I promise I won't let Jack anywhere near the kitchen.'

Smiling, Kate accepted, glad the near-argument had been patched up before it could begin to fester. But Lucy's words stayed with her, pricking at her thoughts like a splinter.

Am I doing the right thing?

There was a commotion from downstairs. Kate hoped a drunk hadn't wandered in. It sometimes happened. She pushed herself back from her desk, and as she did so the raised voices were drowned by sudden thuds and bangs. There was a scream, and then Kate was out of her office and running downstairs.

The door at the bottom of the stairs opened before she reached it and Caroline ran out. From behind her it sounded as though the office was being wrecked.

'They're fighting! They're fighting!' Caroline yelled, wide-eyed. Kate pushed past her. Josefina was at the other side of the office, white-faced. A desk was tipped on its side. Chairs were scattered, and in the middle of the room two figures wrestled. One was Clive. The other was Paul.

'Stop it!' she shouted. They took no notice. Clive flicked her a quick glance, and then grunted as they slammed into a filing cabinet. It rocked, almost falling. Kate ran down to the basement kitchen. A heavy red fire-extinguisher was clipped to the wall. She tugged it free and staggered back upstairs with it. There was another crash from the office. The two men had fallen onto a second desk, still clutching each other. Hugging the extinguisher under one arm, she pointed the nozzle at them and set it going. A jet of water shot out, and Kate moved nearer, directing it into their faces. They spluttered, shielding their eyes, but Kate kept it on them until they broke apart.

'Get away from him, Clive!' she ordered, still keeping the spray on them. Clive hesitated. 'I said get away! Now!'

Reluctantly, Clive moved back. Kate struggled to turn the extinguisher off. The water finally died to a dribble, then stopped. She glared at where Paul and Clive stood, both panting, water plastering their shirts to their chests and dripping off their faces. Around them, the office was in turmoil. At least one chair was broken, and a leg had snapped off the desk they had overturned. Kate glared at them.

'What the *bloody* hell do you think you're doing?' She was shaking, not from fear but with an incandescent anger.

Paul wiped water from his face. One cheek was swollen. He pointed at Clive, sullenly. 'I came to see you, and this prick wouldn't let me!'

'He came in drunk and tried to barge upstairs,' Clive snapped, staring at him. Paul turned towards him again, and before they could restart the fight Kate moved between them.

'Get over there, Clive. Go on.'

Still glowering at the other man, Clive moved across to the other side of the office, where Josefina and Caroline, who had ventured back in, huddled. Kate confronted Paul.

'Well, I'm here! What do you want?'

He seemed deflated by her aggression. It took him a moment to pump up his anger enough to answer. 'I came to give you some good news!' he said, face twisting. 'I've been fired! Satisfied, now, are you?'

Kate felt a pang of sympathy. And guilt, she admitted.

She stamped down on both. 'I'm sorry you've lost your job, Paul. But it's nothing to do with me.'

'No?' He gave a bitter laugh. 'I bet you're heartbroken, though, aren't you, you backstabbing bitch?'

Clive started forward. She shot him a look, stopping him, and turned back to face Paul. Her anger had burned down to a weary impatience.

'I'm going to put this as simply as I can,' she said, trying to speak levelly. 'I'm not interested in you, your job, or your problems. You got yourself fired because you're a self-pitying drunk who always has to blame someone else. I don't want to see you again, I don't want to hear from you again, and I don't want to talk to you again. Now get out of my office before I call the police.'

Paul blinked. He glanced around, and for the first time seemed to notice that other people were watching. He looked bewildered, as though he didn't understand how he came to be there. Then he drew himself up and stared at her.

'You wait. You just wait.' He nodded to himself as he went to the door. 'You just fucking wait.'

He went out, slamming the door. It bounced back on its hinges and swung open again. Kate watched, half expecting him to reappear, but he didn't. She could feel herself beginning to tremble as reaction set in. She looked around the wreckage of the office and felt a lump form in her throat.

'I'm sorry, Kate. It all got a bit out of hand.'

Clive looked shame-faced. He was still soaking wet. Kate saw that his lip was bleeding.

'Are you okay?' she asked.

He touched his hand to his mouth and gave a weak

grin. 'I think so. Been a long time since I've been in a scrap.'

'It wasn't Clive's fault,' Caroline said, coming forward. 'He just tried to stop him when he started going upstairs. Clive didn't start it.'

Kate nodded and managed to give Clive a smile. 'No, I know. But in future—'

The window behind her shattered. She ducked as broken glass struck the back of her head and shoulders, and glimpsed something flying past. She looked up in time to see Clive race to the door and tear it open.

'No, Clive! *Clive!*' she shouted. He stopped, poised on the doorstep. 'Let him go.'

Clive hesitated, then closed the door. Glass crunched under his feet. Kate looked at the window. The vertical blind was hanging half off. Where the name of the company had been stencilled on the glass, now there was only a jagged hole.

There was a moan. Kate turned around and saw Josefina clutching her arm, her face screwed up in pain. Caroline was supporting her, looking if anything even more stricken.

'She got hit by that,' she said, nodding at a half housebrick on the floor.

Kate went over. The Spanish girl slowly removed her hand to reveal a bloody gash on her forearm. Josefina sucked in air with a hiss and sat down.

'It only just missed your head,' Clive said, giving Kate a grim look.

The back of her neck prickled as she remembered how close the sharp-cornered housebrick had come. She pushed the thought aside.

'Get the first aid box, will you?' she told him. 'I'll phone the police.'

Kate cleared up the wreckage of the office by herself after the police had taken their statements and left. Clive had gone to the hospital with Josefina, and she had sent Caroline home early. The girl was too shaken to be of any use, and Kate didn't really want any help anyway. Setting the office to rights was a sort of penance for letting her private life spill over into business.

It took longer than she'd expected, though, and by the time she arrived at her flat that evening she felt exhausted. She poured herself a glass of wine and put some pasta on to boil, before remembering that she'd told Miss Willoughby she would visit her.

Kate looked at her watch. She could still make it before visiting time ended, and she knew the old lady would be expecting her. But the thought of turning out again was too much. With the relief from making the decision only slightly tinged with guilt, she phoned the hospital and was put through to the ward sister.

'I was supposed to be visiting Miss Willoughby tonight,' Kate told her. 'Can you give her my apologies and tell her I'll see her tomorrow instead?'

The sister hesitated. 'Are you a relative?'

'No, just her neighbour.' She guessed from the sister's tone, but still asked, 'Is everything all right?'

'I'm afraid Miss Willoughby died last night.'

Kate felt no real surprise, only a tired sadness. 'What happened?'

'It was heart failure. It was very quick. There's always a

risk at that age, and after the sort of shock she'd had . . .' The sister didn't bother to finish. 'Actually, I'm glad you've called,' she went on, bad news delivered. 'She put down her solicitor as next of kin, but we're not sure what to do with her personal effects. Do you know if she had any friends or relatives?'

'No,' Kate said. 'No, she didn't have anybody.'

CHAPTER 7

It was late afternoon when the train arrived back at Euston. Kate stepped down from the carriage and made her way with the few other travellers towards the exit. Their footsteps echoed in a complicated cross-rhythm. It was strangely deserted on the hot Saturday. With the sunlight suffusing through the high windows, it assumed a hushed, almost dream-like quality, and Kate remembered her anxiety dream of being lost in a crowded station. Now, though, as she walked through the almost empty concourse, she knew exactly what she was doing.

She caught a taxi outside the station. It was an extravagance when the tube was almost as convenient, but she didn't care. She gave the driver Lucy and Jack's address and sat back, feeling her body hum with barely suppressed exuberance.

The taxi dropped her outside the house. She struggled with the gate, which was almost as dysfunctional as hers, and went up the path. After a moment Lucy answered the door, wiping her hands on a towel.

'So how was Birmingham?' she asked, standing back to let Kate inside.

'Oh . . . okay.'

Lucy cocked an eyebrow. 'Judging by the look on your face it went better than okay.' She closed the door. 'Go straight through. We're out back. I'll be with you in a minute.'

She went upstairs. As Kate began to go down the hallway, Lucy leaned over the banister that fronted the first-floor landing. 'And keep an eye on what Jack's up to with the barbecue, will you? He pretends he knows what he's doing, but he hasn't a clue.'

The warped french windows in the lounge were thrown open. Beyond them, the garden was overgrown and unkempt. Someone had made a token effort to cut the grass, trimming a shaved square in the centre of the ankle-deep lawn. Over one corner of the high, crumbling brick wall that screened the house from its neighbours hung the heavy branches of a laburnum.

Emily and Angus ran up to Kate as soon as she went out. Emily, older and more shy, presented her face for a kiss, but Angus, still unsteady on his feet, demanded to be picked up. His mouth was orange from the ice-lolly he clutched in one fist.

Jack was standing by a home-built barbecue, made from bricks. Smoke crept up from the grey-black lumps of charcoal, jerking back and forth as he fanned it vigorously with a piece of wood. He wore a grubby white T-shirt, and his hairy legs stuck out from beneath a pair of knee-length shorts. He grinned at her, red-faced and sweating.

'How you doing, Kate? Grab a beer. Or there's wine in the kitchen, if you want it.'

'Beer's fine, thanks.' Setting Angus down, she went to the plastic cooler beside the barbecue and took out a chilled bottle. She opened it and drank. She hadn't realised how thirsty she was until she tasted the cold liquid.

'Look at you, dressed up to the nines, and swigging beer from a bottle,' Lucy said, as she came through the french windows. 'Oh, God, you've let Angus near you. There's orange lolly all over your skirt.'

Kate glanced down at the stains on the cream-coloured fabric. There was a smear on her sleeveless white top, too. She didn't care. 'It doesn't matter.'

Lucy regarded her. 'My, it *must* have gone well!' She led Kate over to a table and plastic chairs, clustered in the shade of the overhanging laburnum. Emily went with them.

'Go and help Daddy, Emily, there's a good girl,' Lucy told her.

'Angus can help Daddy,' the little girl said, climbing on a chair next to Kate.

'Angus'll get in the way. Go on, you'll have all evening to pester Kate, but Mummy just wants to talk to her now.'

With a *moue* of disappointment, Emily slid off the chair and trudged over to the barbecue.

'I don't mind her staying,' Kate said.

'No, but I do. I've not told her the facts of life yet, and I don't want her suddenly asking what "insemination" means in the middle of Tesco's.' Lucy settled back in her chair. 'So. What happened?'

Kate tried to sound blasé. 'They told me there's no problem.'

'Just like that?'

'More or less. I've got to wait for the results of the blood tests and everything,' she held out her left arm, displaying the plaster the nurse had put over the needle mark, 'but assuming they're okay I can go ahead.'

'And they're willing to use whoever you pick for the donor?'

'They say so, yes.'

Lucy's face showed what she thought of that. 'So they'll basically impregnate anybody who asks, then.'

'Of course they don't.' Kate felt her mood touched by irritation. 'Particularly not anyone single, like me. You have to satisfy them that you're capable of bringing up a child on your own. Emotionally as well as financially. And they wanted to know how I'd cope with working and being a mother.'

The word 'mother' sent a thrill through her. It seemed to take on a whole new context. She cleared her throat. 'I told her – the counsellor – that for a lot of the time I could probably work from home, or even take the baby to the office with me. Then, later, I'd have to think about finding a nursery for some of the time.'

Lucy gave a snort. 'You haven't even had the poor mite yet and already you're farming it out.'

'I'm being realistic. You'd be the first to criticise me if I wasn't. Anyway, the counsellor was satisfied, and they take the child's welfare pretty seriously.'

'So that's it, then? You're going ahead?'

Kate looked away from Lucy's interrogative stare, watching Emily and Angus as they played near their father. 'I don't know. I haven't made up my mind.'

'Are you sure?'

She tried to sidestep the question. 'It's no good deciding anything until I get the results of the tests.'

She could feel Lucy watching her. After a moment Lucy sighed. 'What's this place like, anyway?'

Kate took a colour brochure from her bag and handed it across the table. Lucy studied the photograph of the tree-shrouded building on the cover.

'"The Wynguard Clinic,"' she read. 'Well, that's certainly not NHS, is it?'

'No, it's private.' Kate told herself there was no reason to feel defensive. 'They don't just do DI, though. They carry out all sorts of fertility treatments. And they've got a fully equipped maternity unit.'

It had been a far cry from the first clinic she had visited, air-conditioned and carpeted. Lucy's mouth turned down slightly at the corners as she flicked through the brochure.

'So what's this going to cost you, then?'

Kate noticed that Lucy spoke as if the decision was already made. She didn't correct her. 'It's a bit more than the other place.'

'How much more?'

Kate felt her face going red. 'It's . . . er, five hundred. A cycle.'

Lucy's head came up from the brochure. 'Five hundred *pounds*? Each time you have it *done*?'

Kate nodded, uncomfortably.

'Christ!'

'It isn't that bad, really. You know, considering how few places actually do it. They give you two inseminations per cycle. And they'll continue the treatment for up to twelve cycles, instead of nine, like the other place.'

'I should think they bloody will, if you're paying them five hundred quid a shot!' Lucy stared at her, incredulous. 'Bloody hell, that's ridiculous! I mean, it could end up costing you five, no, *six* thousand quid! And there's no guarantee you'll even *get* pregnant, is there?'

'There's a good chance. And it might work first time.'

'And it might not!' Lucy put down the brochure. 'Look, if you're this serious about having a baby, why don't you just find somebody and . . .' she glanced over to where Angus and Emily were playing, and lowered her voice '. . . and *sleep* with them, for God's sake? There's just as much chance of getting pregnant, and even if you don't, at least you'll have *enjoyed* yourself! This is just . . .' She threw up her hands, speechless.

The last vestige of Kate's good mood disappeared. 'So what do you want me to do? Trawl through singles bars and ask anyone who takes my fancy back for a quickie?'

'No, of course I don't!' Lucy's mouth quirked upwards. 'It doesn't have to be quick.'

Despite herself Kate laughed. But she was still angry. 'Well, that's what it amounts to, isn't it? I mean, to start off with you say that you disapprove of me having a baby, full stop. Now it's okay for me to get pregnant, provided it doesn't cost me anything, even if I have to turn into Supertart to do it!'

Lucy's lips were clamped in a tight line. 'It's your money, Kate, you can do what you like with it. But millions of other women manage to get pregnant without having to pay six thousand quid for the privilege, and I can't see why you have to be any different.'

There was a shriek of laughter from nearby. They looked around as Angus tottered towards them in an unstable run, hands held up in the air, orange-stained face split in a wide grin. Emily was close behind, laughing, and as she caught up with him Angus tumbled and thumped down onto the grass.

Lucy went to pick him up. 'Oh, now you haven't hurt yourself,' she said, as his face puckered uncertainly. She rubbed the grass stain on his knee. 'There, is that better?'

Angus still didn't seem too sure, but Lucy plonked him back on the lawn. Emily hung back, watching her apprehensively.

'I thought I told you that Mummy and Kate wanted to talk?'

'Yes, but Angus started running over, and I was only—'

'You were only chasing him. Now go over and help Daddy, like I said. We won't be long.'

'But Mummy!'

'No buts. Go on.'

Sulking, Emily turned and walked away. Angus ran after her, his fall already forgotten.

Lucy came back to the table and sat down. The interruption had taken the heat out of the argument, but Kate waited until the children were out of earshot before she spoke.

'Look, Lucy, I know you don't approve. But what's the alternative? I don't want casual sex. I don't want any complications. I just want a baby. This way I can have control over who the father is *and* have the legal and medical protection of using a clinic. You don't get that on a one-night stand, do you?'

Lucy looked unconvinced. 'I know, but it just seems so . . . *impersonal*.'

Kate nodded, emphatically. 'That's what I want.'

'But what about when the baby gets older? What will you tell it?'

Kate had asked herself the same question. She attempted an insouciance she didn't entirely feel. 'The truth. It's nothing to be ashamed of.' She believed that, even while she knew it might not be so simple. But the clinic offered advice and counselling on how to deal with it. She would meet that problem when it came.

She leaned forward in her seat. 'Come on, Lucy. This is what I want. Be pleased for me.'

'I am, but . . .' Scepticism remained on Lucy's face. She looked at Kate for a moment longer, then relented. 'I am. Ignore me.' She gave a wry grin. 'Anyway, I thought you hadn't decided anything yet?'

Kate smiled but said nothing. Lucy stood up. 'Come on. Let's go and stop Jack from burning everything.'

They left the shade of the laburnum and went over to the barbecue. Jack had given up fanning the charcoal and was regarding the tray of sausages and marinated meats with a dubious expression, a spatula in his hand. They were still pink and raw.

'Is it hot enough?' Lucy asked, as they came up behind him.

'It should be. I've spent long enough fanning the bloody thing.' His sparse dark hair was plastered to his forehead.

'Why don't you put some of that fluid stuff on?'

He gave Lucy an exasperated look. 'I have.'

'Well, I should put some more on, if I were you. It'll be dark at this rate.'

He held out the spatula to her. 'Do you want to do this?'

Lucy threw up her hands. 'No, thanks, I cook every day. Having a barbecue was your idea. And don't let Angus get too near, he'll burn himself.'

Jack sighed and steered his son away from the bricks.

'I hear you've got refinancing from the bank,' Kate said, hoping to divert a family squabble. 'Congratulations.'

He smiled. 'Yeah. I was sweating there for a while. Ten grand down and another three thousand just gone on new hardware. It was looking a bit grim.' He stopped, suddenly self-conscious. 'Thanks for offering to help out, though. Lucy told me.'

'I'm glad it didn't come to that.'

'Probably as well it didn't,' Lucy cut in. 'Kate might need refinancing herself now, Jack.'

He looked at Kate, surprised. 'I thought the agency was doing well?'

'I don't *mean* the agency,' Lucy said, giving him a look.

'No? Oh, right!' His face lightened. 'So you're going ahead with it, then?'

Annoyed at the way Lucy had introduced the subject, Kate just nodded. Jack grinned at her.

'Good for you.'

'You don't know how much it's going to cost,' Lucy said, pointedly.

'So what, if it's what she wants?' He winked at Kate. 'It's your life. You go for it.'

He turned back to the barbecue, rubbing his hands together. 'Right, let's sort this out.'

He picked up the plastic bottle of barbecue fluid and, holding it at arm's length, squirted it liberally on the charcoal. Nothing happened. He took a box of matches from his pocket and struck one.

'Stand back.'

There was a *whuff* as a sheet of pale flame shot into the air. They flinched from the sudden heat. Jack made darting grabs for the wire tray to lift it off as the fire engulfed it, but after a moment he gave up, blowing on his burnt fingers.

'Do you think you put enough on?' Lucy asked, and they began to laugh as the air above the barbecue shimmered, and the meat started to blacken and curl in the flames.

They ate green salad and takeaway pizza at the table under the laburnum tree. The remains of the barbecue, charred and foul with the taste of the fluid, lay untouched above the still-hot embers.

Angus had become tired and fractious and had gone to bed in tears, while Emily sat on Kate's knee, almost asleep herself. The sun had gone down, but the evening was still warm. Several beer bottles and a bottle of wine sat on the table by the plates. Kate moved slightly, easing Emily to a more comfortable position. The little girl stirred and yawned, hugely.

'Time for bed, young lady,' Lucy said. Emily gave a half-hearted moan of protest. Lucy ignored it. 'Kiss Kate goodnight. Daddy'll take you.'

'I want Kate to take me.'

'No, Kate's going to stay with Mummy.' Lucy motioned with her head at Jack. He took the hint and stood up with a crack of knee joints. Rubbing her eyes, Emily allowed him to pick her up. Her breath was sweet with cherryade when Kate kissed her.

Lucy waited until they had gone inside. 'So have you thought about who you want to be the donor?' she asked, out of the blue. 'Assuming you decide to go ahead, obviously,' she added, ironically.

It was a question that Kate had been avoiding. 'No, not yet.'

'Any ideas?'

'Not really.'

Lucy pushed her glass around on the table with her finger. 'You must have thought about it.'

Kate had started nudging her own glass around, smearing the wet rings on the table top. She took her hand away. 'I haven't got that far yet. I've been too busy trying to find out if I could have it done to worry about anything else.'

'Surely you've got some idea, though?'

'Lucy, I don't *know*, all right? Why are you going on about it?'

Lucy was watching her with a strange expression. 'Not Jack.'

'What?'

'Not Jack. I don't want you asking Jack.'

Kate stared at her. 'Lucy, I . . . I'd never even considered it!'

But as she said it, she knew she had. She liked Jack and, more importantly, trusted him, and the thought of using him as the donor must have been loitering at the edge of her subconscious. It was enough to redden her face now. Both she and Lucy looked away from each other at the same time.

'I'm sorry, but I'd got to say it,' Lucy said, abruptly.

'It's okay.'

'I know it's selfish, but I just couldn't handle that at all.'

'It's all right, really.'

A silence built between them. Lucy cleared her throat.

'So are you going to make a list of possible candidates?' she asked, with forced lightness.

'I suppose so, yes.'

'Who—' Lucy began, then stopped when she remembered they had already gone over that. 'I mean, do you think you'll have any trouble finding someone?'

Kate was as keen as Lucy to leave the brief awkwardness behind. 'I don't know.' She felt obliged to add more. 'I suppose the problem's going to be that I don't know that many men when it boils down to it. Not well enough to ask, anyway.'

'What about Clive? I'd have thought he was an obvious choice.'

Kate had begun sliding her glass around on the table again. She put her hand in her lap. 'He would be, but I don't think it'd be a good idea.'

'Because the baby would be mixed-race, you mean? I wouldn't have thought that would bother you.'

There was a faintly arch note in Lucy's voice. Kate ignored it. 'It wouldn't, but having to work with Clive again afterwards would. And if I asked him and he said no, that'd be almost as bad.'

'Isn't there anyone at the gym?'

'No one I'd want to ask.'

Lucy sighed, though whether in sympathy or exasperation it was difficult to tell. 'Looks like you've got a problem, then, doesn't it?'

'What problem?' Jack asked, coming up to the table. Neither of them had heard him approach.

'Kate can't think of a donor,' Lucy said, and Kate tensed, waiting for him to make some joke about himself.

'Just don't pick anybody with ginger hair,' he said, sitting down. 'Wouldn't be fair to the kid.' He poured himself a glass of wine. 'Who've you got it narrowed down to?'

'Nobody, yet,' Kate admitted.

'Spoilt for choice?'

'Hardly. The only people I can think of, I either wouldn't want to ask or I can't because it'd cause too many complications.'

She had meant Clive, but realised as she spoke that this last point applied equally to Jack. Lucy gave her a sharp look.

'Which really makes a mockery of the idea of a known donor, doesn't it?' Lucy said, with a slight edge. Kate tried not to react to it.

'Not really. Just because I don't think it's a good idea to ask someone who'd see me – and the baby – regularly, it doesn't mean I'm going to settle for someone I've never even met.'

Lucy gave a snort. 'Well, if you don't want anyone you don't know, and you won't ask anyone you *do* know, there's not a great deal left, is there?'

Kate was about to respond, hotly, when Jack spoke.

'Why don't you advertise?'

'Oh, don't be stupid,' Lucy snapped.

'I'm not being stupid,' he said, equably.

'Well, where's she going to advertise? The post-office window?'

Jack gave Lucy a stark glance before turning to Kate. 'Have you thought about putting an ad in the personal columns?'

'Oh, come on!' Lucy exclaimed. 'You can't advertise for a sperm donor in a newspaper!'

'Why can't you?'

'Because you *can't*!'

Jack ignored her. 'You can word the ad to specify the sort of bloke you want,' he said to Kate. 'You know, intelligent, professional, good-looking. Not ginger-haired. Whatever.'

'For God's sake, Jack!' Lucy protested. 'I can't believe you're suggesting this!'

'Why not?' Kate thought he was enjoying his wife's outrage. 'It's only like advertising for a job. What's the difference?'

'What's the *difference*? The difference is you don't have to masturbate at a job interview! I've never heard anything so ridiculous in my life! You could get *anyone* answering!'

'So you check them out. And you're careful which newspapers you place the ad in. Go for something like the *Guardian* or *The Times* rather than a tits 'n' bums tabloid.'

'Or I could place it in professional journals,' Kate said, fired by the idea. 'Target specific groups I *know* are going to be fairly responsible and intelligent. Like teachers or lawyers.'

'I dunno about lawyers,' Jack said.

She laughed. 'Doctors, then. I could advertise in a medical journal. I can't see a doctor being easily shocked or offended. And they'd be more likely to take it seriously.'

Lucy was looking at her, horrified. 'You're not really *considering* it!'

'Well,' Kate said, 'it's worth thinking about.'

She batted at a moth that had blundered into her face. It fluttered off into the growing darkness, towards the still-glowing barbecue.

CHAPTER 8

Kate received her first reply on the same day that Paul Sutherland's case was heard at the magistrates' court. There was a delay on the Underground line, and she was late reaching the court building. A light drizzle was falling when she arrived. Too fine to merit an umbrella, it salted her hair with fine beads of water, misting on her cheeks like sweat in the clammy, windless morning. A middle-aged man and woman stood outside on the steps. She was crying, leaning against the man's chest. He stood with one arm around her, staring at nothing over the top of her head. Kate hurried past and went inside.

She was late, and the case had already been called when she found Josefina and Clive waiting in the corridor outside the courtroom. Only Caroline hadn't been called as a witness, and Kate hoped that the girl would cope at the office by herself. She sat next to Clive on the padded bench, torn between begrudging the wasted time and dreading the moment when she would have to go in and testify.

Predictably, Paul had pleaded not guilty. He had been charged with actual bodily harm – in addition to assault and criminal damage – when the wound to Josefina's arm turned out to be less serious than it had appeared. Until that point, the police had wanted to charge him with GBH, which could have carried a custodial sentence. Kate was glad it hadn't come to that. Despite everything, she didn't want to see him sent to prison.

She had been resigned to a lengthy wait, but after only ten minutes a clerk emerged from the courtroom and approached them.

'Josefina Mojon, Kate Powell and Clive Westbrooke?'

Kate felt her stomach knot as they gave obedient nods.

The man was thin, in a crumpled suit and mismatching tie. He gave a flickering smile that quickly switched off.

'I'm sorry, but I'm afraid we won't be needing you after all,' he said. 'Mr Sutherland decided to change his plea to guilty at the last minute.'

Paul had been fined two hundred pounds and ordered to pay a hundred and fifty pounds' compensation to Josefina and three hundred pounds' damages to Kate, the clerk told them. He gave details of how the payments would be made and then left. They remained where they were, trying to adjust to the anticlimax. Clive spoke first.

'Well, the bastard managed to make us all waste a morning. And I bet that wasn't deliberate.'

Kate didn't bother to dispute it. 'I suppose we might as well go,' she said. They stood up, but before they got any further the courtroom door opened and Paul Sutherland came out.

He glared at them. His face was sullen and accusing, the flesh under his eyes swollen. Kate tensed, waiting for him to say or do something. But he just stared at her before turning on his heel and walking away.

She let out her breath, slowly.

'Not the type to forgive and forget, is he?' Clive said.

'No,' she agreed.

The magistrates' court was in walking distance of King's Cross. Neither Josefina nor Clive made any comment when Kate said she would see them back at the office, but she still felt like a truant as she left them and went into the Underground.

There was a fault on the Victoria line, so Kate took a tube to Piccadilly Circus. The post-office depot was only a few minutes' walk from there, and Kate left the station with the now customary sense of anticipation. The feeling wasn't as intense as it had been the first few times she had been, but it still made her quicken her step as she drew near.

She had always supposed that a post-office box would be like a safety-deposit box, a small locker to which she would be given the key. Some were like that but they were more expensive, and Kate had decided there was no real need for one. She went to the counter and handed her security card to the unsmiling, uniformed woman, who took it without speaking and disappeared through a doorway.

Kate tried not to build up her hopes as she waited. The advert had been running for two weeks now. She had spent hours agonising over its wording before finally settling for a simple, bare statement of fact.

'Professional woman seeks donor for artificial insemination.'

Kate had placed it in a variety of different medical journals, from psychiatric to gynaecological. Some had flatly refused to run the ad, and she had felt a hot flush of embarrassment at each rejection. But most had accepted it without comment, and Kate had begun calling into the depot regularly to check for replies. So far, though, her PO box had remained mockingly empty.

The woman seemed to be gone a long time. When she came back, the white rectangle of the envelope was bright against the blue of her uniform.

Suddenly clumsy, Kate signed for it with a scribbled signature that only faintly resembled her own. Part of her noted that the envelope was thin and floppy, the handwriting untidy, but her excitement overwhelmed the awareness. She resisted the urge to open it until she was outside the depot, and then she stopped and tore open the flap.

There was no letter. Her first impression was that the envelope was empty, but then she saw something crumpled in the bottom. She realised what it was just in time to stop herself from pulling it out.

The condom had been unrolled, and before she snapped the envelope shut Kate saw that whoever had sent it had first cut off the teat. Bile rose high in her throat, from humiliation as much as disgust. Her eyes stung as she walked to a nearby waste bin and dropped in the envelope. She wiped her hands thoroughly on a tissue and dropped that in after it.

Feeling pervasively soiled, she walked back towards the tube station.

The summer passed its mid-way point. Lucy and Jack took the children camping to Brighton. They were worried about leaving the house untenanted, so Kate offered to stay there while they were away. She'd never been wholly comfortable in her own flat after Paul had barged his way in, and since Miss Willoughby's solicitors had put the old lady's up for sale she had felt even less so. Miss Willoughby had left everything to a botanical society, her solicitor had told Kate at the funeral, a sad little affair with only Kate, the vicar and the solicitor in attendance. A lorry had arrived to clear the flat the next day, and Kate still wasn't easy with the thought of living above the empty rooms, with their uncurtained windows and bare floors. Two weeks in Lucy and Jack's rambling house appealed like a holiday.

'You should go on a proper one yourself,' Lucy had commented, when Kate had said as much to her.

'Perhaps later,' Kate had replied, and both of them knew she had no intention of going away.

The house seemed odd, much bigger and less friendly now that she was alone in it. Lying in bed in the spare room on the first night, she had listened uneasily to the unfamiliar creaks and noises until at some point she had fallen asleep. After that, though, she had grown accustomed to the solitude, until it no longer bothered her. Echoes of the family still filled the house, scattered toys and books and clothes, so that it didn't seem empty so much as paused, a Mary Celeste waiting for voices and life to resume. Sometimes Kate felt like a ghost moving through it, living there but leaving no trace of herself. It was a gentle, lulling feeling.

Going there at night became a pleasure, so that she resented having to call at home to feed Dougal and check the post. The evenings were hot and muggy, and she would prepare a salad and eat it outside in the garden. Afterwards she would either just sit, or read until it became too dark to see, and then she would go inside and listen to Jack's jazz and blues collection, head back on the overstuffed sofa as Billie Holiday bared her heart, and the moths bumped and whirred against the lampshade.

It was so long since Kate had felt relaxed that it was an unfamiliar sensation. Only the question of finding a donor still chivvied away at her, but as the weeks had passed with no further response to her advert, she had begun to accept that there was unlikely to be one. She was already considering her next step when the letter arrived.

She had not checked the box in over a week, and it was with a sense of obligation rather than hope that she called in to the depot one lunch-time. When the woman returned with an envelope, Kate felt her day lurch into confusion. She signed for it and took it outside. The memory of the condom made her handle it cautiously, and she superstitiously moved to another spot to open it.

This time there was a letter inside, neatly handwritten in blue ink on a cream vellum. There was an Ealing address and telephone number. Kate saw by the date that it had been posted over a week ago. It had been waiting for her to collect it all the time she had been lotus eating at Lucy's.

The letter began without preamble. 'I am writing in response to your advertisement for a donor for artificial insemination,' Kate read. 'I am a thirty-four-year-old clinical psychologist, based in London. I am single, with no children,' Kate smiled at that, 'average height, slim, with dark hair and blue eyes. If you would like to meet up, please call me at the above number after 6.00 p.m.' It was signed 'Alex Turner'.

Kate had begun walking without having any idea of where she was going. She stopped, looking around. The sunlit street suddenly seemed unfamiliar. Its brightness dazzled her, and for an instant she felt unsure of where she was. Then the sensation had passed. Folding the letter back into the envelope, she set off for the tube station.

She sat in the garden again that evening, but now its peace had been shattered. Her meal had consisted of a mug of tea, which sat cooling and untouched on the table in front of her. Next to it was the letter. She picked it up and re-read it from time to time, as though she might be able to glean something else from the small, careful handwriting.

The thought of meeting the man who had written it terrified her. This was what she had wanted, but now it had actually happened even the thought of telephoning him seemed monumental. She found herself remembering Lucy's warning: he could be anyone. A piece of bark from the laburnum tree lay on the white plastic of the table. Kate nudged it absently with her finger, and the shape resolved itself into the dry husk of a dead moth.

She brushed it off the table, grimacing. Abruptly, she snatched up the letter and went inside. The telephone waited on a bureau in the lounge. Kate strode over and picked it up. She stabbed out the first three digits of the number from the top of the letter before banging down the receiver.

'Come on, get a grip,' she murmured. She wished Lucy wasn't away so she could talk it out, and immediately felt a surge of anger at herself.

She picked up the phone again and quickly dialled the number. There was a tightness in her chest as she waited for the connection to be made. The receiver was clammy in her hand as she heard it begin to ring.

'Hello?'

It was a man's voice that answered. Kate found she had no idea what to say. She quickly checked the letter for his name.

'Can I speak to . . . to Alex Turner, please?'

There was a pause. 'This is Alex Turner.'

Kate swallowed. 'My name's Kate Powell.' Belatedly, she remembered she hadn't intended to give her name. 'You answered my advertisement. For a . . . a donor.' She closed her eyes, squirming.

'Oh . . . Yes.'

'I was wondering – that is, I suppose we ought to meet up.'

Another pause. 'Okay.'

Kate tried not to be discouraged by his lack of enthusiasm. 'So, when's convenient?'

'Whenever.'

Kate wished she had never phoned. 'Well . . . er, how about . . .' She blanked. 'Tomorrow lunch-time?' she gabbled, and immediately regretted it. *Too soon, too soon!* She willed him to say no.

'Yes, tomorrow's fine.'

'Oh, okay. Er . . .' Her memory failed to come up with an obvious place to meet. 'Do you know Chando's brasserie?'

It was the first name that occurred to her, and Kate winced. The restaurant was French, pretentious and expensive. She had never liked it, but she was too embarrassed now to change her mind. She heard him hesitate.

'No. Sorry.'

'It's just off Soho Square,' she told him, and gave directions. 'Will one o'clock be okay?'

'Fine.'

She waited, but there was no more. 'Okay then. I'll see you tomorrow.'

Kate waited until he had hung up before replacing the receiver herself. She looked around the empty room. The need to talk, to tell someone, was like a suppressed shout. But she was on her own.

She phoned the restaurant to make the reservation.

CHAPTER 9

The restaurant was full. Conversation bubbled along, snatches of laughter occasionally surfacing through it. Waiters swirled around the tables like eddies in a stream, trays balanced, pads held at the ready.

Kate flinched as a loud hiss and billow of flame showed through the open hatch into the kitchen. She looked again at her watch. It was five to one. She had been there since a quarter to, long enough to feel as though she'd been waiting a lifetime.

She stiffened as the door from the street opened. A man walked in, dark hair swept back, wearing a bow tie and camel-coloured waistcoat despite the hot day. He spoke to the girl behind the reception desk, who scanned the book in front of her before answering. The man looked imperiously around the room, and his gaze stopped on Kate. Just as she was about to give a tentative smile, he turned away. The girl escorted him to another table, where two men greeted him.

Kate felt a small wash of relief.

She had spent the night before trying to reassure herself. It was no different from a business lunch, really. If they reached an agreement, fine. If not, then what had she lost? It wasn't as though she was committing herself. He didn't know where she lived, and if she didn't like the look of him she didn't have to take it any further. After two of Jack's brandies, she was almost convinced.

But when she had woken that morning, the doubts had descended again. By the time she reached the agency, they had developed almost to full-blown panic. She had gone to her office and drawn on an unlit cigarette, the flame from her lighter dangerously close to the tip, until her nerves had steadied.

The panic had retreated, but not gone entirely away. She could feel it pushing against her will as she waited at the table. It surged up as the restaurant door opened again, but this time it was a man and woman who entered. Kate turned away and stared out of the window. The street outside was bright and sunny beyond the low awning. The sound of it was lost against the restaurant's busy hubbub, so that it was like looking at a silent film.

She looked up as a waitress approached. Behind her was the man who had just arrived. Kate looked beyond him and saw that the woman he had come in with was kissing someone at the far side of the room. Then the waitress was moving off with a smile, and the man was standing by her table, looking uncertainly at her.

'Kate Powell?' he said, hesitantly. 'I'm Alex Turner.'

Kate half rose to her feet, feeling the blood rush to her face. 'Oh, I'm sorry, I thought . . . I saw you come in with someone, so I assumed . . .'

He looked confused for a moment. 'Oh! No, we just arrived at the same time.'

They were both standing, facing each other across the table. 'Please,' Kate said. 'Sit down.'

She tried to gather her wits as they arranged themselves. He didn't look at all how she had imagined. From his voice, she'd pictured someone altogether more like the man she'd seen earlier, all bow tie and arrogance. But he didn't give that impression at all. He looked reassuringly normal; a little younger than she'd expected, slim, with an earnest, unobtrusively attractive face. His hair was thick and wavy, almost as dark as her own, and a blue shading of beard was already colouring the line of his jaw. He was dressed casually, in fawn chinos and a navy blue short-sleeved shirt. It was open at his throat, revealing a glint of thin silver chain around his neck. Kate felt overdressed in her business suit.

He held himself very still, looking around the room before letting his eyes settle on her. With sudden intuition, Kate guessed that he was as nervous as she was. The knowledge gave her confidence.

She smiled. 'You managed to find it all right, then?'

'Yes, no problem.'

He returned her smile, but his tension was almost palpable. Kate's own anxiety diminished even more. She set about trying to put him at ease.

'It's a bit of a funny situation, isn't it?' she said, voicing her thoughts. 'Meeting for something like this?'

'Yes.' He cleared his throat. 'Yes, I suppose it is.' He looked around the restaurant again, as though he was unable to keep eye contact with her for more than a few seconds. She thought about how he'd sounded on the phone the previous evening. He hadn't been arrogant after all. Just nervous.

'So you're a psychologist?' she said. 'Did you see the advert in the *Psychological Journal*?'

'Yes.' He gave an apologetic smile. 'I'd have contacted you before, but it was a few weeks old by the time I got around to reading it.'

There was a faint stumble in his speech, not so much a stammer as a syncopation on certain words. *C-contacted.* Kate took it as further evidence of nerves.

The waitress returned and handed them each a tall menu. 'Would you like something to drink?' she asked.

'Mineral water for me, please.' Kate said. 'What about you, Mr Turner?'

'Oh . . . I'll have the same, thanks.' He waited until the waitress had left before adding, 'And, er, please call me Alex.'

Kate was carefully non-committal. 'Whereabouts do you work?' she asked, as they opened the menus.

'In Ealing. Part of an NHS unit.' He blinked at the French script and glanced up at Kate. 'How about you?'

'I've got a small PR agency,' she said, checking herself as she was about to add where it was.

'Your own?' He seemed impressed.

Kate felt irrationally pleased. 'It's only small.'

'Is it doing well?'

'At the moment.' She smiled, drawing unexpected satisfaction from the simple statement. He smiled back, and for a moment their reserve was gone.

The waitress returned with the drinks, and the moment of contact was broken. Kate ordered a salad. Alex, after a pause, chose a plain omelette.

'So,' Kate said into the silence left by the waitress's departure. 'I suppose I'd better ask you to tell me a little bit about yourself.'

He nodded. 'Okay.' *O-okay.* 'I went to university in Edinburgh, came away with a degree in psychology and a PhD in clinical psychology. Then I worked in a psychology unit in Brixton before I moved to the one at Ealing. Er . . . I'm single, I don't smoke or do drugs . . .' He shrugged. 'That's about it.'

'What about your family?'

Alex had picked up his fork, holding one end with the fingers of each hand, slowly turning it. His fingers were slender, Kate noticed. 'My mother and father are both retired. They live in Cornwall now.'

'Have you any brothers or sisters?'

'Two brothers, both older than me. One's in Australia, and one's in Canada. We're pretty scattered, I suppose. How about you?'

Kate smoothed her napkin on her lap. 'No. I've no family. My parents are dead.'

Alex looked unsettled again. 'I'm sorry.'

'It's okay.' She turned the conversation back to him. 'So what made you want to be a psychologist?'

'Oh . . . I'm not sure, really.' He put down his fork, considering. 'It was just something that's always interested me, I suppose. I'm a better listener than a talker, which helps.' He gave a shy grin. 'And I read the *Foundation* trilogy when I was a kid, so perhaps that had something to do with it. You know, Isaac Asimov?'

'No, I've heard of him, but . . .' She shook her head.

Alex made a throwaway gesture. 'Well, it doesn't matter. I used to read loads of science fiction, and then I came across that, and . . . wow. It was brilliant. There are these "super psychologists" in it, who've developed psychology into such an art that they don't even have to speak to communicate. God, I thought that was great! You know, the thought of being able to *know* people so well. Understand why they do things. And understand themselves, as well. It just seemed—'

He broke off, self-consciously, as the waitress returned with their food.

'What were you saying?' Kate asked, when the girl had gone. She noticed that he waited for her to begin eating before he started himself, which struck her as quaint.

'Oh, nothing. That was all, really.'

His reserve was back. Kate smiled, wanting him to relax again. 'And are you a "super psychologist"?'

He gave an embarrassed smile, rubbing the back of his neck. 'No, I don't—'

There was another loud hiss and burst of flame from the kitchen hatch. Alex jerked, and the piece of omelette he had just picked up on his fork flipped off and landed neatly in his water glass.

'Oh, God! Sorry!'

His expression was so mortified that the laugh escaped Kate before she could stop it. He glanced at her, then grinned. He had a nice smile, she thought.

'It was too hot, anyway.' Blushing, he fished the omelette out of the glass and set it on the edge of his plate. 'So how did you get into PR?'

The blush was fading from his face, now. It made him look very young, Kate thought.

'Oh, I just drifted into it, I suppose,' she said. 'I'd done a couple of years of an English degree, but then my parents died quite close to each other, and I dropped out. I wasn't sure what I wanted to do after that, so I worked at a few places and then got a job at a PR company.'

'How long have you had your own agency?'

'Two years, now.'

'What sort of work do you actually do?'

He was looking at her with genuine interest. His manner had changed, becoming more confident now that he was asking her questions. There was no trace of the earlier hesitancy in his speech.

'Do you mean, who do I work for? Or what does it involve?'

'Both, really. It isn't something I know much about,' he admitted.

'Well, we handle all sorts of accounts, anything from small record companies and publishers, who want to get somebody reviewed in newspapers or interviewed on TV and radio. Or it can be somebody who's got a particular product that they want to publicise. The biggest account we've got is a charitable trust who want us to raise their profile as subtly as possible, but most of our clients want as much publicity as they can get.'

'So how do you go about it?'

'It varies from client to client but generally it revolves around catching people's attention. It doesn't matter if it's a press release you're sending to newspapers and magazines or a poster campaign, it's got to be something that grabs their interest straight away. You've got to make sure you're hitting the right targets, too, and be prepared to keep plugging away at them until they sit up and take notice.' She smiled. 'Or until your budget runs out.'

He had his chin propped on his hand, watching her as he listened. 'Do you enjoy it?'

Kate thought. 'Yes, I suppose so. It has its ups and downs. You tend to find you don't have much time for anything else, though. Sometimes I wish I didn't have all the pressure.'

She stopped, surprised at the admission. Alex was still looking at her, waiting for her to continue. She turned her attention to her salad to cover her embarrassment at being drawn out.

'To get back to your background,' she said, businesslike again. 'Do you have any family history of illness? You know, diabetes, anything like that?'

'Uh, no, not that I know of. My grandmother had arthritis, but not until she was in her seventies.'

Kate nodded, trying to remember what else she needed to ask. The questions she had prepared eluded her. She clutched at one.

'Why do you want to be a donor?'

He appeared taken aback. 'Well, I don't know. It seemed like a good thing to do. It doesn't hurt me, and if I can help somebody, then . . . you know, why not?'

'Have you donated sperm before?' Kate refused to let herself be fazed by saying 'sperm' to a complete stranger. 'Or given blood?'

'N-no, no, I haven't.' The syncopation was back.

'Then what made you decide to now?'

'Uh, well . . .' A flush had crept into his face. 'It, er, it wasn't something I'd even thought about before I saw your advert, really. But I suppose I like the idea of, well, fatherhood without the ties.'

'You could have the same thing by going straight to a sperm bank.'

He seemed flustered. 'I know, but . . . Well, it might sound stupid but that's all a bit too anonymous.' His face was very red now. 'I wouldn't like the thought of letting just anyone have my . . . my child, if you know what I mean.'

It had never occurred to Kate that a man might feel the same way she did. 'You do know that you wouldn't have any of a father's rights, don't you? You'd still only be the donor. The child wouldn't legally be yours, and there wouldn't be any contact between us afterwards. Assuming we go ahead, obviously.'

'Yes, I understand that.'

'And it'll mean a lot of inconvenience. The clinic's in Birmingham, and you'll have to make a lot of trips. They need quite a few . . . quite a few samples.'

He nodded acceptance.

'I'll pay expenses,' Kate went on, briskly, shutting out the thought of what she was discussing. 'For your time as well as travel. I'll pay you either a flat fee or a daily one each time you go.'

Alex shook his head, emphatically. 'I don't want paying.'

'I wouldn't expect you to do it for nothing.'

'I'd be doing it because I want to.'

Kate decided not to argue. She still hadn't decided anything yet, so there was no point. 'You'll have to be tested for things like HIV and hepatitis,' she continued. 'And you'll have to go back for a second HIV test after six months. They won't actually go ahead with the, er the treatment until you've had that.'

He looked startled.

'Is that a problem?' Kate asked.

'Oh, no, it's just . . . I didn't expect it to take so long, that's all.'

'They do the same tests on every donor. It isn't any reflection on you personally.'

'No, no, it's okay, really. I just didn't realise. But it's no problem.'

Kate tried to think of what else she had to say. Nothing came to mind. 'Is there anything you'd like to ask?'

Alex minutely repositioned his knife and fork on his plate. Except for the piece he had dropped into the glass, his omelette was still untouched.

'Are you married?'

Kate stared at him, levelly. 'Why?'

He was disconcerted by her reaction. 'Sorry, I – I know it's none of my business. I just wondered if you were doing this because you were single and wanted to, or whether you were married and your husband was . . . was . . .' he gestured with his knife, stepping around the reference to sterility '. . . wasn't able to have children,' he finished. 'Your advert didn't say one way or the other.'

Her face had become hot. 'Does it matter?'

'No, of course not. I'm sorry, I didn't mean to pry.'

He was so obviously reluctant to offend that Kate relented. 'No, I'm not married. I'm doing this because I want to.'

'Good. I mean, you know, good for you.'

Kate studied him for a few seconds. He picked up his knife and fork and half-heartedly began to cut up the omelette.

'Why are you so nervous?'

She had asked the question without intending to. He shot her a quick look.

'I'm not nervous. Not really,' he amended, as though realising there was no point denying it. 'I've just, you know, never done anything like this before.'

He looked so chagrined that Kate couldn't keep from smiling. 'It isn't something I've made a habit of, either.'

He glanced up at her, then smiled himself. 'No, I suppose it isn't,' he acknowledged. His smile faded. 'I expect you'll have interviewed quite a few other people, though. I mean, I know I won't be the only one and . . . Well, it's a bit nerve-racking, that's all.'

Kate didn't correct him. He had gone back to playing with his omelette. His face was serious again.

'Is this so important to you?' she asked.

He didn't speak for a moment. Kate got the impression he was wrestling with the answer. Then he looked across at her. His eyes were a darker blue than Lucy's.

'Yes,' he said, simply.

'Why?'

He looked down at his plate. 'I want children. I'm just not . . . I'm not the marrying kind. I'm not gay, it's nothing like that. I just can't see myself settling down and having a normal family or . . .' His voice tailed off, as though he had changed his mind about what he was going to say. 'This seems like the next best thing.'

'Even though you'll never see the baby? Not even know if it's a boy or a girl?' Kate felt brutal, but she had to be sure he understood.

All at once his face looked immeasurably sad. He stared at the unlit candle in the centre of the table, but Kate doubted he saw it.

'I'll know it's there, though.'

He came to himself with a little start. 'If you decide to choose me as the donor, that is. I don't want you to think I'm taking anything for granted.'

Now Kate looked away. 'I've been keeping you from your lunch,' she said, going back to her salad.

She asked him for his card as they left the restaurant. 'I'll phone you next week and let you know what I've decided,' she told him, feeling both cowardly and pompous.

He accepted that without complaint. 'It's better if you call me at night,' he said, taking a business card from his wallet. 'I'm generally with a patient when I'm at work, so I wouldn't be able to speak to you. And I don't really want anyone there to know about this,' he admitted, apologetically.

He scribbled a telephone number on the back of the card before he gave it to her. 'I know you've already got my number, but I'll give it you again. I've just moved, and I'm ex-directory now, so if you lose it you won't be able to get in touch.'

They shook hands, both a little awkward. Kate felt the heat and pressure from his even after she was no longer holding it. She watched him walk down the street, a slim figure, already lost in thought, hands shoved casually in his pockets.

Catching sight of herself in the restaurant window as she turned away, she saw she had a smile on her face.

'It looks complicated but there's really nothing to it,' the librarian assured her.

He was an earnest-looking young man, red-haired with a complexion that looked permanently wind-burned. His fingers produced soft clacks from the computer keys, like a stringless piano. 'It's really much easier than dredging your way through piles of books.'

Looking at the messages and text appearing on the screen, Kate doubted that. But the librarian, almost irritatingly helpful, had insisted she use CD-ROM instead of the heavy indexes. Even though it was him doing most of the using.

'Okay, what name did you say it was again?' he asked, without looking up from the screen.

'Turner. Alex – or perhaps Alexander – Turner.'

Kate watched as phrases and letters appeared and disappeared from the screen with bewildering speed. She hoped that this would be the last check she would have to run. Although she knew it was only common sense to make sure that the psychologist was who and what he claimed to be, she still felt underhand for not taking him at face value.

The first thing she had done when she had returned from the restaurant was to look in the phone book. The Ealing Mental Health Centre was listed, with the same address and telephone number as on Alex Turner's business card, although it didn't give the names of any psychologists working there. Kate had considered for a moment, drumming her fingers on her desk. Then she reached for the phone and dialled.

A woman's voice answered. 'Ealing Centre.'

'Hello, could you tell me if you have a Dr Alex Turner working there, please?'

'Yes, we do, but he's out at the moment. Would you like to leave a message?'

'No, it's okay, thank you.'

Kate had put down the phone before the woman could ask anything else, feeling a little thrilled and scandalised by her detective work. She tapped Alex Turner's card on the desk, thoughtfully, then picked up the phone again and dialled Directory Enquiries.

'Can you tell me if there's an Institute of British Psychologists listed, please?' she asked, when the operator answered.

There wasn't. Kate put on her most persuasive voice and asked if there was anything similar. She waited while the operator looked. Would the British Psychological Society do? he asked. Kate said it would.

She dialled the number he had given her before she had time to reconsider. A woman answered. Kate plunged straight in.

'I'm trying to find out details about a psychologist. His name's Alex Turner.'

To Kate's relief, the woman seemed to find nothing odd in the request. 'Is he chartered?' she asked.

'I don't know,' said Kate. She wasn't even sure what chartered meant. 'Does that matter?'

'We only have chartered psychologists registered here. So if he isn't, I won't be able to help you.'

Telling herself she should have known it couldn't be so easy, Kate asked her to try anyway. She spelt out his name and waited as the woman entered it into a computer.

'Here we are. Alexander Turner,' the woman announced, taking Kate by surprise. She scrabbled for a pen as the woman reeled off a list of qualifications. Kate recognised some of them from his card.

'And this is definitely the same Alex Turner?' she asked.

The woman was apologetic. 'I can only verify his qualifications. I'm not allowed to give out any addresses or phone numbers unless you're a member yourself.'

'I've got his work address as the Ealing Mental Health Centre, London. Can you at least tell me if that's the same one you have?'

Kate could feel the woman's indecision. 'Let's say if it wasn't I'd tell you,' she said.

Kate was about to ring off when the woman asked, 'Have you tried Psychological Abstracts?'

'Er . . . no. What's that?'

'It's an index that gives details of any articles a member's had published. Or there's the same thing on CD-ROM called PsychLIT.' She spelt it out. 'Any university library should have it.'

Kate thanked her and hung up. She had no intention of digging around in any library. She was satisfied that Alex Turner was legitimate. There was no need to waste her time on pointless exercises.

But the knowledge that an avenue remained unexplored niggled like a stone in her shoe. After spending most of the previous evening telling herself it was a waste of time, that morning she had phoned Clive to tell him she would be late. Then she set off for the university.

The librarian's wind-burned face frowned in concentration as his fingers lightly patted the keyboard.

'Ah. Here we go,' he said, in a pleased tone. He leaned back so she could see the screen. 'He's got eleven entries. Was it any particular title you were wanting?'

'No, not really.'

The librarian looked momentarily curious, but made no comment. He showed her how to call up a record of each article. 'The articles themselves aren't on CD-ROM, but we should have most of the actual journals on file, if you want photocopies.'

He gave up the chair, reluctantly. 'If you want any more help, just ask. I'll be at the desk.'

Kate assured him she would. She looked at the first record. Some of the information was unintelligible to her, but the title of the article was clear enough: 'The role of upbringing and environment in the forming of obsessional behaviour.' Further down the page was something called an abstract, which she gathered amounted to a brief synopsis:

Obsessional behaviour is frequently attributable to a specific event or events in an individual's background. Frequently, memory of these has been suppressed, so that the root of the obsession is obscured. This paper suggests that the success of therapy for such obsessions may be substantially increased when these seminal events are recognised. Six patients were helped to recall these using hypnosis, with positive results.

There was nothing of interest there, so Kate moved on to the next record. This article had been published by an American journal, she saw, impressed. The title was 'Blood Ties: Impulse-control disorders as an inherited trait?' It meant little to her, and the abstract wasn't much more help, either:

Identical twins, separated at birth and given contrasting upbringings, were convicted of theft within twelve months of each other. This study considers the possibility of an inherited tendency towards impulse-control disorders, and suggests this as a subject of further research.

Her attention wandered before she had finished reading. She called up the next record, this one detailing an article on pyromania but sat back without bothering to read it. Enough was enough. Leaving the monitor switched on, she went over to the librarian.

His wind-burned cheeks grew darker when he saw her. 'Sorry, I'm not sure how to turn it off,' she told him.

'That's okay, I'll see to it. Did you find what you were looking for?'

'Yes, I think so.'

'Do you want any of the articles photocopied?'

'No, it's okay, thanks.'

He looked disappointed. 'Are you sure? It's no trouble.'

'Really, it's okay. I've seen what I needed.'

Then, because her excitement demanded an outlet, she gave him an extra broad smile as she went out.

Lucy and Jack returned that weekend. Kate waited through tales of collapsing guy-ropes, sunburn and ice-cream indigestion, before Lucy wound down.

'Are you going to be free one night next week?' Kate asked.

Lucy was slumped in an armchair. 'I think you'd have to drag me out of the house after the last fortnight. Why?'

Kate couldn't keep it in any longer. 'There's someone I'd like you to meet.'

CHAPTER 10

'This is Alex.'

The four of them stood in Lucy and Jack's living room, stiff smiles on all their faces. The planned barbecue had been rained off. Instead, the big table at the back of the room was now draped with a heavy white tablecloth, and set with Jack's aunt's best cutlery and glasses. Two heavy silver-plated candlesticks stood in the middle, the beeswax candles in them slightly askew.

Lucy gave Alex a bright smile. 'Pleased to meet you.' Kate thought that she was going to step forward and kiss him, but she didn't.

Jack stuck out his hand and gave Alex's a firm shake. 'How you doing?'

There was an awkward lull while everyone waited for someone to speak and no one did.

'Well, isn't this just typical English weather?' Lucy declared. 'If there's one certain way of getting it to rain, it's for us to decide to have a barbecue!'

They laughed, a little more heartily than was strictly necessary. Before the silence could descend again, Jack rubbed his hands together.

'Right, who's for a drink? Kate?'

'Red wine, please.' She reminded herself to drink slowly. She hadn't been able to eat anything all day.

'Alex?' Jack said. 'Beer, wine. Something stronger, if you'd like it?'

Alex looked momentarily lost. 'Er . . . beer, if you've got one.'

Jack's face split into a grin. 'You can have Budweiser, Boddy's or Old Speckled Hen.'

'You can show him your beer collection later,' Lucy said, disguising the sharpness behind a smile. 'I'm sure Alex isn't bothered.'

Jack's smile was just as cosmetic. 'Well, let's let him decide, shall we?'

Kate knew Lucy and Jack well enough to gather that they had been arguing. She had felt anxious enough before she arrived, and the tension between them didn't make her feel any better. She had a sudden presentiment that the night was going to be awful.

'I'll have a Bud, please,' Alex said. Jack gave Lucy a triumphant glance, clearly taking the nickname as proof of a kindred spirit. He went through into the kitchen.

'I'll have white wine, since you've asked,' Lucy shouted after him, sweetly. She smiled back at Kate and Alex. 'You might as well sit down.'

They went to the sofa and chairs set around the unlit fire. As she passed Kate, Lucy lowered her voice.

'New dress?'

Kate nodded. It was plain white, sleeveless and ended well above her knee. Lucy raised an eyebrow at her, but made no further comment as she settled into one of the armchairs. After hesitating by its twin, Kate sat on the sofa with Alex, though at the other side. She was conscious of her dress riding up over her thighs. It was shorter than she was used to.

Lucy gave him a hostess's smile. 'Kate tells me you're a clinical psychologist?'

Alex nodded. 'Er, yes, that's right.'

'You'll have to forgive my ignorance, but I'm not sure what one is. I mean, I know what a psychologist is, but I'm not sure about the clinical bit.'

He cleared his throat. 'Well, it, er, it basically means I work with patients rather than on the, uh, theoretical or research side.'

He sat with his legs crossed and one arm thrown casually over the arm of the sofa, but Kate sensed the same rigidity in him she had noticed in the restaurant. He seemed to be holding himself in the relaxed posture by an effort of will.

'So you treat schizophrenics and people like that, instead of getting rats to run round mazes?' Lucy persisted.

'Ah, no, I wouldn't treat anyone for schizophrenia. That's more a psychiatric condition, really.'

'What's the difference?'

'The difference?' Alex looked discomforted at being quizzed. Kate wished Lucy would change the subject. 'Psychiatry deals with, er, with mental illness. It, uh, it tends to use a lot of drug treatment. Psychology – c-clinical psychology – is more concerned with behavioural problems.'

The faint catch was back in his voice, an almost imperceptible stumble over his consonants. Kate wondered if Lucy could tell how nervous he was. She was beginning to regret the enthusiasm that had led her to take him there. It hadn't been her intention to put him on display, but that was how it must seem.

'What made you choose it? The clinical thing, I mean?'

Kate wondered if she had sounded as inane when she'd first met him. She waited for Alex to tell Lucy about the 'super psychologists'.

'Oh, no particular reason,' he said, dismissively. 'It was just something I liked the sound of.'

He didn't look at her, but Kate was suddenly sure that Alex knew she was conscious of the omission. And, for some reason, she was glad he hadn't told Lucy.

'What sort of—' Lucy began, but Kate never knew what her next question would have been. She broke off as a small figure came into the room. Dressed in a pale yellow nightgown, Emily hung back at the edge of the circle formed by the sofa and chairs. She had a shy smile on her face as she looked up coyly at Alex from under her hair.

'And what are you doing out of bed, young lady?' Lucy asked, affecting sternness.

Emily twirled back and forth on her toes, not taking her eyes from Alex. 'Couldn't sleep.'

'And I don't suppose that's because you wanted to see who was here, is it?'

Emily smiled but said nothing. Lucy sighed and turned to Alex. 'I don't suppose you know anything about child psychology, do you? Like what to do with nosy children?'

He gave an uncertain grin. 'No, sorry.'

As if Emily had been waiting for him to speak, she edged closer. 'Are you Kate's boyfriend?'

'Time for bed, I think,' Lucy said, coming out of her chair and swooping her up so quickly that they were half-way down the hallway before the little girl's objections sounded.

As the noises of protest receded Kate forced herself to smile at Alex. Separated by the width of a cushion and mutual embarrassment, they waited for Jack to return with the drinks.

Lucy had cooked roast chicken, rubbed with lemon and garlic and served with green beans and minted new potatoes from their garden. When she put her mind to it, she was a good cook, but she had obviously lost interest by the time it came to preparing a dessert. The chocolate gâteau she produced was mainly synthetic cream and additives, and misshapen on one side where it had been squashed in the shopping bag. But by that time the drinks had relaxed them enough so they could laugh about it.

Kate felt light-headed, from relief as much as the wine she'd vowed not to drink. The initial awkwardness had slipped away unnoticed during the meal. Alex had unwound and seemed to hit it off with Lucy and Jack, who had either shelved or resolved whatever had been bothering them. Lucy had begun to flirt mildly with him, a sure sign of approval, and he and Jack had found common ground in books.

Lucy caught her eye as Jack began to tell Alex about his business.

'Give me a hand with the dishes?'

Suddenly nervous, Kate helped her collect the dirty plates and followed her into the kitchen. Lucy closed the door behind them and turned to face her.

'Tell me you're not still planning to go through with it.'

Kate had known Lucy was about to give her verdict, but this wasn't what she expected. 'Why? Don't you like him?'

'Of course I like him! He's a bit shyer than I'd have expected, but apart from that I think he's lovely.'

'What's wrong, then?'

'Nothing's *wrong*. Except that you've been lucky enough to meet a really nice bloke, never mind how, and if you're still even *considering* going ahead with that artificial rubbish, then you want your head looking at!'

Kate felt the tension drain out of her. 'I thought you were going to say you didn't approve of him.'

'The only thing I don't approve of is if you still plan to go ahead with this stupid idea of yours. You've really fallen on your feet. Again. I just hope you make the most of it.'

'Lucy, I'm looking for a donor. That's all.'

'Oh, yes?' Lucy arched her eyebrows. 'I suppose you're going to tell me you don't fancy him, either?'

'I don't. I'm glad he's turned out to be a nice bloke and I don't deny I like him, but it doesn't go any further than that.'

Lucy looked pointedly at Kate's dress. 'And I suppose that outfit's just coincidence, then?'

Kate blushed. 'I decided to buy myself something new, that's all.'

'Which just happens to show off your legs and boobs. Come on, I'm not stupid. You didn't put that on for my benefit. Or Jack's.'

Something in her tone alerted Kate. Remembering the tension between Lucy and Jack when she'd first arrived, she asked, 'Is everything okay? Between you and Jack, I mean. I'm not prying,' she added, hurriedly, seeing Lucy's suddenly closed expression, 'but you seemed at bit . . . edgy with each other earlier.'

Kate thought she wasn't going to answer, but then Lucy turned away.

'We had a bit of an argument, that's all.' She paused. 'About you, actually.'

'Me?'

Two patches of colour had entered Lucy's cheeks. She looked at Kate with something like defiance.

'Jack seems to think I'm being too hard on you. He says I should be more supportive. I told him I was only saying what I thought was for your own good, and that I wished he'd be half as bloody supportive towards me.' Her mouth tightened. 'But then I wouldn't look as good in a white mini, would I?'

Abruptly, she squeezed her eyes shut.

'Oh, Christ, I didn't mean that. I'm sorry.'

Kate said nothing. She became aware of a tap dripping, rhythmically, into the silence.

Lucy's forehead was creased in anguish. 'Ignore me, I'm just in a bitchy mood, that's all. It wasn't only about you, anyway. Jack and I have been going through a bad patch lately, the kids have been brats. And to top it off I'm having an absolute bugger of a period – my stomach's swollen like a balloon, I feel yukky, and then you come walking in looking like Audrey bloody Hepburn. And instead of some geeky pervert, the only bloke who replies to your advert turns out to be a gem!' She gave a weak smile. 'Sometimes, you know, things just get on top of you.'

Kate felt as though she'd inadvertently opened a door that should have stayed locked. 'Do you want us to leave?'

'No, of course I don't! Oh, look, please, don't take any notice of me. I'm just in a bad mood and feeling sorry for myself.'

The tap made a metallic *plink* as each drip hit the sink. Lucy reached out and tightened it. The drips slowed but didn't stop. She watched it, her arms folded around herself.

'You'd better go back and rescue Alex,' she said. 'Jack'll have bored him witless about work by now. I'll be through when I've made the coffee.'

Kate opened the door.

'Kate?'

She looked back. Lucy gave a small shrug.

'Sorry.'

Kate went out, letting the door close behind her. The glimpse of Lucy's bitterness had been as unexpected as a mouthful of rot from a wholesome apple. She stood for a while in the dark of the hallway. From behind her in the kitchen came the muted click of a cupboard being opened, the chink of crockery. Ahead of her a spill of light fell through the partly open lounge door. There was no sound of conversation. Kate went in.

Alex didn't look up when she entered. He was alone at the table, his face full of shadows in the candlelight. His expression was lost and faraway as he regarded the small piece of fire swaying from the candle nearest him. Kate hung back as he passed his finger through the yellow tip, halted, then steadily passed it back. The flame fluttered with each passage, leaning towards his finger as though trying to catch it.

Kate moved towards the table. 'Doesn't that hurt?'

Alex's eyes were wide and startled as his head came up. 'What?'

'Running your finger through the flame like that. Doesn't it hurt?'

He stared at his finger and the candle as though he had only just noticed them. 'Uh, no, not really.'

Kate sat down. 'It must burn, though, surely?'

He looked back into the flame. 'Only if you let it.' He smiled at her. 'Try it.'

Kate laughed and shook her head. 'No, thanks.'

'It doesn't hurt. Not if you're fast enough, and don't go too close to the wick.'

She gave him a sceptical look.

'Honest. It won't burn if you do it right.'

They were staring at each other over the candle. Tentatively, Kate held out her finger until it was only a few inches away from the flame.

'No,' she said, with a laugh, snatching it back.

'Come on. Trust me.'

She looked at him and extended her finger again. A slim line of smoke rose from the flame. She could feel the heat against her skin. Her finger quivered.

From the hallway came the sound of Lucy returning with the coffee. Kate quickly drew back her hand, feeling both relieved and cowardly.

'I'll take your word for it.'

They shared a taxi home. Alex insisted on dropping off Kate first, assuring her that it was quicker that way. After a second's hesitation, she accepted. She hadn't planned on letting him know her address but, since he'd just been to Lucy and Jack's, that seemed petty and pointless. They sat next to each other on the back seat. To begin with, they talked easily enough. Alex seemed almost garrulous when she asked him about where he lived, explaining how he was in temporary accommodation after being caught up in a chain of house buyers. After exchanging contracts with the couple who were buying his flat, the people whose house he was supposed to be buying had withdrawn theirs from the market.

'I'd got three days to find somewhere else before the new owners moved into mine,' he told her. 'So now most of my stuff's in storage, and I'm stuck renting a studio flat until I can find somewhere else.'

'Have you seen anywhere yet?'

'Uh, no, not really. I don't have much time to look. You know how it is.' His self-consciousness had returned.

'Well, at least nobody'll know where to find you out of hours,' Kate said, lightly, wanting to draw him out again.

Alex looked confused.

'Patients, I mean,' she explained, feeling stupid. 'I'd have thought being a psychologist was like a doctor, always getting people pestering you at home. Now you've moved, though, and gone ex-directory as well, I don't expect they'll be able to.'

She was beginning to wish she hadn't started. But Alex's frown cleared.

'Oh . . . no, I suppose not.'

They lapsed into silence. Their isolation in the dark intimacy of the cab began to impose an awkwardness on them both. In the confined space, Kate could make out the clean, alcohol tang of Alex's aftershave. Paul had always drenched himself in the stuff, as though the reek of it declared his masculinity. Alex's was more subtle. She liked it.

The taxi lurched round a bend, throwing her against him. Kate reached out to steady herself, and put her hand on his thigh. She jerked it away and straightened, stammering an apology. Her face was hot as she stared fixedly out of the window. Beside her, she sensed that Alex was equally tense. The air between them seemed charged with awareness, so that the slightest movement was magnified.

She slid down the window, letting the breeze splash onto her face, and breathed deeply. *Too much wine.*

'Is it too windy for you?' she asked Alex.

'No, it's fine.'

There had been no mention of the reason they were together. Alex hadn't pushed her for a decision, for which she was glad. They might almost have been out on a date, in fact. Kate quickly put that notion out of her head.

'I hope tonight hasn't been too much of an ordeal,' she said.

'Not at all. I've enjoyed it.'

She nearly said, *So have I*, but stopped herself. She glanced at the taxi driver. He probably couldn't hear through the glass partition, but she lowered her voice anyway.

'I don't want you to feel you've been on trial, or anything.'

'It's okay, really.' He smiled. 'I liked them. They're a nice family.'

They were approaching Kate's road. 'The next corner, please,' she told the driver. She turned back to Alex, lowering her voice again. 'Look, I appreciate how patient you've been, and I don't want to mess you about, but . . . Well, will it be all right if I let you know in a few days? About what I decide?'

He nodded, quickly. 'Yes, no problem.'

'It's just a big decision to have to make. I don't want to rush into anything.'

'No, of course. It's okay, I understand.'

The taxi grated to a halt. Kate reached into her bag and handed the driver a note to cover the fare, against Alex's protests. She put her hand on the door handle.

'Well. Goodnight, then.'

'Goodnight.'

There was a moment when neither of them moved, then Kate pressed down the handle and climbed out.

'I'll be in touch by the end of the week,' she told Alex, through the open window.

She phoned him the next evening.

It was a doctor they saw, not the counsellor Kate had met on her first visit to the clinic. The three of them sat in her office around a low, claw and ball-footed table in comfortable leather chairs. Beside them, unused for the moment, was an antique cherrywood desk, dark and rich with the scent of beeswax. Sunlight striped the carpet through the horizontal bars of the fabric blinds. The window itself was closed, but air-conditioning made the office pleasantly cool. The entire hospital seemed to exist in an environment completely separate from the outside world.

'The thing you have to remember, and I really can't stress this enough, is that legally "donor" and "father" are two different entities,' the doctor was saying to Alex. Dr Janson was an attractive woman in her forties, with carefully styled blonde hair and clothes that supported the hospital's charges. She had told them that scheduling problems had meant she would see them instead of another counsellor, but Kate wondered if it wasn't more because she wanted to handle an unusual case herself.

'It doesn't matter whether the donor is anonymous or, as in this instance, known to the patient,' she continued. 'Your responsibility begins and ends with the donation of the sperm. It's very important that you understand that.'

Alex nodded. He was leaning forward in his chair, listening to what the doctor said with an intent, almost anxious expression. He had been silent for most of the journey from Euston, but then Kate hadn't felt like talking either.

Satisfied that the point had been made, Dr Janson continued. 'Before we go any further, I should say that we're obliged to offer counselling before you give your consent for your sperm to be stored and used. Not everyone feels they need it, but it's there if you do. It's important you fully understand the implications of becoming a donor.'

She waited, a polite smile on her subtly made-up face. Alex glanced uncertainly at Kate.

'Er . . . I don't think that's . . . I mean, no, it's okay, thanks.'

The doctor inclined her head. 'As you wish. Just so long as you're aware that the offer has been made.' She took a gold-plated fountain pen from the top pocket of her white coat and unscrewed its cap. 'Now, I'll have to ask you a few questions about your general health and medical background.'

Kate let their voices wash over her as the doctor read out questions and Alex answered. Through the window she could see a small ornamental pond. A miniature willow hung its branches forlornly over the water's surface. Beyond it, the grounds were set out like a park, a tame landscape of trees and shrubs. *This is what I'm paying for*. The thought was obscurely disturbing.

She turned away from the window as the doctor handed Alex a sheet of paper.

'We need your consent to contact your GP, in case we have to find out more about your medical history, so if you could just fill in this form, please.'

Alex took the form. 'I, uh, I don't have a pen.'

Dr Janson handed him her gold fountain pen. He began to write, then stopped.

'Sorry, I don't, er, I don't know the surgery's address.'

His face had gone red. The doctor smiled reassuringly. 'Don't worry about it. Just put your GP's name and then sign it. You can give us the address next time you come. Provided there's no problem with the blood tests, we probably won't need it anyway since you're a known donor.'

Alex wrote quickly and passed back the sheet. The doctor put it to one side and handed him another.

'This is a consent form for us to store and use your sperm. Read it carefully before you sign it, and please ask if you have any questions.'

She handed Kate another sheet of paper. 'And while he's doing that, you might as well be filling in your consent form for the treatment.'

It was surprisingly uncomplicated. Kate filled in her name and address, and gave Alex's name as the donor, then signed it at the bottom. She gave it back to the doctor.

Alex looked up from his own form, frowning. 'It says here about giving my consent for my, er, my sperm to be used after my death.' He stumbled a little over *consent*.

'That's so we can carry on using your samples in case anything happens to you before the treatment is concluded,' the doctor answered, smoothly. 'You don't have to give it, and we hope it won't be necessary. But if it was, without your consent we wouldn't be able to continue. There was a court case not long ago, if you remember,' she said, including Kate now, 'where a young woman had sperm taken from her husband when he was in a coma, so she could be inseminated with it after he died. Even though he was her husband, it caused all sorts of problems because she hadn't got his written consent. It's usually just a formality, but unless you have any strong objections, it's best to be covered for it.'

Alex still looked uncomfortable. 'What happens to any . . . any samples that are left over? Afterwards, I mean?'

'That's entirely up to you.' She smiled. 'Obviously, though, the clinic is grateful for any donations. So if you've no objections, we'd like to keep them frozen as part of our donor panel.'

'So they can be used on someone else?'

'At some point, possibly, yes.'

Alex shook his head. 'No. No, I don't want that.'

The doctor's smile never slipped. 'That's your prerogative, of course. You can stipulate on the form that you only want them to be used for treating a specific person.'

Alex gave a short nod and began to write. The office was silent, except for the scratching of the pen nib. He rested on the low, glass-topped table. Incongruous in the centre of it was a modern, fluid-filled ornament, like a rectangular spirit-level. Inside it, pink globules drifted sinuously in a viscous-looking red liquid. When enough had gathered at one end, it slowly tilted, forcing them to float up to the other. It looked vaguely obscene. Kate wondered which reflected Dr Janson's taste the most – the antique furniture, or the disturbing ornament.

Alex finished writing. He straightened and considered the form for one last time before passing it across to the doctor. She put it with the others on the clipboard.

'Right,' she said, smiling with easy confidence. 'The next step is for you to give us a sample, so we can check that you aren't azoospermic. That means you either have a very low sperm count or no sperm at all,' she explained, when Alex looked doubtful. 'It's a routine test, but we obviously have to make it. You can book an appointment with the receptionist on the way out.' She tilted her head. 'Unless you want to make a start straight away?'

'Now, you mean?' Alex looked horrified.

'The sooner you start the better, really. And there's no point in having to make any more journeys than you have to, is there?'

The doctor's expression was bland, but Kate wondered if she wasn't taking a subtle revenge for Alex's insistence over the consent form.

'If you'd rather leave it till next time it's okay,' Kate said, seeing him flounder.

'Uh, yes, I – I think I would.' His face had gone crimson.

Dr Janson smiled.

Kate telephoned from the clinic for a taxi to take them back to the station. The gravel drive crunched under their feet as they went out to the main gate to wait for it. After the hospital's air-conditioned chill, the sun's heat was smothering. Kate could feel the hot prickle of sweat breaking out. They walked in silence to the shade of the horse-chestnut that overhung the stone-pillared gateway. The spiky yellow nuggets of conker shells were already visible among the splayed, leathery leaves.

'You okay?' Kate asked.

Alex nodded, without looking at her. 'Fine.'

They fell silent again. Patches of bright sunlight dappled through the leaves, like hot coins where they fell on Kate's bare arms.

'You don't mind, do you?' Alex asked, suddenly. 'I just wasn't expecting to have to . . . you know, to start today.'

'It's all right, I wasn't expecting you to either. Just come whenever it's convenient for you.'

She realised the *double-entendre* as soon as she had spoken, and went on quickly to cover her embarrassment. 'I mean, I know you'll have to fit the trips in with work and everything. I don't want you to go to any more trouble than you have to.'

'It won't be a problem.'

The drone of a car engine became audible. A taxi was pulling up the hill towards the clinic. They moved out from beneath the tree as it approached, but it went past without stopping. The sound of its engine trailed away in the heat. They stood for a second or two on the pavement edge, staring after it, then went back to the tree's shade.

'What do your parents think about this? About what you're doing?' Kate asked.

'My parents?' Alex seemed startled. 'Oh, I haven't told them.'

'Are you going to?'

'No, I don't think so.'

'Wouldn't they approve?'

He looked up through the leaves, squinting into the light. 'No.' Then, as if he felt this wasn't enough, he added, 'They aren't prudish, I don't mean that, and they've always been really supportive. But something like this is . . . Well, you know.'

'So you aren't going to tell anyone?'

He was silent for a moment. 'I'd tell my grandmother, if she was still alive. She'd be pleased. No one else, though.'

Kate saw a small piece of twig caught in his hair. She almost reached out and removed it before she stopped herself. 'Were you very close?'

Alex nodded, absently. Then he looked at her, concerned. 'Not that I'm not close to my parents as well. I don't want to give that impression. It's just that my grandmother was . . .' He was self-conscious now. 'Well, she was special.'

Another taxi was approaching the clinic. This time they watched until it indicated and pulled to a stop.

'I think this one's ours,' said Kate.

They were quiet for most of the journey back to London. Alex sat opposite her, staring out of the window, swaying slightly with the movement of the train. His eyes were sleepy, half-lidded against the sunlight angling into his face through the glass. He looked vulnerable, Kate thought, much younger than the thirty-four she knew him to be.

A sudden lurch roused him. He turned and caught her staring before she could look away. She smiled.

'There's a piece of twig stuck in your hair,' she said.

He looked bewildered. She pointed. 'You've got a twig caught in your hair.'

'Oh. Right.' He pulled it out. 'Thanks.'

He looked around for somewhere to put it. She could see him considering the seat, the table and the floor before he dropped it in his pocket.

'No bin,' he explained, with an embarrassed smile.

Kate hid her amusement by searching in her bag. She pulled out a white envelope and passed it across to him.

'There's a cheque in there for your expenses,' she said. 'I've based it on train fares for fifteen visits to start with, plus taxis to and from both stations.'

Alex held the envelope without opening it.

'If you want to work out how much you think I'll owe you for your time, I'll be happy to pay that in advance as well,' she offered, seeing his expression.

'No! I didn't mean . . .' He hurriedly put the envelope down on the table. 'I told you, I don't want paying for this.'

'I don't expect you to do it for nothing.'

He shook his head. 'I can't take money from you.'

'In that case we'd better forget about the whole thing.'

She had meant it lightly, but Alex looked as though she had slapped him. 'It's only your travel expenses,' she said, smiling to show she hadn't been serious. 'We can discuss a fee later, if you like. But I can't let you be out of pocket.'

She pushed the envelope across the table towards him. 'Now, please, no arguments. I insist.'

He was clearly unhappy, but after a second he picked it up. 'Okay. If you're sure.' He put the envelope in his pocket, still unopened.

Kate glanced out of the window. 'We'll be at Euston in a few minutes.' She cleared her throat. 'Look, I don't quite know what to say, but . . . well, I really am grateful for what you're doing. Thank you.'

Alex kept his head averted. 'I'm glad to do it.'

Kate hid her embarrassment behind a no-nonsense tone. 'All the same, I really appreciate it. And I'll find out from the clinic how many extra visits you have to make, and send you a cheque.'

He looked up, sharply. 'Aren't we . . . I mean, won't I see you again?'

'I don't think there's any point.' She was unprepared for how blunt that sounded. 'If there are any problems, or anything you want to ask, you can always ring me. You've got my number. But I don't expect there will be. And the clinic'll keep me notified with how things are going.'

'Oh . . . yes, I suppose . . . yes, you're right.'

They didn't speak again for the rest of the journey. When the train pulled into the shadow of the station, they avoided looking at each other as they left their seats and filed out of the carriage with the rest of the passengers. The platform was hot and airless. Kate turned and held out her hand.

'Well. Thanks again.'

Alex took it. His palm was hot and dry, and she remembered the other occasion on which she had shaken it, outside the restaurant the first time she had met him. She pushed the memory to one side.

His blue eyes were troubled as he looked at her. He seemed about to say something, but then he dropped his gaze.

''Bye.'

Kate let go of his hand with a last polite smile, and set off down the platform. She wished she had waited until they had reached the concourse to say goodbye, because now they both had to walk in the same direction anyway. But there was no sound of his footsteps following hers. She told herself it was the claustrophobia of the busy platform and the diesel fumes that suddenly seemed depressing, and determinedly walked faster.

She heard someone running only a second before the shout.

'Kate!'

She turned around. Alex slowed as he reached her, and the urgency on his face gave way to confusion.

'Look, I was just wondering . . .' he began, breathlessly, 'I mean, if not, it's okay, but . . .' He seemed to gather himself. 'Well, I – I just wondered if you wanted to go for a – a drink some time?'

Kate didn't even need to think of reasons why she shouldn't. It was far better to make a clean break now, rather than invite complications later. There was no point delaying it.

Alex stood in front of her, nervously waiting for her answer. She smiled.

'I'd like that.'

CHAPTER 11

The summer burned itself out. The days were bleached by a sun that scorched grass and cracked the earth, while the nights hung unmoving in a breezeless haze. Newspapers ran features on global warming and droughts, and garden hoses were sneaked out after dark to sprinkle desiccated lawns and plants away from the censorious eyes of watchful neighbours.

Kate began to see Alex regularly, once a week to start with, but then more often as the reserve between them slowly dropped away. The results of his first sample and set of blood tests came back clear, and he began his trips to the clinic, going once or twice a week as far as Kate could tell. He still hadn't cashed the cheque for expenses, though, she saw when she received her bank statement.

'I said I'd take it, I didn't say anything about cashing it,' he told her with a grin, when she confronted him. She argued, but this time he was insistent. 'We can sort it out later,' was as far as he would commit himself.

He rarely alluded to the visits, and Kate didn't press for details. She knew he was sensitive about them, and didn't want to risk embarrassing him. She had spoken to Dr Janson after Alex's first session at the clinic. It had not gone well. 'Non-productive' was the term Dr Janson used.

'Nothing to worry about,' she had told Kate. 'It happens to quite a lot of men. They find the whole idea of masturbating to order a bit off-putting at first. Especially in a hospital cubicle.'

Kate had decided against asking Alex about it, realising that was probably the last thing he needed. He made no mention of what had happened, but cried off from meeting her as they'd arranged, claiming he had too much work. He sounded tired and depressed, and the faint stammer, which had become hardly noticeable, was more pronounced than ever.

Her relief when the clinic told her there had been no problems with his next sample was as much for his sake as for her own.

They continued to go out together. They would meet in some pub or wine bar, generally one with a garden, where they could sit outside in whatever cool there was. One night Alex convinced her to go to an arthouse cinema in Camden, where they sat in sweltering discomfort and watched *The Wicker Man*. Afterwards, Kate joked that in the final conflagration scene Edward Woodward had probably been cooler than the audience. They spent the rest of the evening good-naturedly arguing the point in a Chinese restaurant.

She didn't admit to herself how much she looked forward to seeing him. It was one thing to appreciate her luck at having found a donor she liked and respected, but Kate veered away from considering the extent to which she enjoyed his company. When she thought about it at all, she rationalised that it was only natural to want to know him better, so that she could one day tell her child (and the thought of her *child* still gave her a little dip of vertigo) what sort of person its father was. There was nothing wrong in that, she told herself.

But she didn't think about it too often.

Only once was there a slightly discordant moment, and at the time Kate thought little of it. She had met Alex for a drink, and as they found a table in the pub's beer garden she noticed a smear of black on the back of his Levi's.

'Have you got decorators in at work?' she asked.

'No, why?'

She grinned and nodded at the patch. 'You've got paint on your jeans.'

'Where?' He craned around to see.

'At least I think it's paint,' she said. 'It might be ink.'

Her grin faded. Alex was staring at the black patch. His face was drained of colour.

'What's the matter?'

He quickly straightened. 'Nothing. I – I just . . .' The colour was coming back into his face now. He sat down. 'I d-didn't know it was there, that's all.'

His stammer was noticeable again.

'It might come out,' Kate said. 'You might be able to buy some sort of cleaning solvent if it's ink—'

'It isn't ink.'

She was surprised at his vehemence. He dropped his eyes. 'I mean, I think it's p-paint. I – I must have leaned against something.'

Kate gave an uneasy nod of acceptance as she sat down. She regretted having pointed it out to him, although she couldn't see why it mattered what it was, or why it should have upset him so much. But the brief awkwardness raised between them by the incident soon faded in the warm evening. It was probably just embarrassment at meeting her in paint- or ink-stained jeans, she decided.

She never saw him wear them again.

They saw quite a lot of Lucy and Jack. Alex enjoyed playing with the children, and he and Jack would preside over barbecues in the back garden with varying degrees of success. Lucy was pleased but exasperated by Kate's relationship with him, even though Kate insisted she didn't have one.

'You don't have to justify seeing him to me,' Lucy said once, when Kate grew defensive. 'I think it's great. I just can't understand why, since you obviously like the bloke, you're still intent on using the poor bugger as a donor. I mean, what's wrong with having it draught, like everybody else?'

'Lucy!'

'Well, I'm sorry, but it seems odd to me. I mean, have you slept together yet?'

Kate's face grew hot. 'That's none of your business!'

'So you haven't,' Lucy said, blithely. 'Why? What's wrong with him? He's not queer, is he?' She held up her hands before Kate could object. 'All right, sorry. I mean gay. But he isn't, is he?'

'No!'

'So why don't you sleep with him, then?'

'Because we're just friends!'

It sounded trite, even to her, but she doggedly refused to admit there was anything more than friendship between them. The ground rules of their relationship had been set at the beginning, by her, and since Alex seemed content to abide by them, Kate didn't let herself so much as consider an alternative.

One hot and restless Sunday, though, Kate broke with routine and phoned him to suggest they go for a picnic. She was mildly surprised to feel nervous in case he said no, but he didn't. They caught a train to Cambridge, where they bought a bottle of wine and baguettes filled with cheese and salad, and queued on the steps of the river for a punt. They took turns in poling the unwieldy, flat-bottomed boat upstream, laughing at each other's clumsiness, until they reached a relatively quiet spot in which to picnic. Kate almost overbalanced climbing onto the bank, and when Alex grabbed her arm to steady her, the sudden contact embarrassed them both. She busied herself unwrapping the sandwiches, while Alex uncorked the wine and poured it into paper cups.

He had taken a camera with him, and unobtrusively snapped Kate before she knew what he was doing.

'Right, in that case I'm going to take one of you,' she said, and, over his protests, took the camera from him. She caught him in the frame, grinning and flushed from the sun, looking absurdly boyish in his white T-shirt and faded jeans. The fine silver chain he wore around his neck gleamed in the sunlight. Kate had been meaning for some time to ask what he wore on it. She was about to now, but before she could phrase the question a middle-aged Japanese man detached himself from a family group and came over.

Smiling, he pointed to himself, then to Kate and Alex, and mimed taking a photograph.

'I think he's offering to take our picture,' Kate said. The man nodded, still smiling as he reached for the camera. A little uneasily, Kate relinquished it and moved next to Alex.

The Japanese man motioned them to stand closer together. They edged nearer to each other. Kate felt her bare arm brush Alex's. He smelled of sun-heated flesh, deodorant and, ever so faintly, of fresh sweat. She remained aware of the contact as they both grinned, self-consciously, at the camera.

The Japanese man pressed the shutter and handed the camera back.

'Thank you,' Kate said. The man smiled again and bobbed his head, then went to where his family, a woman and two teenage boys, stood waiting.

The camera went back in its case, like a dangerous toy, while the two of them ate their picnic.

It clouded over as they took the punt back. The first fat drops of rain began to spatter on the steps leading up from the small wooden quay. They took cover in a nearby pub as the drops became a downpour, and other people ran inside for shelter. They managed to find a table overlooking the river before the pub became too full, and watched as the water's smooth surface splintered into fragments. A flash of light lit the copper-coloured sky, followed by a crack of thunder a few seconds later.

'Don't suppose you've got an umbrella handy, have you?' Kate asked Alex, and for some reason that struck them both as funny. They laughed helplessly as the other customers gave them curious glances, and the storm clamoured overhead.

Afterwards, Kate was always to think of that as the end of summer. The sun returned in the wake of the rain, but now with that subtle change in light that comes when the season has peaked. The mornings became fresher, and the evenings were shattered by more storms that spiced the air with ozone and the mustiness of rain on hot pavements. In the space of a week it was autumn.

The trees began shedding leaves, stirred by breezes that carried a chill hint of winter. Nights grew darker, afternoons dusky and seasoned with the smokiness of autumn. On bonfire night, Kate and Alex arranged to go to a firework display with Lucy, Jack and the children. But the day before, Lucy phoned to say that both Emily and Angus had been stricken with chickenpox.

Alex sounded disappointed when she told him.

'There's no reason why we can't still go,' she said. 'Is there?'

They met in a pub near the park where the display was being held. Kate laughed when Alex presented her with a packet of sparklers.

'God, I've not held one of these since I was a kid.'

He smiled, pleased with her reaction. 'That's the point of bonfire night. We can pretend we're kids again without anyone thinking we need locking up.'

They left the pub and made their way through the park towards the fire. The night was hazy with woodsmoke and sulphur. Exploding rockets peppered the sky with sounds like tearing cloth. As they drew nearer, the pungent smells of the hot dog and burger stalls threw their weight into the atmospheric stew.

They bought jacket potatoes and mulled wine, and made their way through the crowd towards the bonfire. It towered behind a cordon of ropes, throwing a stream of sparks into the sky. A lifelike guy was slumped in a chair balanced at the top, smouldering but not yet alight. One gloved hand, buffeted by the heat, moved disturbingly up and down, as though trying to beat down the flames.

Kate grimaced. 'It's a bit gruesome, when you think about it, isn't it?' she said. 'Pretending to burn someone. Even if he did try to blow up Parliament. Not much reason to call it a "good" fire, is it?'

Alex was watching the guy. It seemed to take a second for what she said to register. He looked at her with a quizzical expression.

'Bonfire,' she explained, feeling stupid, 'At school they said it meant "good fire". You know, as in *bon*, French for "good".'

A smile touched his face. 'That isn't where it gets its name from. It's derived from "bone fire". Because they used to burn bones.'

Kate gave a horrified laugh. 'God, it gets worse! I thought it was bad enough celebrating someone being executed!'

Alex shook his head, turning back to the flames. 'That wasn't what it was about originally. To start with it was a Celtic fire festival called Samhain, when people used to build fires to mark the beginning of winter. It wasn't even on November the fifth, it was on the first. But after the Gunpowder Plot people were encouraged to burn effigies of Guy Fawkes on the fires, and the whole idea was hijacked.'

'You sound like you don't approve.'

He didn't answer at first. His face was jaundiced with reflected flame.

'It was something pure to start with,' he said. 'People celebrating fire as a counter to winter. Then it was turned into a political sham, a warning from the government to any other malcontents. Fawkes was a scapegoat. He was just a mercenary, an explosives expert hired to handle the gunpowder. Robert Catesby was the real leader, but no one hears about him. He was killed when they arrested the actual plotters, so they played up Fawkes's role instead. And the real reason for lighting the bonfires became lost.'

He stopped, giving her a chagrined grin. 'Sorry. Lecture over.'

'You sound like you've read a lot about it,' Kate said. It was rare to hear him speak at such length.

Alex seemed about to say something else when a detonation above them lit the sky with a stuttering *crack!* Kate looked up and felt the pressure of the rocket's percussion on her face as the display began.

They were forced closer together as people pushed forward for a better view. Kate was conscious of him standing slightly behind and to one side as the firebursts boomed and flowered overhead. She swayed back, involuntarily, but in the moment before her shoulders brushed against him, a sudden waft of hot smoke stung her eyes. She turned away, blinking, and as she wiped them there was a commotion at the opposite side of the fire.

Through streaming eyes she saw a man duck under the rope cordon. A steward made a grab for him, but the man jinked around his outstretched hands like a rugby forward. He ran straight at the blazing stack of wood, and as Kate watched, still not believing what he was going to do, the man launched himself into it.

The steward's cry was drowned in the bang of another explosion overhead. He dodged back, throwing up his arm to shield himself as the bonfire collapsed in a frenzy of sparks.

Behind him, the horrified, pale faces of the people standing by the ropes began to turn away, like lights blinking out. She heard one or two screams above the clatter of the fireworks, but most of the crowd were unaware of what had happened. A cooing *ahh* went up at another extravagant rocket-burst as stewards ran towards the fire.

Kate quickly turned away as two of them pawed with long poles at a smouldering shape in the edge of the flames. She clutched hold of Alex's arm.

'Let's go.'

Now more people were turning to look. A low murmur, almost a moan, went up from the crowd at some further movement from around the bonfire.

'Alex . . .'

He was still staring at the cluster of stewards. She tugged at him. He didn't move.

'Come on, Alex.'

His face was blank with shock as he let her lead him away. They pushed against the flow of a crowd that was now moving towards the fire to see what had happened. She almost lost her grip on Alex's arm, but then the crush thinned and they could move freely.

Kate gagged at the smell of cooked meat as they passed the hot dog and burger stalls. She held her breath until they had left them behind, and glanced at Alex. His eyes were unfocused. He walked loosely, as though he were concussed.

'Are you all right?'

Kate had to repeat the question before he responded. For a moment he looked at her without recognition, then he nodded.

'Yes, sorry, I . . .' His voice tailed off.

'Do you want to go for a drink?' Kate asked. They had reached the park exit. In the light from the street lamps she could see how pale his face was.

'No . . . no, I think I . . . I'd just like to go home.'

Kate flagged down a taxi. They rode in silence. Alex seemed to have withdrawn into himself. He sat in a corner of the cab, staring out of the window. Lights from the street played over his face like a slow-motion strobe.

'Why would someone do that?' Kate said, unable to keep quiet any longer.

Alex shook his head.

Kate saw the figure leap into the flames, the fire collapse again. She gave an involuntary flinch. 'Even if he wanted to kill himself, why pick such a – a *horrible* way?'

She found that her teeth were chattering a little as she spoke, although it wasn't cold in the cab. Alex continued to stare out of the window.

'Perhaps it didn't seem horrible to him.'

His face was in shadow. Kate couldn't see his expression. She knew she was beginning to sound ghoulish, but couldn't stop herself. 'But why do it like that? In front of all those people?'

She felt rather than saw Alex stir.

'It was a way of getting attention. Showing everyone he was there. Perhaps he wanted to hit out at them. Or at someone in particular. Like saying, "Look what I'm doing, this is your fault. You made me do this".' He was silent for a moment. 'Or perhaps he wanted to punish himself.'

Kate tried to shut out the memory of the steward's face, paralysed with horror and disbelief as he was forced to watch.

She knew that no matter how bad her nightmares might be, his would be worse.

'It seems . . . I don't know. Selfish, somehow.'

'Selfish?' Alex had turned to look at her.

'Doing something like that in front of so many complete strangers. Not caring what it would do to them afterwards.'

'Would they have cared about him if he hadn't done it?'

'No, probably not, but—'

'So why should he care about them?'

The bitterness in his tone was like a rebuke. She didn't answer.

Alex sighed. 'I'm sorry.'

'It's all right.'

'No, I . . .' He gestured, helplessly. 'It just got to me a bit, that's all.'

Kate was already regretting what she'd said. Alex rarely talked about his work, but she felt clumsy and insensitive for not anticipating how this might have affected him.

Tentatively, she asked, 'Have you known someone like that?'

'Once,' he said, looking back out of the window.

Lucy and Jack asked Kate over for Christmas Day, as they usually did.

'Ask Alex, too,' Lucy added. 'Unless you've both got other plans?'

Kate tried not to sound too evasive. 'I haven't. I'm not sure what Alex is doing, though.'

'Is he thinking about going to his parents'?'

'He might be, I don't know.'

'You don't *know*? Haven't you asked him?'

'Uh . . . No, not yet.'

'Not yet? Don't you think you're leaving it a bit late?'

Kate wouldn't meet Lucy's eye. 'I just haven't got round to it. Anyway, I expect he's already got his own plans.'

'And I expect he's thinking exactly the same about you. God, you're as bad as each other!' Lucy went to the phone, looking exasperated. 'All right, what's his number? If you're not going to ask him, I will!'

'Don't you dare!'

Lucy smiled, the receiver held ready.

Kate threw up her hands. 'All right, all right! I'll ask him.'

'Now?' Lucy offered her the phone.

'Tomorrow,' Kate said, firmly.

She told herself it was ridiculous to feel nervous, but that didn't make her feel any less so as she waited to broach the subject the next night. The theatre bar they were in was festooned with gaudy green and red baubles and tinsel. Christmas was inescapable, no matter how much you tried.

'Are you going to Cornwall for Christmas?' Kate asked finally, giving up any attempt at subtlety.

'Cornwall?'

'To your parents.'

'Oh! Oh . . . yes, probably, I expect.' He gave an unenthusiastic smile. 'Have to carve the turkey and listen to the Queen's speech, and everything.' He paused. 'What about you?'

Kate tried to sound unconcerned. 'Lucy and Jack have

invited me over. They wondered if you wanted to go as well, if you hadn't already got something lined up. But I said you probably would have.'

'For Christmas Day?' He sounded surprised.

'Yes, but it's all right. We thought you'd be spending it with your family.'

The chime sounded for the start of the next act. Kate finished her drink. 'We'd better go back in,' she said, and blamed the flatness she felt on the poorness of the play.

It was two days later when Alex phoned.

'Looks like I've been ditched at Christmas,' he told her. 'My mother rang last night and asked if I minded if they went away instead. A last-minute offer from friends in Spain.'

Kate kept her voice neutral. 'So what will you do now?'

'Oh, I don't know. Probably just spend a quiet one on my own.'

Kate could almost hear Lucy's prompting, *Oh, for God's sake, just ask him!*

'You can still come over to Lucy and Jack's,' she said, trying to sound off-hand. 'I know they'd be pleased to see you.'

Christmas morning was bright with a crisp winter sun that struggled to melt the white frost garnishing the pavements. The big house smelled of cooking and mulled wine. Nat King Cole vied for precedence with the TV as Jack took their coats and gave them both a steaming glass. Alex had taken a carrier bag full of presents, and Emily and Angus delightedly shredded the garish paper from theirs, carried away more by the orgy of opening rather than the gifts themselves, which were an expensive but unimaginative doll and a toy car that Angus was too young to appreciate.

There was a bottle of whisky for Jack, Chanel perfume for Lucy. Her eyes widened when she saw it.

'Oh, my God, now that's what I call a present!'

She kissed Alex on the mouth. Kate felt a quick jab of something that could almost have been jealousy, and then Alex came over to her.

'Happy Christmas.'

Almost shyly, he handed her a small parcel, and she suddenly wished she had bought him more than the bottle of Irish whiskey.

She took the parcel from him and unwrapped it, aware of the others watching her. Inside was a long box. Kate opened it and took out the plain gold chain and locket.

'I didn't know what size socks you took,' Alex said. The quip sounded rehearsed.

'It's beautiful,' Kate said. 'Thank you.'

She stepped forward and kissed him. The kiss was no longer than the one Lucy had given him moments before, but it was their first, and Kate felt acutely aware that Lucy and Jack were watching. When they moved apart she made a show of fastening the chain around her neck to hide her confusion.

They drank a dry Spanish sparkling wine with the enormous turkey Lucy had cooked, and then various bottles of whatever Jack produced during the afternoon. By early evening Kate was pleasantly light-headed, and the pressure of anticipation that had been building in her all day finally found a focus.

She and Alex were in the kitchen, washing the stack of congealed dishes. She handed him a wet glass to dry, and as their hands touched, the thought came without warning.

Tonight.

Flustered, Kate turned away, briskly scrubbing at a greasy plate to conceal her sudden tumult.

She pushed all thought of the decision to one side, but the awareness remained on a subliminal level for the rest of the evening; a faint breathlessness, a tensing in her lower stomach. And then she and Alex were saying goodnight to Lucy and Jack and climbing into the taxi, and all at once it confronted her with the suddenness of a slamming door.

Alex seemed to sense her tension. The atmosphere in the cab became strained. Familiar landmarks went past the windows like a countdown, and then the taxi was pulling into Kate's road. It stopped outside her flat.

Her heart thudded. The words felt clumsy in her mouth. 'Would you like to come in?'

She saw understanding dawn on his face. He looked away quickly.

'I'd, er . . . I'd better not. It's late.'

The rejection was so unexpected she felt nothing.

'Oh. Okay,' she heard herself say, and then she was climbing out of the cab. The cold night air didn't penetrate any deeper than her skin. 'Goodnight, then.'

Alex didn't look at her. 'Goodnight.'

The taxi pulled away, leaving behind a fading blueness of exhaust. The street was deserted. Kate walked up her path. Her keys were in her hand, although she had no memory of taking them out. She reached up to unlock the front door, and then it hit her.

She squeezed her eyes tight against the pain of it, hand still outstretched towards the lock. For a long moment she stood, rigid, unable to make herself move. There was a miaow at her feet. She looked down as Dougal twined himself around her ankles. The cat stared up at her, wide-eyed and indifferent.

'Happy Christmas, Dougal,' she said, and let them both into the empty flat.

CHAPTER 12

The letter from the clinic arrived on a February morning when the rain lashed against the windows and daylight was a grudging, sepia non-event. Kate knew what it would be, but that didn't make her any less nervous as she slit open the envelope, crested with the hospital's logo, and took out the letter.

Alex's final blood test, taken six months after his last donation, was clear. The clinic asked her to contact them so that they could make arrangements for her first treatment.

Kate set down the letter on the breakfast bar. She didn't realise she was staring into space until the toast popped up, making her jump. Ignoring it, she went to her bag in the hallway and took out her diary. She had been keeping a temperature chart and testing her urine every day to time her menstrual cycle. It was so regular that she didn't really need to check when she was next due to ovulate, but she did all the same.

It was just over two weeks.

Kate went back into the kitchen and absently spread sunflower margarine on the toast. It had gone cold, and the first bite clogged in her mouth. She washed it down with tea and dropped the rest of her breakfast into the bin.

Although she wasn't supposed to make her appointment

for the first treatment until her period had actually started, she couldn't wait. She called the clinic as soon as she arrived at work. The receptionist, polite, with only the barest trace of Birmingham in her voice, booked her in for a little over a fortnight's time and told Kate to telephone the day before to confirm. It was curiously undramatic, almost like making a dental appointment. The excitement was there, a taut anticipation, like sitting in a plane as it gathered speed to take off. But the knowledge of what she had to do first overlay any pleasure she felt.

She had continued to see Alex after Christmas, accepting the apology he had made on Boxing Day, a stammered account of over-indulgence and indigestion. She had even managed to convince herself that she had narrowly avoided a stupid mistake. But she had deliberately begun to tail off the number of times they met, preparing herself for the moment she now faced.

It didn't make it any easier.

Kate didn't phone him until that evening, feeling a sneaking relief that he had asked her not to ring him at work. His phone rang on, monotonously, and she was about to hang up when he answered.

'Yes?'

He sounded breathless, as though he had run to get to it.

'It's Kate, Alex.'

'Oh, hi! I wasn't expecting you to call tonight.'

She steeled herself against the pleasure in his voice. 'I've heard from the clinic. Your final blood tests are okay.'

'That's great! I knew they would be, but . . . well, you know.' He laughed, happy. 'So you can go ahead now?'

'Yes. The thing is . . .' She shut her eyes. 'I don't think we should see each other any more.'

There was a pause. 'Oh.'

'It isn't anything personal. But we always knew this was going to happen some time, and – and I think now's the time to do it. It's only going to complicate things if we don't, and I don't think that'll do either of us any good. Or the baby.'

The words sounded false.

'It's for the best . . . You can see that, can't you?' It was almost a plea.

'Uh . . . yeah, yes, I . . .' She heard him clear his throat. 'Yes, I suppose you're right.'

'I don't want you to think I'm not grateful for what you've done,' she said, knowing she was only making things worse, but unable to stop. 'I'll send you a cheque for the rest of the money I owe you, and—'

'No!'

The word was spat out. Kate recoiled from the heat in it.

'No,' he repeated, more calmly. 'I told you I didn't want paying.'

The conversation was over, but Kate couldn't bring herself to end it. She said the one thing she had determined not to say.

'I'm sorry.'

'Yeah.'

Kate kept the receiver to her ear, waiting for him to say something else or break the connection. But the line remained silent.

She hung up.

*   *   *

Her meal lay untouched on the coffee table. The CD had finished playing, but she didn't get up to put on another. She sat on the settee, her legs curled under her, idly stroking Dougal who was slumped asleep on her lap.

She told herself she had no reason to feel miserable. The whole point of what she was doing was because she didn't *want* a relationship. Alex had known from the start what the situation was. This would be *her* pregnancy; *her* baby. It would be cruel to let their relationship – or non-relationship, she thought, remembering Christmas – go on any longer.

With a sigh she slid Dougal onto the cushion and stood up. She picked up the plate of cold pasta and took it into the kitchen. As she was scraping it into the bin, the phone rang.

Expecting it to be Lucy, she went to answer it. 'Hello?'

'It's me. Alex.'

The sound of his voice brought a rush of mixed emotions. He went on before she had time to sort them, not giving her a chance to speak.

'Look, I've been thinking. You're right, we should stop seeing each other, but, well, the thing is, I thought it would be nice to meet one last time. Perhaps after you've been to the clinic, or something . You know, for a sort of farewell good-luck dinner.'

The words had come out in a rush. Now he stopped. When he spoke again it was more haltingly.

'It seems a shame to – to just end it like this. Without, well, without saying goodbye properly.'

His voice held a note of hope. Kate found her mood had lightened.

'Yes,' she said, smiling. 'I suppose it does.'

*   *   *

WHERE THERE'S SMOKE

The oak tree by the clinic's gate was bare and black. Kate passed under it and walked up the drive. The gravel, dry and bleached the last time she had been, was dark and shiny with rain. Although it was only mid-afternoon, the day was reduced to a foggy twilight. Wind tugged at her hair and chapped her cheeks, and then the automatic doors slid open to let her pass into the warmth and light of the clinic.

The smiling receptionist took her name and asked her to take a seat. Kate sat by the window. Outside, the February bleakness blustered silently behind the double glazing. She unfastened her coat, already feeling the central heating dispel the chill.

After a few minutes a young nurse, smart in a tailored pale grey and white uniform appeared and led her over to a lift. Kate had only been on the clinic's ground floor before, but the first floor seemed little different. Their feet were silent on the wide, carpeted corridor. Weeping figs and yucca plants provided a green and healthy contrast to the dead vegetation outside. Soft, piped classical music followed them from hidden speakers.

'The residential area's down there,' the nurse said, as they passed another corridor. Concealed lighting cast a gentle glow along the double row of well-spaced, limed wooden doors. It could have been a hotel.

'The rooms are all private, obviously,' the nurse added. 'There's a six-month waiting list for them, but I don't suppose you'll have got as far as thinking about the birth yet.'

Kate smiled dutifully. 'I'll think I'll get this bit over first.'

A woman in a crisp white maternity smock came towards them, the only other patient Kate had seen so far. Her stomach bulged, taut as a drum against the smock, but she was beautifully made up. She nodded in return to the nurse's hello and her glance took in Kate's damp hair, clothes and left hand. Her smile was perfunctory.

The nurse opened a door and stood back to let Kate enter. The room was windowless and small, but not claustrophobically so. A chair stood at one side, and a small rail at the far end held a row of coat hangers. A dressing mirror was fastened to a partly open door, beyond which she could glimpse a sink and lavatory. Another door, closed, was opposite the chair.

'You'll find a gown and paper slippers for you to change into. There's no rush. Just press the buzzer when you're ready,' the nurse told her, indicating a button by the light switch, 'and someone will come and get you. Okay?'

Kate said it was. She waited until the nurse had left with a final smile, then looked around. A single white gown was hanging on the rail. She went over and touched it. It was a soft paper. She remembered how the counsellor at the other clinic had told her that there would be no need to take off her clothes. The Wynguard Clinic clearly took a different view.

She sat on the edge of the chair. Her dislike of hospitals made her shiver. Turning, she caught sight of herself in the mirror, nervously perched with her thighs pressed together, her hands clamped between them. She stood up and began briskly to undress.

Kate didn't hear any buzzer when she pressed the button, but one must have sounded because almost immediately the inner door was opened. The same nurse smiled at her.

'All ready?'

She moved to one side, letting Kate into the next room. It was bigger than the one she had changed in, but also windowless. A couch stood against the wall. Beside it was what looked like a computer console and monitor. A young woman in a white coat sat by it.

'You've had an ultrasound scan before, haven't you?' the nurse asked. 'So you know what the drill is.'

Kate nodded. She had been given a scan when she had first gone to the clinic. She lay back on the couch while the technician put a condom over the end of the scanner's probe. The nurse pulled on a pair of surgical gloves.

'I'll need a mucus sample first. So if you can move your legs apart and raise them a little, please?'

Kate did. The clearness and texture of her vaginal mucus was another indication of whether or not she was ovulating. She had checked it herself that morning, along with her temperature and urine. She was as sure as she could be that she had got the timing right, but she was still anxious to have it confirmed by the clinic. After a few seconds, the nurse stepped away.

'Okay, I'll just get this checked out.'

She left the room and the young woman took her place at the foot of the couch. She gave Kate an encouraging smile.

'Right, just relax.'

That was easier said than done. Kate tried to concentrate on the black and white images on the screen. They were unintelligible to her, but the technician studied them intently as she manipulated the probe. Finally, she gave a nod of approval. Kate felt the probe being withdrawn.

'Super. The follicle's a good nineteen millimetres. Should be ready to rupture any time, I'd say.' The technician peeled off the condom from the probe and dropped it into a bin with her gloves. She wheeled away the scanner. 'You can sit up again, if you like. Dr Janson'll be along in a few minutes.'

She went out. The piped classical music drifted on in the background without relieving the loneliness of the empty white room. Kate swung her legs off the couch. The sheet of tissue paper covering it slid around slightly on the underlying vinyl. She looked down at her feet as they dangled above the ground, ridiculous in the elasticated paper slippers. She wondered if she would have had to wear them at a less expensive clinic.

The door opened and Dr Janson walked in. The nurse followed her. Dr Janson's grey-blonde hair was pinned up in a thick French pleat, immaculate as ever. Her white lab coat seemed incongruous over the elegant clothes she wore underneath.

'Hello,' she greeted Kate, brightly. 'Everything all right?'

'I think so, yes.'

'Good. Well, you'll be glad to know that the timing's fine. You're about to ovulate, so we can go ahead with the first treatment as planned.'

Dr Janson smiled. She was wearing a pair of gold-rimmed glasses. She looked like a model from an optician's catalogue, Kate thought.

'Nervous?' the doctor asked. Kate nodded. 'There's no need to be. You won't be able to feel very much, and it doesn't take very long. Just try to relax. Now, if you can lie back on the couch . . .'

Kate lowered herself down again, positioning her legs as before. She could feel the knots of her gown digging into her bare back where they pressed against the mattress. She clenched her hands together by her sides.

There was a snap of surgical gloves. Glancing down, Kate saw the nurse sliding a small orange plastic straw into the stainless-steel tube. She gave it to the doctor, who turned back towards the couch. A speculum was in her other hand.

'Can you raise your legs a little more, please? That's it.'

Kate stared resolutely at the featureless ceiling. She tried to breathe slowly and steadily, but she still tensed as she felt the first touch. The metal of the speculum had been thoughtfully warmed, and there was no real discomfort. It was no different from having a smear. Even so, the knuckles of her clenched hands were white. Her heart thudded and raced.

She concentrated on the piped music. It was familiar. She had a version herself on CD. Vivaldi. *The Four Seasons – Le Quattro Stagione.* She tried to remember which movement it was. 'Spring'? Or 'Winter'?

At the end of the couch, Dr Janson straightened.

'Right. There we go.'

Kate lifted her head to see the nurse step forward, holding out a stainless-steel tray. Dr Janson put the inseminator and speculum into it and smiled down at Kate.

'How do you feel? All right?'

Kate nodded.

'Good. Just lie still for a few minutes, and then you can get dressed and go home.'

'So I can carry on as normal?'

'Completely as normal. I'll see you tomorrow for the second insemination, and then that's it for this cycle. It's just a matter now of keeping your fingers crossed and waiting to see if you have a period or not. If you do, then we'll try again next month.' She gave Kate another smile. 'The nurse will bring you a cup of tea or coffee, so just relax for a few minutes. There's no rush.'

She left. The nurse asked Kate what she wanted to drink and then left also, carrying the tray containing the instruments and the doctor's latex gloves, crumpled on the gleaming metal like a beached jellyfish.

Kate lay back on the couch.

I've done it!

The thought was a silent, exultant cry, setting her down on the other side of a barrier from the fears and uncertainties of a pre-insemination existence. She felt drunk on the knowledge that she was irrevocably committed. Even if she didn't become pregnant this cycle, there was always the next. Or the one after that. She had finally made the leap. Now it was simply a matter of continuing.

The nurse returned, carrying a china cup and saucer and a plate of biscuits.

'Another five minutes and you can get dressed,' she said.

Kate pushed herself upright as the woman set the tea and biscuits on the table at the bottom of the couch. She turned to go, but then bent and picked up something from the floor.

'Is this yours?'

She held out the gold chain and locket Alex had

bought Kate for Christmas. Kate's hand went to her throat.

'I must have caught it when I was getting changed. Thanks.'

Though the chain was light, Kate felt a heaviness at its cold touch as she fastened it back around her neck.

Subdued music, played on unfamiliar stringed instruments, was playing in the Thai restaurant. The dining room was dark, but each table was lit by two fat candles so that walking down the aisles between them was like being in a temple. The air smelled of burning candle wax, lemon and garlic.

Alex was already at the table when Kate arrived. She had thought it best if they made their separate ways there, rather than share a taxi as they had in the past. The candlelight gave his face a melancholy cast as he stared into it, reminding Kate with a pang of the first night they had gone to Lucy and Jack's. Then he looked up and saw her, and she pushed the memory away.

'Sorry I'm late,' she said, as the white-jacketed waiter pulled back her chair. 'The taxi didn't turn up so I had to order another.'

'That's okay.' Alex smiled at her. 'You look . . . ah, you look great.'

Her hair was up in a chignon, and she wore a plain black long-sleeved dress. The locket hung around her bare neck.

'Thank you.'

They fell silent.

'So—' they began at the same time, and stopped.

'Sorry. You first,' Kate said.

'I was just going to ask how it went.' He lowered his voice slightly. 'You know, at the, er, at the clinic.'

She had finished her second insemination the day before. 'Oh, okay. I've just got to wait and see what happens now.'

'Well. I hope . . .' Alex struggled. 'Well, you know.'

She nodded. 'Thanks.'

The bubble of tension around them seemed to tighten, choking any chance of conversation. Kate looked at the other tables, islands of intimacy with their burning candles. The conversations were low but animated, a murmuring counterpoint to the tinkle of cutlery. No one seemed miserable. She drew a deep breath.

'Perhaps this wasn't such a good idea.'

He looked hurt. 'Why?'

'It just might have been better to leave it as it was.' She shrugged. 'This is only dragging things out, isn't it?'

Alex nudged the warm wax pooled at the base of the candle with his finger. He didn't look at her. 'Do you want to go?'

'No,' she said, after a moment.

The waiter returned. Giving a short bow, he handed them each a menu.

'They serve saki. Why don't you have a flask?' Kate asked, brightly.

'Aren't you having any?'

'I'm not drinking alcohol.' She glanced at the waiter, who was waiting patiently by the table. 'But don't let that stop you.'

Alex looked momentarily bewildered, then understood. 'Okay.' He sounded apathetic.

They ordered, but lapsed into silence again once the waiter had gone. There was a disturbance on the other side of the restaurant, where the head waiter, distinguished by a black jacket instead of a white one, was having a controlled but heated debate with the occupants of a table hidden by a bamboo screen. Finally, with a terse nod, he strode towards the kitchen. The distraction over, Kate tried to think of something to say.

'So how's work?' she asked.

'Oh . . . okay, thanks.'

She cast around for another conversational gambit, but they all skittered out of reach. The waiter arrived with a truncated flask of saki and a bottle of mineral water. He filled their glasses and withdrew.

'Well. Cheers,' Kate said, raising hers. The bubbles from the water tickled her tongue. She noticed that Alex hadn't drunk from his glass.

'Look, Kate . . .' he began, slowly, and she stiffened at the seriousness of his tone. 'I, er . . .' He swallowed. 'I just wanted to say . . . I'm glad . . . uh, glad it was me.'

He broke off, his voice husky, and looked away quickly. Kate felt her eyes sting. But she was saved from having to respond by the return of the waiter. He put a metal warming tray in the centre of their table, and lit the four alcohol lamps inside with a taper he first held in a candle flame. Another waiter appeared and set out a series of small steaming bowls on top of the tray. They bowed again and left.

'Smells delicious,' Kate said. Her appetite had vanished.

Avoiding each other's eyes, they served themselves with portions of rice and subtly scented meat and vegetables. They both reached at the same time for the small bowl

of satay sauce. Kate smiled and motioned for Alex to take
it first, and as she did there was another commotion from
the other side of the restaurant.

The head waiter was standing beside the screened table
again. This time he was shaking his head, emphatically,
talking in a low but firm tone against the more strident
voice that was raised against him. Kate couldn't make out
what either was saying, but the hidden speaker grew louder
and more angry, and there was just time to register that the
man's voice was familiar when there was the scrape of chairs
being pushed back.

The screen shook as the couple who had been sitting
behind it stood up. The girl was heavily made up, large-
breasted and drunk. The man with her had his back to Kate
but then he turned, and she felt the shock of recognition as
she saw his profile.

She ducked her head, stared down at her plate.

'Kate? What's the matter?' Alex asked. She shook her
head without looking up. The exit was behind her, she
realised, sickly.

'Are you all right?'

She nodded. Now she could hear them approaching, his
heavier footsteps chased by the staccato tap of the girl's
heels. She lifted her chopsticks, made a show of interest in
the food.

The footsteps stopped by their table.

'Well, fancy seeing you here.'

She looked up. Paul had halted by the table. He had a
lopsided smirk on his face as he stared down at her. The
girl stood behind him, looking on with blowsy confusion.

'Hello, Paul.'

Even in the candlelight, she could see how flushed he was. His face was bloated and puffy. He looked from her to Alex.

'Aren't you going to introduce us?'

She felt surprisingly calm. 'Alex, this is Paul.'

Alex gave him an uncertain smile. Paul's grin was unpleasant.

'You haven't introduced us to your friend,' Kate said.

'Sorry, no, I haven't, have I? Forgetting my manners.' Paul motioned with his head at the girl, who was swaying with the effort of standing still. 'This is Kim. Kim, meet Kate. Kate's an "old friend" of mine. This is Alex, her "new friend". So what do you do, Alex?'

Alex glanced hesitantly at Kate. 'I'm, uh, I'm a psychologist.'

'A psychologist!' Paul's voice was growing louder. Kate was aware of heads turning in their direction. 'Don't tell me you're finally seeing a shrink, Kate? Or is this just a social thing? One way of getting treatment without paying for it, I suppose.'

More people were turning to look now. Kate felt a cold detachment. 'You were on your way out. Don't let us keep you.'

'Yeah, I'm on my way out, all right.' His smile was a thin mask. 'Freud here doesn't know what he's letting himself in for, does he? You watch your back, mate,' he said to Alex, without taking his eyes from Kate. 'Little Katie here's always mixing business with pleasure. Until she's got what she wants out of you, and then boom! You're out!'

Alex's face was pale, except for patches of colour on his cheeks. 'I think you'd better g-go.'

He said it quietly, and the syncopation was barely audible, but Paul picked up on it.

'You thu-think I'd buh-buh-better guh-go? Why, so you can psychoanalyse her with your dick?'

The surrounding tables had fallen quiet. Kate saw the head waiter coming towards them. Alex clenched his fists on the table.

'Ignore him,' she said, but now both men were focused on each other. Alex seemed to be almost quivering.

'G-get out!'

Paul leaned towards him. 'Fuh-fuh-fuck off.'

'Alex, no!' Kate said, reaching across to restrain him as he began to stand. He glanced at her, and while he was still half in, half out of his seat, Paul hit him.

The punch caught him on the cheek and knocked him sideways, sending him sprawling almost full length onto the table. It tipped up, toppling Alex off in a cascade of candles, food and breaking crockery. The noise seemed to go on forever as dishes, trays and glasses crashed to the floor, and then, abruptly, it stopped.

A plate spun, lazily, in the ensuing hush, spiralling to a gradual standstill. The restaurant was utterly silent. Then Kate was out of her seat and kneeling beside Alex, and white-coated waiters were converging on them from everywhere.

Alex let her help him sit up. His mouth was bleeding. Broken plates crunched underneath him.

'Are you all right?' she asked. Dumbly he put his hand to his mouth. He blinked, staring at the blood on his fingers, and then glared up at Paul. Kate felt him tense.

'Don't, Alex! Please!'

She kept tight hold of his shoulders. Some of the tension went out of them, and then other hands were helping him to his feet.

Paul was surrounded by waiters. He looked surprised himself by what he'd done as he allowed himself to be hustled towards the exit. The girl, who hadn't spoken throughout, tottered along behind on her high heels. Kate saw Alex staring after him with a look in his eyes she hadn't seen before. Then Paul was roughly pushed out of the room, and the doors had closed and shut him from view.

One waiter brushed the worst of the debris from Alex's clothes while another neatly stamped out the small puddles of blue flame that had spilled out from the alcohol lamps. The table was swiftly righted and Kate and Alex were politely ushered along the aisles to the door as waiters set about repairing the mess. Some people stared openly at them as they passed, others ostentatiously kept their eyes averted.

There was no sign of Paul or the girl in the foyer. The head waiter solicitously sat Alex in a chair and had hot towels brought to wipe him down. Alex held a napkin to his mouth, saying nothing. A taxi was ordered, and the head waiter smilingly refused Kate's offer to pay for the meal and damage. He was polite, but clearly wanted them to leave. Kate glanced back into the dining room as the door swung open. Their table was already fully set and covered with a fresh white cloth, candles glowing sedately as though nothing had happened.

She tried to persuade Alex to let the taxi go straight to his home, but he refused.

'I'd rather take you home first,' he said. His voice was thickened slightly by the swelling on the side of his mouth from where Paul had hit him. Something in his tone told Kate not to press.

Neither of them spoke again during the journey. Alex sat bunched in the corner, staring out of the window. Occasionally he dabbed at the corner of his mouth with the bloodstained napkin the head-waiter had insisted he take. Kate sat at the other side. There could have been a glass wall between them.

The taxi pulled up outside her flat. Alex continued to stare through the window as she opened the door.

'I'm sorry,' she said. He nodded. He looked as dispirited and dejected as a schoolboy who had lost a fight. Abruptly, she turned to the taxi driver.

'We'll both get out here, thanks.'

Alex turned to her, alarmed. 'No, I'll go home—'

'No, you won't. I can't let you go like this. The least I can do is let you get properly cleaned up.'

'No, really—' he began, but she was already on the pavement, the taxi door standing open as she paid the driver. After a moment Alex got out.

He waited behind her, silent, as she unlocked her flat and led him up the stairs.

'The bathroom's through there. If you want to change your sweater, I've got a T-shirt that'll probably fit you.'

Leaving him, she went into the kitchen and set the coffee percolator on to boil. Then, rummaging in a drawer until she found a baggy T-shirt, she went to the bathroom and knocked on the door. Alex opened it a crack. He had taken off his sweater, and through the gap in the doorway she could see how white his skin was. The silver chain lay pale around his neck.

'Can't promise much for the style,' she said, passing him the T-shirt. He smiled, a little nervously, as he took it.

Kate went back to the kitchen. The coffee hadn't started to bubble. She set out two cups. Then, taking a tumbler from a cupboard, she went into the lounge and poured a large brandy into it.

There was a noise from the doorway. Kate turned as Alex came in, pausing uncertainly in the doorway. It was strange seeing him in her lounge, wearing her T-shirt. She held out the tumbler.

'I thought you could do with this. Coffee's on its way.'

He accepted the glass with mumbled thanks. Kate sat in one of the armchairs. Alex went to the other. He took a sip of brandy, and winced. Gingerly he touched his mouth again.

'How is it?' she asked.

'Okay.'

She looked down at her hands. 'I'm sorry about tonight. About what happened.'

'It doesn't matter.'

'It does. You got dragged into a situation that . . . well, it wasn't your problem.'

'You don't have to tell me.'

'Yes, I do, I owe you an explanation, at least.' Kate felt the need of a brandy herself. But she was determined to abstain. She wasn't going to risk anything interfering with the chances of becoming pregnant. 'I used to be involved with Paul. We were at the same agency for a while, but then things got unpleasant and I left. I didn't see him for years, but then I won a pitch he wanted, and he lost his job, and now he blames me.'

Alex looked into his glass. 'How involved were you?'

'We lived together for over a year. I thought . . . well, I was thinking in terms of marriage and babies. I must have been stupid.'

'Why?'

'Oh, it isn't really worth going into.'

To her surprise, though, she found she wanted to. 'I just didn't see what sort of person Paul was, that's all. He was the agency's marketing director, and I was the new girl. I suppose I was flattered that he took an interest in me. It took a while for me to realise he was taking an interest in half the other girls in the office as well. And anybody else that took his fancy. By the time I did, we were living together.'

Kate swallowed. She could feel Alex watching her.

'Anyway, eventually I confronted him. He denied it, and like a fool I believed him. But then something else would happen, and I'd confront him again, and he'd deny it again. That went on for a while, and then one night we had a blazing row. You know, a real vase smasher. And he didn't deny it any more. He said – he said it was my fault. That I drove him to it.'

She stopped, remembering the crushing lack of self-respect. She shook it off and went on.

'I should have left him then, but . . . well, I didn't. We made up. But now he knew he could get away with it, he didn't even try very hard to hide what he was doing any more. And then—'

She broke off.

'What?' Alex asked.

'Nothing. I just left him.'

'What were you going to say?'

'Nothing,' she repeated, but there was no conviction in her voice. She could feel Alex watching her.

'He gave me VD.'

Part of her couldn't believe she was telling him this. Only Lucy knew, and she never alluded to it. Kate could feel the rawness and shame surfacing again, but also a relief at telling someone. Telling Alex.

'The doctor at the hospital told me it was nothing serious, only gonorrhoea, and that a course of antibiotics would clear it. So then I told Paul. And he . . . uh, he blamed me. Called me a slut and a whore, and accused me of giving it to him. He knew I hadn't, but it was easier than accepting he was in the wrong. And I suppose he was upset because he knew he'd have to go for treatment himself, and get in touch with all the girls he'd slept with recently. He'd got to take it out on somebody. So he threw me out of the flat we were sharing. You know, physically pushed me out, and started throwing all my clothes out of the window. The neighbours called the police, and when they came he started telling them what a whore I was, and what I'd given him. I think he'd almost started to convince himself by that time. And I looked at these two policemen, and I could tell they believed him. They didn't say anything, but they looked at me like I was . . . dirt.'

She noticed she was plucking at the chair arm. She folded her hands back on her lap like an unwanted book. 'Anyway, he refused to let me back in. I didn't know anywhere else to go, so I phoned Lucy. She and Jack had only just had Emily, but they let me stay with them until I found a flat. I was in quite a state. I couldn't go back to work, not with Paul there. I suppose I had a sort of breakdown. I cut myself off from all my friends, except Lucy. I couldn't face seeing any of them. I started chain-smoking, bursting into tears for no reason. Then Lucy got me some freelance work with someone Jack knew. I did a few more jobs like that and ended up starting my own agency.' She shrugged. 'Instant work therapy.'

Alex was listening with an intense expression.

'What about Paul?' he asked.

'I'm not with you.'

'Was tonight the first time you've seen him since then?'

'I wish.' She told him, briefly, about the pitch for the Parker Trust account, and its aftermath. When she finished she took a deep breath. 'So that's what you ended up in the middle of tonight.'

Alex didn't say anything. Kate tried to phrase another apology, when a smell she had been peripherally aware of for some time finally registered.

'God, the coffee!'

She leapt from her chair and ran to the kitchen. The odour of burnt coffee became much stronger. The espresso percolator was blackened around its base. It was hissing threateningly as Kate turned off the gas. She picked it up by the black plastic handle and hastily set it down again, shaking her hand.

'Damn!'

Heat radiated from the metal as Kate used a cloth to pick it up this time. She turned a tap on and tentatively held the percolator under the stream of water. The sudden burst of steam almost made her drop it.

'I'd just leave it to cool. You'll crack the metal doing it that way.'

She hadn't heard Alex come in. Kate poured a little coffee into one of the cups, and wrinkled her nose at the sharp odour. She set the percolator back on the cooker.

'Looks like coffee's off. I've got instant, though. Or tea?'

'It's okay. I ought to phone for a taxi, really.'

His edginess was contagious. 'Okay.' She turned away. 'The phone's in the hall.' She went to pour the coffee down the sink and, without thinking, picked up the percolator by the hot metal.

With a cry, she dropped it and boiling coffee splashed out as it struck the cooker. Kate jumped back, but the scalding liquid spattered her bare wrists. She gasped at the pain of it, and then Alex was beside her, pushing her to the sink.

'Here.' He was spinning the cold tap on full. 'Put them under.'

She recoiled from the force of the cold water, but he kept both her arms in the stream, turning them so that the water gushed over her burnt hand and scalded wrists. Red patches had already formed where the coffee had landed on her skin, and Alex kept them under the tap until her entire forearms started to ache from the cold.

'I think that'll do it,' she said.

Alex shook his head, still holding them in the icy water. 'Not yet. If you keep them in long enough it'll stop them from blistering.'

She glanced at him. He stood pressed against her, his hands gripping her arms at the elbow, face intent. At last he turned off the tap.

'Is there a clean towel?'

'In that drawer.' Kate motioned with her head. Alex took

one out and gently dabbed her arms dry. The livid patches were not as angry as they had been, and no longer hurt. Her arms felt numb from elbow to finger tips.

'Have you got any E45 cream?'

Kate didn't even know what it was. 'No. Savlon?'

Alex gave a terse shake of his head, still patting her arms with the towel. 'Anything you use for sunburn?'

'There's some aloe lotion. On the shelf in the bathroom.'

He nodded approval. 'What about pain-killers?'

'It doesn't hurt.'

'It will, once the numbness has worn off.'

'I think there's some aspirin in the bathroom.'

He went to fetch them. Kate stayed where she was, a little bemused by it all. Her arms were beginning to tingle.

Alex returned and gave her three aspirins. He began to fill a mug from the draining board with water.

'Don't bother,' Kate told him. 'I'll chew them dry.'

He looked at her for the first time since she had dropped the coffee pot.

'It was a habit I got into,' she explained, seeing his expression. 'I used to get a lot of tension headaches.'

He handed her the mug anyway. 'It still won't hurt to get some fluid inside you.'

As Kate used one hand to drink, he delicately smoothed the lotion onto the burnt palm and wrist of the other. She put down the mug and watched him.

'I thought you were a psychologist, not a burns specialist.'

He kept his eyes on what he was doing. 'You'd be surprised what you pick up.'

He gently smeared lotion onto her other arm. His fingers were light on the tender skin. 'There. That should take the worst of the sting from it.'

He was standing close in front of her.

'Thank you,' she said, and without planning it leaned forward and kissed him.

He stiffened. Kate could feel his sudden tension, and for a second thought he was going to pull away. Then, hesitantly, he relaxed.

The contact between them was only slight, little more than a brushing of lips, and Kate dimly wondered what she was doing. She closed her eyes. She could taste the brandy on his mouth, feel the slight hardness where his lip was swollen. She touched it with the tip of her tongue. His breath feathered against her skin. She kissed him again, her tongue softly tracing the line of his lips. Moving closer, she brought her arms up around his neck, awkwardly, because they were sore. His went tentatively around her. She kissed him more deeply, feeling his tongue begin to respond to hers. His arms tightened around her waist. She dug her fingers in his hair, pulling him to her, no longer aware of the pain in her arms. His hands dropped to her buttocks as he pressed himself against her. She drew away, leading him towards the hallway.

Alex didn't take his eyes from hers. He seemed almost drugged as they went into the bedroom. It was dark, with only the light from the kitchen spilling through the open door. She kissed him again, stroking his back. When she slid a hand inside his T-shirt she felt him give a small quiver. She took hold of one of his hands and moved it to her breast. He cupped it lightly, and she felt the quiver spread through him. He was trembling as she undid his belt, then the top button of his trousers. She could feel him suck in his stomach slightly as the backs of her hands touched his bare flesh. There was a crispness of hair beneath them. He gave a low moan and clutched her more tightly, his own hands fumbling at her dress. She reached behind herself to unzip it. The dress tumbled slowly to her ankles. She stepped out of it.

'Oh God,' he breathed, looking at her, and then they were kissing and she was dragging off his T-shirt, scarcely aware of the ripping sound as it came over his head and shoulders. The skin of his chest and stomach was hot against hers. She heard the faint rasp of it against the fabric of her bra as he groped behind her, struggling with its catch. She unfastened it for him, and Alex gave a little whimper as he bent his head and took one of her nipples in his mouth. She tugged his trousers over his hips, running her hands inside the back of his underpants to grip the roundness of his buttocks before peeling off the thin fabric.

He wasn't fully erect, so she took hold of him, squeezing lightly. She felt him throb and harden, the shaft smooth, almost silky, in her hand. He gave a low gasp. With her other hand, Kate pushed off her own pants, letting them whisper down her legs to the floor. She put her arms around his neck, kissing him, feeling his erection pressing against her stomach, and stepped back towards the bed. Alex was shivering as he went with her. She sank onto it, pulling him on top of her, opening her legs so he lay between them. He lunged at her clumsily straight away, missing and gliding over her lower belly. She reached down between their bodies, guiding him, lifting her hips slightly, and then she felt him sliding inside her.

She raised her legs, snaking them around him as their bodies wedged tight together. Suddenly he was thrusting frantically, his head arching back as he spasmed and gave a strangled moan. He hung for a moment, jerking and rigid, then went limp. Kate felt his full weight settle on her as he buried his head in the angle of her neck and shoulder, gasping. She gently stroked the back of his head, adjusting to the abruptness of it being over.

After a while she felt him stir. He pushed himself off her and lay on his back.

'Sorry.'

Kate could barely see him in the darkness. 'What for?'

'You know. Being so quick.'

'It doesn't matter.' She meant it. Her initial disappointment had ebbed now.

'I'm not . . . I'm not very experienced.' The confession was blurted out.

Kate hid her surprise. She rolled onto her side, so that her body was touching his, aware of the cooling wetness between her thighs.

'That's nothing to be ashamed of.'

She put her hand on his chest. She could feel his heart beating under it. The chain he wore around his neck felt cold as she stroked her fingers through the hairs.

'Sorry,' he said again, and Kate lightly tapped him.

'Stop it. There's no need to keep apologising.'

Turning, she reached for the bedside table and switched on the lamp. Blinking in the sudden light, she looked back at Alex. His eyes were wet, she saw with alarm.

'Hey, come on!' She moved so she was lying half on top of him, propping herself up on her elbows. Her breasts brushed against him. She smiled. 'It wasn't *that* bad, was it?'

He smiled back but didn't meet her eyes. 'No. It's just that . . . I'm not very good at this sort of thing.'

'You seemed okay to me.'

He gave her a quick look and, with sudden intuition, Kate understood much of his past nervousness. The tenderness she felt for him closed up her throat.

'What's this?' she said, deliberately changing the subject. She fingered the disc hanging on the chain around his neck.

'It's just a St Christopher.'

Kate casually slid one of her legs over him as she examined it. The medal was about two centimetres in diameter, and the design of the man carrying the child across the water was crude and stylised, not at all obvious at first glance.

'It looks old,' she said, lifting it from his chest. It was thick and heavy.

'Uh, yes, I suppose it is.' He looked down at it. 'It was my grandmother's.'

'Did she leave it to you?'

Alex paused before answering. 'No, she gave it to me before she died. She said it'd bring me good luck.'

Kate laid it back on his chest. 'And has it?' She moved her leg gently up and down.

'I, uh, well, yes, I suppose it has.'

He was smiling now. Kate could feel him beginning to harden again under her thigh. The St Christopher was a cold disc between her breasts as she slid on top of him.

'It's a good job you said that.'

CHAPTER 13

At times during the next three weeks Kate would feel an almost superstitious distrust of being so happy. It would come over her without warning, a pessimistic conviction that this couldn't last, that there would have to be a price to pay. Then the feeling would pass, a brief cloud over the sun, and she would be caught up again in the pleasure of the present.

The sex had quickly improved. Alex was an enthusiastic if not experienced lover, and they coupled like eager teenagers, delighting in each other until both of them were sore and aching. It seemed strange at first. Even after almost four years, Kate found that her body remembered the contours and smell of Paul. He had been heavier and hairier than Alex, with a blunt, bludgeoning approach she had at first mistaken for passion, before realising it was only selfishness. But it didn't take long before the tactile memories of her former lover were supplanted by the new.

They didn't go out often. Kate would hurry home at night, open a bottle of wine and start chopping meat and vegetables. Alex would go to her flat straight from work and they would cook the meal together in an intimate awareness of the other's presence. Sometimes they would prolong the anticipation until afterwards, but often their clothes would be scattered over the floor, and they would make love while the pots bubbled unnoticed on the cooker.

There were times, though, when Alex would fall into a quiet mood, lost in some internal world. Kate liked watching him then, seeing his face take on an unguarded, almost melancholy cast. But while she enjoyed being able to study him in these moments as she would a picture, at her leisure, there was also a muted sense of exclusion. Once he looked up without warning and caught her watching him. For an instant his face seemed blank of recognition, and in a weightless second of panic Kate felt a sudden conviction that she didn't know him, that this was some stranger.

Then he blinked and smiled, and was Alex again.

'What?' he said.

Kate went over and hugged him. 'You were miles away. What were you thinking about?'

'Nothing much. Just miles away, like you said.'

The moment had passed, but not without leaving a faint trace of itself, diminished but lingering like the smell of coffee in a room. To dispel it, Kate asked something she had been meaning to for some days.

'Why don't we go to your flat sometime?'

Alex hesitated. 'Why?'

'Because I'd like to see where you live. You know, see if you're messy or tidy. What sort of books you've got.'

'I can tell you.'

'It isn't the same. What's the matter? Are you hiding something there?'

It was meant as a joke, but Alex didn't laugh. 'No, of course not.'

She felt a rekindling of unease. 'Why not, then?' she asked, serious now.

'It's just . . .' He was frowning, not looking at her. Then he sighed. 'Well, it's a bit of a dump, that's all. I haven't bothered doing anything to it, because I wasn't planning on staying there very long. I suppose I'd be embarrassed for you to see it.'

The stirrings of alarm that Kate had begun to feel receded. 'There's no need to be. I wouldn't mind.'

'No, but I would.' He smiled. 'If you want to go there, we can do. But give me a few days to tidy up first, okay?'

She grinned. 'Okay.' Relieved, she put it from her mind. She wasn't in any hurry.

There was plenty of time.

Besides, she enjoyed being in her flat with Alex. The first weekend there they had spent almost entirely in bed. They had ventured into the kitchen occasionally to prepare a snack, and once they had taken the quilt into the lounge, where they spread it on the floor to watch *For Whom the Bell Tolls* while rain lashed the window, and the gas fire murmured its blue dance. The familiar surroundings, which had once felt so lonely, now seemed intimate and cosy. Often they would just lay and talk. Alex was a good listener, and she found herself opening up to him more and more, sometimes about incidents she had almost forgotten. One evening she told him about going alone to the cinema when she was a little girl. She had intended the story to be funny, but Alex seemed to see past the humour.

'How long ago did your parents die?' he asked, when she had finished. They were lying on the settee, naked after sex. Kate's head was resting in the crook of his arm.

She counted back, lightly tracing a pattern on his chest. 'My mother died when I was nineteen. My father died a year before that, just after I'd gone to university.'

'Do you miss them?'

The question sobered her. She found she couldn't give a simple answer. 'I'd have liked them to meet you,' she said. Alex didn't comment. Kate watched the hairs on his chest spring back up in the wake of her fingers. 'No, I don't suppose I do miss them, in the conventional sense. Not in the way I'd miss someone like Lucy. I loved them, and it was a jolt when they died, but we didn't see much of each other once I'd left home. And we didn't know what to talk about when we did.'

'Didn't you get on with them?'

It wasn't something Kate let herself think about very often, but now she considered it. 'It wasn't that we didn't get on, so much. It was more that we just didn't understand each other. We didn't seem to have anything in common. I always felt I was never who or what they wanted me to be.' She gave a quiet laugh. 'I sometimes wondered if there hadn't been some mix-up at the hospital and they'd been given the wrong baby by mistake. They'd wanted a boy, for a start. Then my mother found out she couldn't have any more children after me. So I was a big disappointment all around.'

'Did they actually say that?'

'Not in so many words. But sometimes my mother used to act like she resented me, because I wasn't the boy she'd wanted to present my father with. Everything had to fall in with what he wanted. It was like there was only one person in the house who counted. He expected to have his own way, and my mother saw her role as making sure he got it. And I was expected to go along with that as well. It was probably a relief for everybody when I left home.'

She looked up at Alex. 'What about you?'

'Me?'

'What was your childhood like?'

She felt him shift slightly.

'Nothing exceptional. Abroad every year for holidays, bikes at Christmas. Boringly normal, I suppose.'

'How about your brothers? Did you get on with them?'

'Oh, yes. I mean, there was a bit of tormenting went on, with me being the youngest, but it was always good-natured. They were quite protective, really.'

Kate fingered the solid coldness of the St Christopher on his chest. She could feel it sometimes during their lovemaking, its coolness tracing rhythmic patterns on her breasts. 'Tell me about your grandmother.'

'My gran? What about?'

'Just what she was like. You said you were close.'

Alex was quiet for so long she thought he wasn't going to reply. When he did his voice had softened. 'She was great. If I'd cut myself, or got in trouble, or . . . or whatever, I could always go to my gran and tell her, and she'd listen. And when I'd done something wrong, she'd tell me, but she'd never get cross, or shout or hit me. She was always there.'

He stared at the ceiling. His eyes were bright.

'How old were you when she died?' Kate asked.

'Fifteen. She gave me this,' he touched the St Christopher, 'the week before she died. It'd belonged to my grandad, and she said I should wear it because it'd bring me luck. It was almost like she knew she wasn't going to be there to look out for me for much longer.'

He stopped. 'You were saying about your parents,' he went on in a brisker tone. 'Did you get on any better with your mother after your father died?'

Kate let him change the subject. 'There wasn't really any difference. I hoped that she might come out of his shadow, you know? Start living her own life. But she never did. It was like she lost interest in everything. Every time I came home from university, I could see how she'd deteriorated. It was horrible. It was like she was winding down, as though she'd no reason to carry on living without him. She kept all his clothes, all his things, and talked about him as if he was still there. She'd even cook his favourite meals, even stuff she didn't like, right up to when she died.' She paused, remembering. 'I still can't make up my mind if it was love or not. It never seemed healthy. I always told myself I'd never let anyone dominate me like that.'

'You nearly did, though.'

She glanced at Alex. Two patches of colour burned on his cheeks.

'You're not jealous of Paul, are you?' she asked.

He tried to sound dismissive. 'No, of course not.' He avoided her eyes. 'I just don't like to think of you with someone like that, that's all.'

Part amused, part annoyed, Kate wriggled around until she was facing him. 'That's not a very professional attitude, is it? I thought psychologists were above such things?'

'Perhaps . . . perhaps I'm not a very good psychologist.'

She had the impression that he had changed his mind at the last second about what he was going to say.

'I'd have thought you'd be pretty good,' she said. 'You're a good listener. That's a lot of what psychology's about, isn't it?'

'Oh, yeah. There's plenty of listening, but that's about all. Psychologists don't actually *do* anything.'

His tone was uncharacteristically bitter. Wanting to pull him out of his suddenly dark mood, Kate bent her head and lightly nipped the flesh of his chest in her teeth.

'I'd better keep you busy, then.'

The phone rang later that same evening. Usually she ignored it when Alex was there, letting the answering machine take the message, but this time she was passing when it trilled out. She wavered, tempted to walk past, then reluctantly picked up the receiver.

'Hi, Kate,' Lucy said, cheerfully. 'Just thought I'd give you a ring and make sure you weren't dead.'

Kate felt a prod of conscience. She hadn't spoken to Lucy since telling her she was meeting Alex for the final time. She glanced involuntarily towards the bedroom.

'Sorry, I've been meaning to, but—'

'I know, I know, you've got a lot on at work. Never mind. Anyway, what happened the other night? Did you see Alex?'

'Uh . . . yes.'

'How did it go?'

'Okay, I suppose.'

'So that's it, then? You told him you're not going to see him any more?' Lucy's disapproval was obvious.

'Er . . . he's here now, actually.'

There was a pause.

'Oh, really?'

Kate could almost hear her smirking.

'The farewell dinner didn't work out quite as you'd planned, then?' Lucy said.

'Not exactly.'

'Well, I *was* going to invite you over for lunch tomorrow, but I dare say now you'll be busy. Unless you wanted to bring Alex as well?'

'Thanks, but I think we'll pass.'

'I thought you might. Well, give Alex my love – if you've any left – and I'll talk to you next week. Oh, and, Kate?'

'What?'

Lucy was laughing. 'Don't forget to use a contraceptive.'

The irony of her timing wasn't lost on Kate. She wasn't sure if waiting until she'd started the donor insemination treatment before sleeping with Alex qualified as perversity or just karma. Whichever, it changed everything.

Kate knew there were issues that had to be faced; about the clinic, about her relationship with Alex. But she couldn't bring herself to worry about them. Her life, at last, seemed to have achieved its natural, pre-ordained balance. She felt a *rightness* about it all, a certainty that this was how things were meant to be, that now everything would fall into place.

It seemed inevitable that she would miss her period.

She waited several days before mentioning it to Alex.

'You said when I first met you that you liked the idea of fatherhood without the responsibility,' she said. 'Do you still feel the same way?'

They lay folded around each other in bed. His arm was draped over her in the darkness.

'Why?'

She toyed with the St Christopher on his chest, winding the silver chain around her finger, then off. 'It isn't definite, but I went to the doctor's today for a pregnancy test.'

She waited.

'When will you know?'

'Sometime next week.'

She could have found out sooner, by buying a kit and testing herself. But even if it had been positive, she wouldn't have entirely believed it. She didn't want to risk the disappointment of making a mistake. Having it confirmed by a doctor would somehow make it more official. More real.

Kate looked up towards Alex's face, almost invisible in the dark. 'I just want you to know that you're not under any obligation. This – us – doesn't change anything.'

It seemed a long time before he spoke.

'It does for me.'

His voice was throaty. Kate let go of the chain. Unable to speak, she laid her head on his chest, glad he couldn't see the dampness on her cheeks.

She was never sure why she didn't tell him exactly when the result of the test would be through. The doctor had told her which day to phone in, but something made her hold that back from Alex. She told herself that she wanted to surprise him, to let him believe they wouldn't know until later in the week. But she knew there was a more selfish reason.

She wanted to keep that much for herself.

On the morning she was to phone for the result they ate breakfast together at her cramped breakfast bar in the kitchen. Alex had to leave before she did, and Kate kissed him and watched him go down the stairs to the front door. At the bottom he turned and waved, and seeing him there, grinning, his dark hair tufted, Kate almost gave in and told him. Then he went out and closed the door, and it was too late.

She went to work in a strange mood of hope and near-terror, the two blending until they became indistinguishable from each other. She was hardly aware of her surroundings, getting on and off the tube automatically, letting her body take her through the familiar routine without consciously thinking about it. Only when she came up from the Underground into the morning furore outside King's Cross was she jolted from her internal world as a fire engine blared past in a cacophony of noise and colour. Looking after it, Kate felt a disquieting tug of *déjà vu*. But even as she tried to grasp the memory, it drifted tantalisingly out of reach, insubstantial as smoke.

She had been told to call the doctor's surgery after eleven. She waited until two minutes past, and then picked up her office phone and dialled the doctor's number. The receptionist took her details and put her on hold. A cheery electronic jingle filled the line. Kate tensed when it stopped, but it had only reached the end of its loop. A second later it started up again, as bland as the chime from an ice-cream van. The tune played through twice, then was abruptly cut off.

'Miss Powell?' the receptionist's voice broke in. 'Your test's positive.'

Kate's mouth had dried. 'Positive? So I'm pregnant?'

'According to this.' There was a pause before the woman added, 'Congratulations.'

It was said without real feeling, but Kate didn't care.

She thanked the receptionist and hung up. She sat back, examining how she felt. No different and yet, at the same time, utterly changed. An emotion so strong rose up in her she couldn't have put a name to it.

All at once, the need to tell Alex was unbearable. She had never called him at work before, not since he had asked her not to when they first met. Now, though, she took his card from her wallet and dialled his office number.

A woman answered. 'Ealing Centre.'

'Can I speak to Alex Turner, please?'

'Dr Turner's with a patient at the moment. Would you like to leave a message?'

Kate hesitated. 'No, it doesn't matter. Thank you.'

She put down the receiver. But the urge to share the news with him was too strong to ignore. Taking a fax coversheet from her drawer, she considered what to say. She wanted to phrase the message so that Alex would understand, but not anyone else who happened to see it. Grinning, she picked up a pen. 'Your grandmother's St Christopher worked!' she wrote. 'Phone me! Love, Kate.'

Pleased with herself, she went downstairs and faxed it off.

Alex didn't call that afternoon. Kate guessed that he hadn't got her fax, and debated sending another or phoning him again before deciding not to do either. She would see him that evening. Now she had waited this long, she could wait a little longer to give him the news.

On the way home, she stopped off and bought a bottle of champagne. Alex rarely arrived before seven, and Kate put salmon steaks in the oven and set the table in the lounge with candles and a white tablecloth. She poured herself a glass of milk and put on a CD, humming along to it while she changed into a navy blue mini-dress. She smiled as she studied the flat-stomached reflection in the bedroom mirror.

'Enjoy it while it lasts,' she said out loud, and laughed.

It was almost seven o'clock. Kate went into the kitchen and turned on the heat under the vegetables. The CD had finished, so she went into the lounge and put on a Nina Simone collection, knowing it was one of Alex's favourites. She made a minute adjustment to the napkins she had folded neatly into the glasses on the table and lit the candles.

Switching off the lamp, she sat in the candlelight and waited for Alex.

At eight o'clock she remembered the food. The kitchen was full of steam as she turned off the oven and gas rings. The bubbling pans subsided. The new potatoes broke apart like puffballs when she touched them with a fork, while the broccoli had disintegrated into pale, swollen florets. They bobbed on the surface, slowing sinking to the bottom as the water settled down.

Kate stared down at the ruined vegetables, then abruptly turned and went into the hall to the telephone. She called the Ealing Centre first. An electronic crackle hissed in her ear. She tried again, with the same result. She broke the connection and dialled Alex's home number.

The phone rang on and on, hollowly. Each pause between rings seemed to take longer, then the next one would trill out, a fresh announcement of loneliness and vacant rooms. Kate hung up.

She went back into the lounge and turned on the lamp.

WHERE THERE'S SMOKE

The table waited, the glasses and cutlery reflecting back the light from the candles. One had dripped red wax onto the tablecloth. Kate looked down at the dark circles on the white surface, and then leaned over and blew out the flames. The wicks sent thick ribbons of smoke towards the ceiling. Its pungent, cloying odour filled the room.

The phone rang. Kate gave a start, then ran into the hallway and snatched it up.

'Hello?'

'Hi, Kate, it's Lucy.'

The leaden ball settled back in her stomach. 'Oh, hi, Lucy.'

'Well, don't sound so pleased. What's the matter?'

'Nothing, sorry. Well, Alex is a bit late, that's all.'

Lucy laughed. 'Got to that stage already, has it? Rolling pin behind the door?'

Kate concealed her irritation. 'No. I'm just worried. He should have been here over an hour ago.'

'I wouldn't worry. He's probably stuck on a tube somewhere. So how's it going?'

'Okay.' She felt no desire to tell Lucy she was pregnant. Not until Alex knew.

Lucy sighed. 'I can tell you're not in a chatting mood. Look, I'm sure he's fine. He'll turn up with some excuse. They always do.'

But he didn't.

By next morning Kate felt dulled with worry and fatigue. She had slept fitfully, sometimes jerking awake convinced that the doorbell or the phone had rung. Then she would lie with her heart thudding in the aftermath of the adrenaline

209

rush, conscious of the cold space beside her in the bed as she listened to the meaningless night-noises of the flat.

At one point she thought of the table, still set in the lounge, and the prospect of seeing it unchanged in the grey light of morning was unbearable. She got out of bed and cleared it without turning on the light, stripping it in the near-dark so she wouldn't see what she was doing.

Daylight and the normality of the rush-hour crowds was reassuring. Kate walked quickly out of King's Cross, the rain drumming against her umbrella and spattering her legs. She had promised herself that the first thing she was going to do was contact the centre again where Alex worked. The phone was bound to be working by now, and someone there would surely know what had happened to him, would at least be able to tell her if he was all right. She hurried along the rain-drenched streets, driven by a fearful eagerness.

The door to the agency was unlocked. She opened it and backed in, shaking off the water from her umbrella outside. Closing the door, she turned and saw Clive looking at her. Two men were in the office with him.

'There's somebody to see you,' Clive said in a voice that was oddly flat. One of the men stepped forward.

'Miss Powell?'

He was a big, heavily built man in his fifties, with bristly grey hair, thinning on top, and startlingly thick black eyebrows. His tweed overcoat smelt like a wet dog. The other man was younger and wore a blue nylon anorak. He remained in the background.

Kate glanced at Clive, but his face was expressionless. 'Yes?' she said.

'I'm Detective Inspector Collins. This is Sergeant Daikin. I wonder if you could spare us a few minutes?'

A hollowness had settled in her stomach. 'Come up to my office.'

She led them upstairs, remembering herself enough to ask if they wanted tea or coffee. Both declined. They sat opposite her across her desk, the older of the two opening his overcoat to reveal a creased brown suit. His shirt was stretched drum-tight across his heavy stomach.

The younger man took a sheet of paper from the folder he was carrying and handed it to him. The Inspector glanced at it and held it out for Kate.

'Can you tell me if you sent this?'

It was a photocopy of the fax she had sent to Alex the day before. She fought down a rising panic.

'Yes, I sent it yesterday.'

'So you know Dr Turner?'

The hollowness in her gut had contracted, squeezing so she couldn't breathe. 'Yes. Look, what's happened?'

'What's your relationship with him?'

'I'm a – a friend. Please, tell me, is he all right?'

The Inspector spoke matter-of-factly.

'I'm sorry. He's dead.'

It was as though the air pressure in the room had suddenly altered. There was a roaring in her ears. She saw the older man watching her, a concerned expression on his face, and realised she was swaying in her seat. She put both hands on the desk to steady herself.

'How?' She wasn't sure if she had spoken out loud, but she must have because the Inspector answered.

'He was found in his office last night. There was a fire, and when the fire brigade went in, they found him.'

He hesitated.

'We've not got the post-mortem results yet, but it looks like he'd been beaten to death. Then whoever did it tipped out all the paper from the filing cabinets and tried to set fire to the room. Luckily, it was a rush job and the building's got a sprinkler system. They don't always work in old buildings, but this one did. It doused the fire before it got a hold.'

Kate felt a great detachment. There was no pain, no sensation at all. She wasn't really sitting here, hearing this. This wasn't Alex they were talking about. When she spoke the words seemed unreal, as though she was taking part in someone else's play.

'Who did it?'

The Inspector shifted slightly in his seat. It creaked under his weight.

'We're not sure yet. But we know Dr Turner was staying behind to see one of his patients. Unfortunately, with the computers shorted out by the sprinkler system and the office in turmoil, everything's still a bit confused. We're hoping to have a better idea about that later this morning.'

He nodded at the photocopy Kate still held in her hand. 'That was underneath him. Or rather, the original was. You didn't sign your surname, but the agency's address is printed on it. So we thought we'd come and see if you knew anything that might help us.'

Kate looked down at the piece of paper. 'Your grand-mother's St Christopher worked! Phone me! Love, Kate.'

She became aware that the policeman had asked her something.

'Sorry?'

'I said, can you tell me what it means? It seems a cryptic sort of message, if you don't mind my saying.'

The two policemen waited. Kate felt the paper in her hands, but didn't look down at it again.

'It was just a joke. A private thing.'

The Inspector gazed across at her. 'Can you elaborate on that? What's this reference to his "grandmother's St Christopher", for instance?'

It jolted her to hear the words from his mouth. 'It's sort of a lucky charm he wears. He never takes it off.'

She saw the two men exchange a look.

'Can you describe it?' the Inspector asked.

'It . . . it's silver, about this big.' She held her thumb and forefinger apart to show them. 'It's heavy. Old.'

She could still feel its cool heft, as if she were actually holding it. She lowered her hand as the policemen's reaction penetrated. 'Why?'

The Inspector seemed to weigh up whether or not to tell her.

'He wasn't wearing anything like that when we found him.' He shrugged, as if not wanting to place too much importance on the fact. 'There'd been a struggle, so it's possible it might have fallen off. We're still examining his office. It could be in there somewhere.'

He went on, quickly, leaving the subject behind. 'How long have you known each other?'

Kate had to think. 'I don't know. Eight, nine months.' The numbers meant nothing.

'Could you tell us when you last saw him?'

'Yesterday morning. About . . . about quarter to eight.' She remembered Alex grinning up at her from the bottom of the stairs. His dark hair was tufted.

'Where was that?'

'At my flat.'

The Inspector's eyebrows raised slightly. 'Bit early, wasn't it?'

'He stayed the night.'

His disapproval showed in a faint pursing of his lips. 'I take it you live alone?'

'Yes.'

'And you didn't see or speak to him after that?'

She shook her head.

'Can you tell me where you were yesterday evening?'

'I was at home. Waiting for Alex. He . . . he was supposed to be calling round.'

'Did you see anyone else during that time?'

'No. A friend phoned, but that's all.'

'What time was that?'

She tried to remember. Her thoughts were scrambled. 'I don't know. Eight o'clock.'

'And what's your friend's name?'

Kate realised with mild surprise that he was checking her out. It didn't seem to matter. She gave him Lucy's name and address.

The sergeant's pen scratched as he made notes.

'What did you do when Dr Turner didn't arrive?' the Inspector asked.

For an instant she felt disoriented, as an echo of the fear she had felt the previous night overlapped with the impossibility of the present.

'I didn't know what to do. I tried calling the Centre, but there was something wrong with the phone.'

Comprehension came like a blow. She broke off, looking across at the policeman.

'The phones all went down when the sprinklers cut in,' he said. 'That was between half past seven and eight, as far as we can tell.'

He was already dead then. He was lying there, dead, when I phoned. The thought was too immense to take in.

'Did you do anything else? Phone anyone else?'

'After I'd called the Centre I tried phoning him at home. But there wasn't . . . there was no answer.'

The Inspector's face was impassive. 'There wouldn't be. His wife was visiting her mother. Otherwise we might have known he was missing sooner.'

Kate stared at him.

'His wife?'

He gave her a quizzical, disbelieving look. 'Dr Turner's married.'

She shook her head. 'No . . . No, he isn't.'

'I've just spoken to his wife. I can assure you he is. I'm sorry, I assumed, as his mistress, you'd know.'

A wind of dizziness was blowing over her, like nausea. *Mistress.*

'He can't be!' The denial was wrung from her. 'I'd have known! I've been seeing him for – for *months*! He gave me his home telephone number! He wouldn't have done that if he was married!'

'What number did he give you?'

Kate struggled to clear her thoughts enough to remember. The sergeant wrote it down as she stammered it out. He leafed through his notes, then looked at the Inspector.

'Different number, sir. That isn't his home phone.'

He avoided Kate's eyes. She turned back to the Inspector. There was something that might have been pity in his eyes now.

'Did you ever go to his home?' he asked.

'No.' It was a whisper. 'He – he said he was living in a studio flat until he found somewhere to buy. He told me it was a dump, and he'd be embarrassed at me seeing it.' She remembered his reluctance, how he had always insisted on dropping her off first when they shared a taxi. It was a physical pain in her chest.

The scratching of the sergeant's pen had stopped. There was an uneasy silence.

'I'm sorry,' the Inspector said. 'I know this must all have come as a shock.'

Kate didn't respond. She stared down at the surface of her desk. There was a scratch on it she had never noticed before.

The policeman coughed.

'I don't suppose Dr Turner made any mention to you about who he was seeing last night?' he asked.

It was an effort to shake her head. 'He doesn't talk much about his work.'

Or anything else.

'So there was nothing out of the ordinary at all?'

She gave another shake of her head.

The Inspector took out a crumpled handkerchief and

216

blew his nose. The handkerchief was returned to his pocket.

'Can you think of anyone who might have had a grudge against him?' he asked. 'Dr Turner, I mean?'

'I thought you were looking for one of his patients?'

'We certainly want to question whoever he saw last night, but we're not ruling out any other possibility either.'

Kate began to say no, then stopped.

'Yes?' the Inspector prompted.

'I had . . . well, a run-in with an old boyfriend in a restaurant. He hit Alex. But I don't think . . . .'

'When was this?'

'About . . . about three, four weeks ago.' It seemed an age now.

'What's his name, please?'

'Paul Sutherland. Look, I don't want to cause any trouble for him,' she added, seeing the sergeant write down the name.

'Don't worry, we'll just check it out. Can you tell us anything more about him?'

Kate told him about the court case. The detachment had returned, sealing her off as she spoke. When she had finished there was a pause. The Inspector rubbed his nose.

'There's one more thing,' he said, slowly. 'The body hasn't been formally identified yet. His wife isn't really in any fit state to do it, so I wonder if you would?'

The sergeant glanced up from his book. He looked unhappy. 'We could ask someone else, though, couldn't we, sir?'

Collins stared him down. 'We could, but now we're here

I'd like Miss Powell to do it.' He turned back to Kate. 'If you don't mind.'

She answered from within a core of unnatural calm.

'All right.'

The mortuary was part of a 1970s concrete and glass building. Kate walked between the two policemen down tiled steps into the basement. The smell was similar to yet subtly different from a hospital's. They came to a row of plastic chairs in a corridor. Kate stayed there with the sergeant while the Inspector disappeared through a nearby door.

She tried to remember the sergeant's name, but couldn't. She could tell he was uncomfortable, and felt distantly sorry for him. But other than that nothing penetrated the numbness that surrounded her.

Only once had the actuality of Alex's death seemed real. During the car journey she had been sitting in the back, staring out of the window, when the knowledge had come to her like a scream. *Alex is dead*. There was an instant of terrible loss, like falling, but then the feeling of unreality gripped her again, putting an anaesthetising screen between her and her feelings.

She almost welcomed it.

Collins came back out. He spoke in a subdued voice.

'Are you ready?'

Kate rose to her feet. She moved towards the door he was holding open for her. She could see through into the room beyond. Facing her was a large window, looking into yet another room.

And suddenly it hit her. Where she was. What she was doing.

She didn't know she had stepped backwards until she bumped into the sergeant.

'Come on, love.'

He spoke softly and took her arm. Her legs were weak as she let him lead her towards the window. She kept her head down as she took the last few steps up to it. Her feet seemed a great distance away.

'All right.'

She wasn't sure who had spoken, but she looked up. On the other side of the glass was a steel table. A body lay on it, covered by a sheet.

That's Alex, Kate thought. *That's him, that's Alex.* She closed her throat on a moan.

The sheet covering the body was perfectly still, unruffled by breath. A woman in a white coat, whom Kate hadn't noticed till now, took hold of it at the top and pulled it back.

Kate looked.

His dark hair was singed and matted, clotted with blood. She could see where his skull under it had been crushed. One eye was swollen shut, the flesh around it discoloured, but the other was partly open, a thin sickle staring up at the ceiling, seeing nothing.

Kate felt a pulse throb in her temple. She took a breath, forced herself to speak.

'No,' she said. 'That's not him.'

CHAPTER 14

The police took her to her flat. They asked for a
photograph of Alex. The only one she had was from
their picnic at Cambridge, when the Japanese man had
taken one of them both together. Alex had mounted it
in a clip-frame and given it to her a few days later, a
little nervous but obviously pleased about making a gift of
it. Kate looked at the colour print before handing it over
to the Inspector. She and Alex stood side by side, smiling
self-consciously at the camera. Behind them was the river, a
corner of the punt just visible under an overhanging willow.
They looked tanned and happy.

She watched Collins put the photograph into his overcoat
pocket. 'I will get it back, won't I?'

'Just as soon as we've finished with it.'

The policemen left. They had offered to take her back to
the office, but she had declined. She needed time alone. The
relief she'd felt at discovering it wasn't Alex's body had been
replaced by reaction, and now she felt drained.

She called Clive to tell him that she wouldn't be in. He
had made no comment when she had left with the police,
but she had seen the concern in his face. It was in his voice
now, when he asked, 'I know it isn't any of my business,
but is everything okay?'

221

She began to formulate a polite response, then abandoned the attempt.

'No, not really.'

'Is it anything I can help with?'

'Thanks, but no, I don't think it is.'

He didn't speak for a second or two. 'Let me know if you want to talk about it.'

She said she would and rang off. She stood in the hall for a while. There seemed no particular reason to go into either the lounge or the kitchen. Finally, with the vague idea of making something to eat, she went into the kitchen. Without bothering to see what flavour it was, she took out a tin of soup from one of the wall cupboards. It was only when she looked for a saucepan that she remembered they were still on the cooker from the night before.

Kate stared down at the cold vegetables, and then grabbed the pans and tipped them down the sink. The potatoes had dissolved into the water. It formed a scummy tidemark on the stainless steel. She scooped out the congealed lumps that were too big to drain down the plughole and dumped them into the bin, then turned on the tap and rinsed the sink sides. Leaving the water running, she pulled open the oven door and pulled out the foil-wrapped salmon, dropping that into the bin too.

The water had begun to run hot. Kate squirted washing-up liquid onto the saucepans and scoured them until her arms ached. When they were dripping on the draining rack, she looked around for something else. She took the heavy metal frames from around the gas rings and plunged them into the soapy water. Then she started on the cooker itself.

Her confusion was like dark water under thin ice. Only

by moving could she hope to keep from plunging through, so she scrubbed and wiped and polished, moving from the kitchen to the bathroom, then down the hall to the lounge. She was vacuuming the lounge carpet when the doorbell rang.

The sound was thin and reedy over the howl of the cleaner. Kate froze, then switched it off. The doorbell rang again as it whined into silence. She flew into the hall and down the stairs, but the hope sagged out of her when she saw two figures through the stained-glass panel.

The Inspector's bulk filled the top step when she opened the front door. This time he had a uniformed policewoman with him.

'Sorry to bother you again, Miss Powell. Can we come in?'

Kate led them upstairs into the lounge. They picked their way around the vacuum cleaner and sat down. All three sat on the edge of their seats. Collins told Kate the policewoman's name, but it made no impression. She wouldn't think about why he might have brought a woman officer with him this time.

The Inspector sat with his meaty hands dangling between his legs. His stomach pushed out towards his knees.

'There've been some further developments,' he said.

Kate couldn't wait any longer. 'Have you found him?'

There was a minute hesitation. 'No. No, not yet. But after you failed to identify the body, we took one of Dr Turner's colleagues to the mortuary. We thought there was a chance he might recognise the dead man as a patient.'

He rubbed his hands slowly together. They made a dry, rasping noise.

'He positively identified him as Alex Turner.'

Kate looked at him, blankly. 'He can't have.'

Collins locked his hands together, as though to keep from rubbing them any more. 'He's known Dr Turner for ten years. He wasn't in any doubt.'

'I don't care how long he'd known him, that wasn't Alex! For God's sake, don't you think I'd have recognised him if it was? You've only got to look at the photograph to see it was nothing like him!'

The Inspector took the photograph out of his jacket pocket. 'Actually, we showed this to Dr Turner's colleague. I'm afraid he didn't recognise the man in it.'

She felt the dark water seeping up around her. 'He must have!'

Collins continued as though she hadn't spoken. 'After that we also showed it to Turner's secretary.' His eyes were mournful as he looked across at Kate.

'She identified him as one of Dr Turner's patients.'

The ice broke. The waters closed over her.

'His real name's Timothy Ellis,' Collins went on. 'He's a schizophrenic. He's been Turner's patient for the past two years. Since the last time they let him loose, apparently.'

As if on cue, the policewoman pulled a large photograph from a file and passed it to Kate. Kate automatically reached out and took it. It was black and white and divided into two halves, one a full-face picture, the other a profile. The man in it was younger, with shorter hair, but still recognisably Alex.

'He's twenty-six, and has had a history of arson since he was a kid,' Collins was saying. 'Which would explain the attempt to set fire to the office. We don't have full access to his psychiatric file yet, but we know he's had a police record as an incendiary since he was ten. He was recommended for psychiatric assessment when he was fourteen, after he set fire to his school. Can't have done much good, though, because a year or so later he set fire to his home. Killed his parents and two older brothers.'

'No!' The cry was wrung from her. 'No, his parents are alive, they live in Cornwall! He told me!'

Collins looked almost regretful. 'Timothy Ellis's parents and brothers died in the house fire that he started. He's been in various institutions ever since. He came out two years ago, and since then he's been employed part-time in a printer's through a community care programme. The latest psychological reports said he was adapting well.' He gave a wry grimace. 'They obviously got it wrong.'

There wasn't enough air in the room. 'No!'

'I'm sorry, Miss Powell—'

'Do you think I don't *know* him?'

'You know Timothy Ellis. You never met Alex Turner.'

'I don't believe you!'

'We checked the telephone number you gave us. It's listed in the phone book under Ellis's name. You can look it up for yourself, if you like. He just told you it was ex-directory because he didn't want to risk you phoning Directory Enquiries and being given the real Alex Turner's number. And the reason he kept you away from where he lived was because his "studio flat" is actually a grubby, one-room bedsit. You'd have known straight away that no professional man on a decent wage lived there. It's only a ten-minute walk from the printer's where Ellis worked, though, so I suppose it was convenient for him.'

Kate shook her head, denying it. But the policeman's

words had triggered a chain reaction of connection that she couldn't stop. The memory of the black stain on his jeans came back to her, terrifyingly clear. Not paint. Ink. Printer's ink. She didn't want to hear any more, but Collins was relentless.

'Alex Turner is dead, Miss Powell. You saw his body at the mortuary this morning, and it seems increasingly likely that Timothy Ellis killed him. We know now it was Ellis who Dr Turner was staying behind late to see. He told his secretary about it, and although he didn't say why, I think we can assume that it had something to do with the fax you sent. We've also spoken to Ellis's boss at the printers. He's told us that there was a phone call for Ellis yesterday afternoon, and that after it he seemed moody and upset. I think that call was from Dr Turner, telling Ellis he wanted to see him. Now one of them is dead and the other is missing, and we need to find out what happened between them, and why. And I believe you can help us with that.'

She was suffocating. 'You think this is my fault?'

'No, I don't think that at all. But Ellis seems to have gone to great pains to make you think he was Alex Turner, and what happened yesterday seems to have been sparked off by your fax. To understand why, we have to know more about your relationship with Timothy Ellis.'

Kate shivered. She folded her arms around herself. A signal must have passed between Collins and the policewoman, because now she stood up.

'Would you like a cup of tea?' she asked.

Kate shook her head.

'I can make one. It's no trouble.'

'I don't want a bloody cup of tea!'

The policewoman's face hardened. She sat down again.

Collins let out a heavy sigh. 'Look, Miss Powell, I know this isn't easy, but I'd like you to bear in mind that, while we're sitting here with you, Alex Turner's lying on a mortuary slab, and his widow is having to come to terms with the fact that the baby she's carrying will be born without a father because he had his head stoved in by a man he was trying to help. So, while you have my sympathy, my main priority is locating Timothy Ellis before he destroys any more lives. I'm sure you can appreciate that.'

He spoke in a tone of patient weariness, but Kate felt her face flush as if she had been rebuked.

'His wife's pregnant?'

'Eight months,' Collins said. 'That's why I didn't ask her to identify the body.'

The last of Kate's resistance leaked away. 'I didn't know.'

'No reason why you should have. I didn't see any point in telling you yesterday. But I thought it might help put things in perspective now.'

She nodded, chastised. 'I'm sorry.'

'No need to apologise,' Collins said. 'But I think it's time you told us a little bit more about the fax. And what its significance was to Ellis.'

There was a last reluctance, a protest that these strangers should be the first to be told. Then it had gone.

'I'd just found out I was pregnant.'

The words fell into the room's silence. Collins turned to the policewoman.

'I think perhaps we could do with that tea now.'

*   *   *

'So. What are you going to do?'

Lucy sat with her legs drawn under her on the sofa, leaning back on Jack. The children were in bed, and the three of them sat in the darkened lounge, close to the fire. It spat and growled behind the mesh guard. Kate stared at the flames, stretching yellow arms up the chimney, and thought of lies and arson.

'I don't know.'

A bottle of whisky stood between them. Kate held a tumbler of it in both hands. She hadn't drunk from it yet.

'Are they sure, though?' Lucy asked. 'I mean, it seems so . . . so . . .' She threw up her hands, speechless.

'They say there's no doubt.'

'But how can they be certain he killed him? The psychologist, I mean. For all they know, it could have been, I don't know, a burglar, or something. It's not forced to have been Alex.'

'Ellis,' Kate said, not taking her eyes from the flames. 'His name's Timothy Ellis.'

Lucy didn't say anything to that. Jack sat, grim-faced, looking at his lap.

'No wonder he looked so young,' Lucy went on, after a while. 'Twenty-six! I mean, it's the cheek of it that gets me!'

'I don't think "cheek" comes into it,' Jack commented.

'No, I know, but . . . Well, he just seemed so *nice*. Although, now you look back, you can see that some things weren't right, can't you? I always thought he was a bit shy to be a psychologist. And, when you think about it, it was pretty odd that he never let you see where he lived.'

Kate wanted to shout at her to shut up.

228

'At least he didn't get any money out of you,' Lucy went on, oblivious. 'I bet he was pig sick that he couldn't cash your cheques. Makes you wonder how he could afford all those trips to Birmingham and everything, though, doesn't it? I mean, he wouldn't get much working part-time in a printer's, would he?'

That seemed irrelevant now. Kate had to rouse herself to answer. 'The police found a cardboard sign for Birmingham in his bedsit. They think he must have hitched.'

Lucy greeted the information with a wondering shake of her head. 'Well, to say he's supposed to be mentally ill, he'd got it all worked out, I'll give him that.' She looked at Kate again. 'What *are* you going to do, though?'

'Lucy, for God's sake, I don't *know*. I can't even think straight at the moment. I just feel . . .' The effort of putting it into words defeated her.

'I know, but you're going to have to decide sooner or later,' Lucy persisted. 'About the baby, I mean.'

'Lucy . . .' Jack said, warningly.

'Well, she *is*.'

'Decide what about the baby?' Kate asked. Lucy looked at her.

'If you're going to keep it or not.'

The crackling of the fire seemed to grow very loud, blending with the rush of blood in Kate's ears. The room tilted, as if not even the floor were stable any more. She put her glass on the coffee table and gripped the chair arms, feeling a greasy slide of nausea. Lucy and Jack's voices went on around her.

'For Christ's sake, Lucy!'

'Well, she's got to face up to it!'

'Give her a bloody chance! She's had enough shocks for one day!'

Jack was crouching in front of her, raising the whisky to her lips. She could smell it, and the wave of nausea rose. Then it passed. She pushed away the glass without drinking.

Jack set it on the coffee table and went back to his seat. 'You okay?'

Kate nodded. She wasn't, though. She felt weak, as though she was convalescing from an illness.

'Look, why don't you go and see a doctor tomorrow?' Lucy asked.

'I don't want tranquillisers.'

'I don't mean that. I just think you need to talk to someone. Get some expert advice.'

'About what?'

Kate saw Jack give Lucy an incredulous look. Lucy ignored it.

'You know what about. I'm sorry, Kate, but I think you've got to accept that abortion's a serious consideration now.'

'Oh, for Christ's sake, leave it alone, Lucy!' Jack snapped.

'No, I won't! I'm as pro-life, or whatever, as anybody, but there have to be exceptions! And, let's face it, being made pregnant by a deranged murderer has got to be one of them!'

Kate felt buffeted by the words. Lucy pressed on.

'You've got to face facts, Kate. I liked him too, I admit, but the man's a lunatic. Apart from anything else, he got you pregnant under false pretences. They do emergency terminations for rape victims, and I don't see that this is much different. But the longer you leave it, the worse it'll be. The sooner you—'

'Please, Lucy.' Kate shut her eyes. 'Just . . . don't. Please.'

'I know but—'

'Leave it, Lucy.' Jack spoke firmly, putting a restraining hand on his wife's shoulder. Lucy hesitated, then sat back.

'Okay.' She threw up her arms with a sigh. 'Okay.'

Behind the mesh screen, the coal fire blazed, indifferently. Hands clenched, Kate stared into the depth of the flames.

The message light was flashing on her answerphone when she arrived home. She stood in front of it, looking down at the insistent pulse, then quickly reached out and stabbed the play button. Only a bristle of static came out of the speaker. She thought she could make out faint breathing before the final clatter of disconnection, but she wasn't sure.

There was one other message, a sales pitch from a double-glazing company, then the machine rewound with a whir. As it clicked into readiness, Kate went into the bathroom, stripped off and showered. It was her third of the day. She stood under the flow of hot water until the tank emptied and it began to run cool. Climbing out, she saw there wasn't a clean towel and padded into her bedroom. As she pulled one out of the drawers, something else flipped into view. She looked at it, blankly, before there was a dip of recognition.

The child's mitten was shockingly red against the white towels. The sight of it stabbed at her. Kate had forgotten about it, and its sudden appearance now seemed deliberately mocking. Snatching it up, she took it into the kitchen and threw it into the bin.

CHAPTER 15

The red-haired librarian remembered Kate. His wind-burned cheeks seemed to redden even more when he saw her. She would have been flattered at another time, but now it barely registered.

'It was several months ago,' she said. 'You helped me with something called—'

'Don't tell me . . .' He snapped his fingers. 'A PsychLIT search, wasn't it?'

'You said that I could have photocopies of the actual articles. Can I still do that?'

He nodded, pleased to be helpful. 'There's a fee, but provided we've got the journals they appeared in on file, no problem.'

He led her to an unused monitor screen. She gave him Alex Turner's name again, and he accessed the CD-ROM records.

'Which was it you wanted?' the librarian asked.

'All of them, please.'

The librarian ran a print-out and asked Kate to wait. She sat at a table near the computer consoles. Around her, students and one or two older individuals stared at screens with degrees of absorption. It seemed a long time before the librarian returned. He had a sheaf of photocopies with him.

'Take you a while to wade through this lot,' he said, cheerfully. 'One or two were in obscure American journals that we don't stock, but we'd got most of them on file.'

Kate waited until he had gone before flicking through the photocopied articles. She'd asked for all of them, but there was one in particular she wanted to see. It was half-way down the pile.

''Prometheus' Children: Case Studies of Pyromania.'

This had been the last record she had looked at when she had checked out Alex Turner's credentials. She had only glanced at it before giving up, but the title had obviously lodged. At least, the fact that it was about pyromania had. She didn't know what, if anything, it would tell her. But pyromania was an obsession with fire. And Inspector Collins had called Timothy Ellis an incendiary.

She began to read. The first section came under the heading 'Classification'.

It is stating the obvious to say that different people raise fires for different reasons. Financial reward, political gesture, revenge, and vandalism are all motives for fire-setting. Numerous systems of classification have been put forward in an attempt to categorise the different types of arsonists, all of which are subject to a degree of overlap. But for the sake of this study the two broad group headings suggested by Faulk will be used:

Group I: Fire serves as a means to an end.
Group II: Fire itself is the phenomenon of interest.

Examples such as arson for insurance claims or to cover evidence of another crime fall into Group I. For the most part, pathological fire-setting, or pyromania, falls into Group II. Pyromania (an older term is incendiarism) is an impulse-control disorder characterised by a recurrent failure to resist impulses to set fires, and a fascination with watching them burn. The fire-setting is typically undertaken without any obvious monetary, revenge, or political motivation, and is frequently accompanied by increased tension before starting the fire, and intense pleasure or release during and afterwards. In extreme cases this gratification may take the form of sexual excitement (pyrolagnia, or erotic pyromania).

According to Greek mythology, Prometheus stole fire from the gods using a hollow stick. Freud and Jung said this could equate to both the male and female organ, and indicated a degree of identity/gender confusion which they thought characteristic of fire raisers. Subsequent studies seem to bear out this observation, showing that most pathological arsonists are young adult males, many of whom have serious social and sexual relationship problems (a trend which also applies to arsonists in general). Pathological fire setters frequently suffer from considerable psychosocial disadvantages as a result of personal inadequacies (actual or perceived) and adverse social conditions. Studies have noted that nearly all children who raise fires experienced inadequate relationships with their parents, and there is evidence that a high proportion have some form of minor physical abnormality, such as obesity or harelip.

Pyromania may be thought of as an addiction wherein the short-term 'benefits' (i.e., excitement, gratification) take precedence over the negative long term consequences.

There were four case studies, simply referred to as A, B, C, and D. Kate began to read the first closely, but skipped to the end when it was obviously unfamiliar. The second she also skimmed. When she reached the third, she found what she had been looking for.

C is a twenty-five-year-old white male, of above average intelligence and from a middle-class background. The family group was dysfunctional, with frequent violent arguments between the parents that would often extend to verbal and physical attacks on C and his two brothers, followed by periods of neglect when the parents entered a reconciliation stage. As the youngest and therefore lowest in the family hierarchy, C was often subjected to sibling bullying. When C was five years old he had his fingers put into a lighted gas fire by one brother. This would bear out Jackson's observation (1994) that some arsonists have been victims of fire themselves at some point. Although it is not possible to say that this experience was the direct cause of C's later obsession with fire, the trauma subsequently left him with a speech impediment in the form of a severe stutter, which exacerbated his sense of personal inadequacy and contributed further to his growing isolation from family and peer group. It should be noted that neither of his two brothers exhibited any corresponding dysfunction, although the elder may have had a latent inclination towards kleptomania, indicated by an arrest for shoplifting shortly before his death.

C's history of fire setting began at the age of ten, when he set fire to a curtain in the family home. His subsequent beating by both parents, and later his brothers, appears to have had the opposite effect to deterring him, forcing him into a spate of fire raising that culminated six months later in his burning down a shed in the local park. This resulted in the first police involvement, following which he was recommended for psychological assessment.

There followed a period of relative stability, lasting for eighteen months, when C started no fires. However, this also coincided with his going to stay with his paternal grandmother, when his father was imprisoned on a fraud charge. Away from the family home, his condition appears to have improved markedly, and it was only after his return there, following his father's release from prison, that his fire setting resumed.

At fourteen he was caught after setting fire to school outbuildings. This time he was referred for psychiatric treatment, following which he was recognised as exhibiting negative symptoms of schizophrenia, such as withdrawal from social contact, intense apathy, and being acutely ill at ease in the presence of other people. However, C's pyromania was ascertained to be a pathological problem rather than a symptom of his schizophrenia. At no time did he claim to have 'heard' voices telling him to start fires, or report any other delusional ideas, as is typically the case when the fire setting is a result of an organic psychiatric disorder. His compulsion to start fires, and his obsession with watching them, seems instead to have stemmed from an unconscious urge to purge himself of negative emotions. This frequently took the form of setting fire to an object associated with them (as, for instance, the attempt to burn down the school outbuildings, where he had been beaten by a gang of boys several days earlier). However, C's intense guilt following each incident of fire setting would generally result in his becoming even more withdrawn and isolated, thereby creating a need to start further fires.

C's schizophrenia appeared to respond well to treatment with anti-psychotic drugs, and once again his pyromania appeared to be under control. However, he was badly traumatised by the death of his paternal grandmother when he was fifteen. This came shortly after an argument between the grandmother and C's parents, in which his welfare was the central issue. On the evening of his grandmother's funeral, C set fire to his home, killing both his parents and brothers. Even now he still appears unclear over his intentions in setting this fire, and it is possible that it was set with no real regard for the consequences. He was interrupted by the emergency services in the act of pouring petrol over himself outside the burning house, clearly with the intention of self-immolation.

C was sectioned under the Mental Health Act, 1983, and transferred to a young person's secure unit, where he was treated with therapy and the anti-psychotic drug

Clozapine. In addition, C also received speech therapy to alleviate his stammer. He responded well, and was discharged after eight years into the supervision of a psychiatric social worker and clinical psychologist. He currently seems to have adapted well to living in the community once more, and has been found supervised work within it. To date there has been no recurrence of fire setting, and he expresses a strong understanding of his condition, and a desire to overcome it. Although he remains under psychiatric social worker monitoring, and bi-monthly psychological assessment, there seems a good possibility that, in time, this can be reduced.

The article went on to the next case study, but Kate stopped reading. The edges of her vision darkened. She felt a tingling light-headedness, and gripped the edge of the table until the faint receded. When it had, she grabbed the photocopies and began cramming them into her bag. Her hands were clumsy and several sheets spilled onto the floor. She bent to retrieve them, and then froze.

The man she had seen on the mortuary slab stared out at her from the top of one of the articles. The photograph was passport-sized and black and white, the face smiling in life, not stiff and disfigured, but it was unmistakably the same man. His name was printed underneath.

Dr Alex Turner.

Kate made it to the toilet before she was sick.

The receptionist tried to convince her to make an appointment for later in the week but finally relented and grudgingly told Kate that she could wait to see a doctor that evening.

Kate sat on one of the hard plastic chairs in the waiting room, avoiding eye contact with any of the other patients. An elderly man sat wheezing opposite her, one leg held out stiffly in front of him. Next to him a teenager pored over a women's magazine in silent absorption. Nearby, a young mother read quietly to a pale-looking toddler on her knee.

Kate picked up a magazine from the table in the centre of the room, but the words and pictures made no sense. When she came to an article on miscarriages she put it down.

The fluorescent lighting took the life out of everything. The waiting room was oppressive in its silence, so that the slightest sound was amplified. The young mother's voice murmured on in a deafening whisper. The old man's coughs boomed from the depths of his chest while the teenager's magazine announced each turned page in a rustle of glossy paper. Kate stared at the top of the receptionist's head, bent over behind the glass partition, and tried to think of nothing.

One by one the other patients were called in, until she was the last one left. The old man came out and walked stiffly to the door. It squeaked shut behind him, leaving Kate alone once more.

'Kate Powell.'

She stood and went over to the receptionist's counter. The woman slid her notes under the glass.

'Room three.'

Kate walked down the corridor and tapped on the door. A man's voice spoke from inside. She couldn't tell what he had said, but went inside anyway.

It was a different GP from the ones she had seen before. He

was an elderly man, small, with grey hair and gold half-moon glasses. Without looking up from what he was writing he held out his hand for her notes. Kate sat down and waited.

Finally he gave a small sigh and looked up. 'What can I do for you?'

Kate had rehearsed what she would say. Now it all vanished.

'I want an abortion,' she blurted.

The doctor looked at her over the top of his glasses. He took out her notes from the manilla envelope and read the more recent entries without answering.

'You're not quite five weeks' pregnant. Is that right?'

Kate nodded. The doctor pursed his lips and unhurriedly flipped back through her notes. She waited, her hands clenched and white on her lap. When he saw nothing that interested him he turned back to her.

'Why do you want an abortion?'

She told him. He listened without comment, legs crossed, looking at a notepad on his desk, on which he occasionally wrote. Kate tried to keep the quaver from her voice, but by the time she had finished she was shivering uncontrollably. She had hoped that telling someone, from beginning to end, would prove cathartic. It didn't.

The doctor made one or two more notes.

'And what does the clinic that carried out the insemination say about this? I presume you've told them?'

'They . . . they say it's nothing to do with them. When I asked them about termination, they said I should contact my own GP.'

Dr Janson had been appalled when Kate had phoned her, and while she had tried hard not to sound unsympathetic, it was obvious that her main worry was absolving the clinic of responsibility. The choice of donor had been entirely Kate's, she hastily pointed out, scrambling to distance the clinic from any hint of scandal. But Kate hadn't needed anyone to tell her where the fault lay.

The doctor's expression was unreadable as he put down his pen and faced her.

'So what you're basically saying is that, after going to great lengths to become pregnant, you've now changed your mind.'

His matter-of-factness took Kate's breath.

'No!' she exclaimed. 'Not just like that!'

The doctor took off his glasses, letting them dangle on the cord around his neck.

'But that is, essentially, what you're saying, isn't it?' Taking a tissue from his pocket, he began wiping the half-moon lenses. 'I'm not unsympathetic. I know this must have been very traumatic. But what we've got to look at is why, exactly, you want to terminate your pregnancy?'

Kate stared at him, unable to believe he had to ask. 'Isn't it obvious?'

He examined the lenses before letting the glasses hang on the cord again. 'It's obvious that you're very upset, which is understandable. What I'm trying to establish is whether you no longer want a baby. Or if you just no longer want this particular one?'

Kate opened her mouth to answer, then closed it. The doctor continued.

'It's only natural for you to feel confused and frightened. And angry, I daresay. You've been lied to, cheated, and found out in possibly the worst way imaginable that the man you trusted to be the father of your baby is not who he claimed. But perhaps you should be looking at counselling to help you cope with those feelings, rather than rushing into an abortion.'

'I don't want counselling!' The confusion she thought had been resolved surfaced again. She shook her head. 'I just can't go through with this!'

'Why can't you?'

'*Why*? Because he's mentally ill!'

'Is that the only reason?'

'Isn't it *enough*? He lied to me about who he was. He – he killed his own family! He's just killed somebody *else*, for God's sake!'

'The baby hasn't.' The doctor looked at her, calmly. 'The child you're carrying hasn't done anything, except be conceived. Is it fair to blame it for something its father's done?'

Again, Kate couldn't answer. She hadn't expected an argument, and the issues the doctor raised penetrated her decision like spikes.

'But how can I have his baby now?' Her voice was anguished. 'How do I know it won't be like him?'

The doctor kneaded the bridge of his nose tiredly. 'If every family with a history of mental illness passed it on to their children, sooner or later we'd all be affected.' He sighed. 'Yes, schizophrenia can sometimes run in families, but it isn't like eye colour. It isn't passed on directly. I think something like one child in ten may, *may*,' he stressed, 'develop it if one of its parents is schizophrenic. Which gives a ninety per cent chance that it won't.

'As for the arson . . . Well I'm not an expert on psychology, but I doubt very much that something like that is hereditary.

I think compulsive behaviour of that sort is more a matter of environment and upbringing than inheritance.'

'So you're saying you won't recommend me for an abortion,' Kate said, coldly. She was on the verge of walking out.

'No, I'm saying it's a serious decision, and before I refer you to have your pregnancy terminated I need to satisfy myself that you're not doing it for the wrong reasons. I don't want you to do anything you'll regret.'

She remembered Lucy saying the same thing at the beginning, when the idea had seemed full of hope. It wasn't a welcome memory, and she didn't respond. The doctor watched her.

'No one would argue that it isn't an awful situation,' he said, when it was obvious she wasn't going to speak. 'This man is obviously a very disturbed individual, and you've undoubtedly suffered a type of abuse. Which is all the more reason why you should reconsider counselling. At the very least I suggest you wait a while before making any decision about your pregnancy.'

'I don't want to wait.' The need to undo what had happened shrieked inside her. Everything else was blotted out.

The doctor inclined his head. 'It's your decision, but once you go ahead with this, it's something you'll have to live with for the rest of your life. You need to think carefully if it's what you really want.'

He looked steadily at her.

'Is it?'

Kate felt she wasn't really in the room, that this wasn't her abortion they were discussing. She gripped tight to her resolve.

'Yes.'

*   *   *

It had begun to rain as she unlocked the door to her flat, a fine drizzle that fogged the yellow glow from the street lights. She trudged upstairs, absently bending to stroke Dougal when he appeared and wound himself around her ankles. She went through the flat, turning on lights and lamps until there was at least the appearance of warmth. The television provided a background of noise and life.

She fed Dougal and made herself a cheese sandwich. The fridge was almost empty, she noticed. She supposed she would have to go shopping soon, but the thought lacked urgency. As she was about to close the fridge door, she saw the bottle of champagne, still waiting unopened. The sight of it brought a sudden pang, piercing the numbness that surrounded her. She picked it up and quickly dropped it in the bin. The cold, wet touch of the glass burned her hand, and she wiped it on a towel until the sensation had gone.

Taking her sandwich through to the lounge, she saw that the answerphone light was flashing. There were two messages. The first was from Lucy, asking what had happened at the doctor's. The second was a low hiss of an open line before the click of disconnection.

Kate stood there, listening to the tape rewind. Then she put down her plate and quickly dialled Lucy's number. The recorded message from Lucy's answerphone replied. She waited until the beep before speaking.

'It's Kate.' There was nothing she wanted to say. 'Call me when you get in,' she finished, and was about to hang up when there was a high-pitched squeal as the answerphone was interrupted at the other end.

'Sorry about that,' Lucy said, breathlessly, 'We were half-way through tea, so we thought we'd see who it was before we answered.'

'I'll talk to you later, if you like.'

'No, it's okay. I want to hear how you went on.'

Now she had called her, Kate felt a reluctance to talk. 'I'm having it. The abortion.'

She heard Lucy breathe out, relieved. 'It's for the best, Kate, it really is. How soon can you have it?'

'I don't know yet. Soon, though.'

'You've done the right thing. I know it wasn't an easy choice, but—'

'Look, Lucy, I – I don't want to talk about it just now.' The urge to put down the phone was almost overpowering. 'I'm sorry, I'll give you a ring tomorrow.'

'Are you okay? Do you want to come over?'

'No. Thanks, I'll be fine, I just . . . I'll talk to you tomorrow.'

She hung up. The effort of communication left her shaken, and when she went into the lounge she realised she'd left her sandwich in the hall. She went back out. As she reached it the phone rang.

Kate stared at it. It rang again. She waited until the last second before the answerphone cut in, then picked up the receiver.

'Hello?'

There was a silence at the other end. She swallowed.

'It's you, isn't it?' Still no answer. 'For God's sake, *say* something!'

'I'm sorry.'

It was almost whispered. She leaned her forehead on the wall at the sound of his voice.

'Kate? A-are you there?'

'Yes, I'm here.'

'I phoned before. You w-weren't in.'

Kate wiped her eyes.

'Where are you?' she asked.

He didn't answer.

'I've seen the police,' she told him. She could hear him breathing. 'They told me what you did.'

Silence.

'Why? Why did you do it?' she burst out.

'I – I'm sorry.'

'*Sorry?*' The cry was wrung from her. She wanted to hammer the receiver against the wall. '*Sorry?* I don't even know what to *call* you!'

'Kate . . . p-please. I didn't m-mean this to happen.'

'You didn't *mean* it to happen? What the hell did you think was *going* to happen?'

'I – I'm sorry, I—'

'*Stop fucking saying you're sorry!*'

She stopped. She felt breathless, as though she had run upstairs. In a calmer voice, she asked, 'Why did you do it?'

The silence went on for so long she thought he wasn't going to answer.

'I saw your advert.' His voice sounded wet, as though he was talking through tears. 'I was in his waiting room, and there was this m-magazine and it was in it. And then, when I went in to see Dr T-Turner, he had to go out for a few minutes, and I saw his jacket on the back of his chair, so . . . so I t-took his wallet.'

Kate sank down onto the floor, her back against the wall. '*Why*, though? I don't understand.'

She heard him sniff. 'I kn-knew you wouldn't want *me*! But if . . . if you thought I was somebody else . . . I didn't know it was g-going to go on for so *long*! I thought . . . I thought you'd n-never know, and that you'd have m-my baby, and look after it, and love it, and – and it'd be like *me* having a second chance!'

Oh, God. She caught her bottom lip between her teeth.

'And then I met you, and you told me it would t-take months . . . and I was glad. You looked so . . .'

Kate squeezed her eyes shut. *Don't. Please, don't.*

'I just wanted you to *like* me! I didn't kn-know it'd go on like it did. I . . . I kept *wanting* to tell you, but I couldn't. I knew you w-wouldn't want to see me any more . . . I *couldn't*!'

'Is that why you killed Alex Turner?'

It seemed strange, saying the name to him, meaning someone else. He didn't answer straight away.

'He got the fax.' He spoke softly. 'He phoned me and said it was important, and I'd g-got to go round straight after work.'

'After work? The printer's, you mean, or is this some other career you've invented?' She felt ashamed as soon as she'd said it.

He faltered, 'The p-printer's. Kate, I—'

'Just go on.'

She heard him draw a shaky breath. 'He was there by himself. When I went in, he just showed me the f-fax and then said, "Who's Kate?" I – I just couldn't *think*! He said he'd thought it'd b-been me who'd taken his wallet, but he hadn't been certain. B-but when he saw what you'd put about my g-grandmother's St Christopher, he knew then, because I'd told him all about her and what she'd said about it. And he said, "Tim, don't you think you'd b-better tell me what you've done?" So I told him, and all the time I k-kept thinking about you being pregnant, and that it was our baby, and – and I felt so *happy*!'

There was a pause. She could hear him breathing, reliving it. His voice when he continued was low, close to breaking.

'And then when I'd finished, he said, "You've c-caused quite a mess, haven't you?" And then he said it'd got to be sorted out, and he was going to have to t-tell you. I said I'd tell you myself, but he said he c-couldn't let me, it had gone too far for that. He w-wouldn't l-*listen*!'

His stammer had grown worse, like a machine shaking itself apart.

'He started telling me to c-calm down, but how c-could I when he was going to spoil everything? If he'd just let me *tell* you it would have b-been all right, but he wouldn't, he told me to sit down, and started saying everything w-would be okay, but I knew it wouldn't be, I kn-knew he was l-lying. Then he told me not to *push* him, but I *hadn't*, I – I'm sure I hadn't, and then he started going towards the d-door, and I knew he was going to f-fetch them to come and get me, and I'd n-never see you again, so I – I tried to *stop* him. I just wanted to *explain*, to m-make him *see*, and then—'

He stopped. Kate was rigid, every muscle tense. She could hear his breathing, rapid and laboured.

'I didn't m-mean to,' he said. 'It was only because he was g-going to tell you, but there was so much *blood*. I just didn't want him to t-*tell* you, that was all, I couldn't stand the thought of what you'd think about me, Kate, I . . .'

Don't. She wasn't sure if she'd spoken it or not.

'. . . I l-love you, Kate . . .'

No.

'P-please, Kate, I'm s-sorry—'

'No.'

'– Please don't h-hate me, I didn't m-mean to hurt anyone—'

'Shut up.'

'– Don't be upset, I wouldn't hurt you—'

'Shut *up*!'

'– I only did it because of the b-baby—'

'*There isn't any baby*!'

It was a reflexive cry. There was a silence.

'What do you m-mean?' His voice held a barely suppressed panic. 'K-Kate, don't say that!'

'I mean there isn't any baby!'

'There is, I saw your f-fax, you s-said it—'

'It's *dead*! I've had an abortion!'

Distantly, she felt herself recoil from the words, but there was a savage exultation in lashing out, hurting him back.

'No.' The denial was hushed.

'I had it this morning.'

'N-no, I d-don't believe you!'

'They killed it.' The words ran away with her.

'You're lying!'

'They cut it out—'

'Oh. God, no, oh, G-God, no—'

'– and then they threw it in the incinerator and burnt it!'

She stopped, appalled with herself. She heard him moan.

'Don't,' she said. 'I didn't mean it.'

'No, no, God, no, oh, no—'

'Listen,' she began, 'I haven't—'

'*No, no, no no nonono*—'

The sound of his pain cut through her own. 'Please, don't! You were right, I was—'

'*Bitch!*'

The word hit her like a fist.

'*M-murdering fucking bitch!*'

'No, listen to me—!'

'*I'll kill you! I'll fucking k-kill you, you murdering BITCH!*'

The line went dead.

The receiver hummed in her ear. Slowly, Kate lowered it. She became aware of a weight on her lap. Looking down, she saw that at some point Dougal had come and sat on her knee without her noticing. A noise from the phone made her start, and she almost dropped it as a recorded voice pipingly instructed her to replace the handset. She dislodged Dougal and climbed stiffly to her feet. Her neck and shoulder muscles ached as though she had overworked them in the gym. She replaced the phone in its cradle and looked around the hallway as if she didn't recognise it. But it appeared no different from how it had ten minutes before.

From the lounge, the quiz show still buzzed with gleeful laughter. Kate walked away from the sound. She went downstairs and checked that both doors were locked. Then she came back up and phoned the police.

CHAPTER 16

It was nothing like the clinic at Birmingham. For one thing, she was fully clothed, sitting on a hard plastic chair instead of lying on a couch. The room was a dull cream colour, NHS instead of private, and lit by a harsh strip light that buzzed like a trapped fly. The doctor was short and plump, and the nurse's uniform nothing like so crisply ironed. But for all that, Kate couldn't help but be reminded of the other place. Perhaps it was because one had been a beginning while the other was an end.

She had come a full, futile circle.

Her hand went instinctively to her throat, feeling for the gold locket that was now in a drawer in her flat. She lowered it again.

'The procedure for an early medical termination's quite simple,' the doctor said, and again Kate was faced with a ghost of that other time, the other clinic. 'Effectively, what we're doing is inducing a miscarriage. The drug we use is called Mifegyne, and what it basically does is stop the lining of your womb forming. You'll have to stay here for an hour after you've taken it to make sure there aren't any side effects, but there rarely are.'

The doctor gave a reassuring smile. She was a pleasant-faced woman in her fifties. 'After that you can go home again. Then you'll have to come back in a couple of days, and we'll give you a pessary to make you pass what's in your womb.'

'Will I be able to see anything?' Kate could hear the tremor in her own voice.

'You'll probably see what you pass, yes. But it won't be much different from a heavy period. There won't be anything recognisable, if that's what you mean. At this stage it's still only cells.'

Cells.

Kate pushed the image out of her mind. 'What . . . what happens to it? Afterwards, I mean. What do you do with it?'

Her eyes went to the yellow cardboard cylinder on the window-ledge. It had stylised drawings of flames on it. The doctor saw where she was looking and gave an understanding shake of her head.

'That's only for wipes.'

She gave Kate a small plastic container, like a miniature cup. In it was a single white pill. Kate looked down at it. The tiny object seemed bland and innocuous. The nurse held out a glass of water for her. Kate took it. The tremor in her hand caused a faint rippling of the water's surface. She raised the plastic cup with the pill in it to her lips. Over its rim she could see the doctor and nurse watching her. She held it poised, tensing herself. One swallow and it would be done. Seconds passed.

Kate lowered the cup.

'I can't.'

She shook her head. 'I'm sorry, I just can't.'

She held out the container, suddenly wanting to be rid of it. The doctor took it from her.

'That's all right, you aren't under any pressure to go through with this.'

Kate felt her eyes begin to swim. 'I'm sorry. I should never have come.'

'Don't worry. You're not the first one who's got this far and then changed her mind.' The doctor gave her a smile and patted her arm, although the nurse was stony-faced as she emptied the glass into the sink. 'Better to find out now than later.'

Kate felt weak and washed out as she went out into the corridor and down to the waiting area. Lucy looked up in surprise from a magazine.

'That was quick.'

'I haven't had it.'

Lucy lowered the magazine. 'Why, what's—?'

'Please, let's just go.' Kate glanced at the other women in the waiting room. They looked away, but were obviously listening. 'I'll tell you outside.'

A thin skim of brown mush lay on the pavement from the snow that had fallen that morning. A few flakes still drifted down. They expired against Kate's cheeks like cold sparks.

'What happened?' Lucy asked, as they walked away from the hospital.

'Nothing. I just couldn't go through with it.'

'You mean you just walked out?'

Kate nodded. Lucy made an exasperated noise in her throat. 'Kate, what are you *thinking* of? Look, perhaps if you went back in and—'

'I'm not going back.'

'Don't be silly. I know it's difficult, but you've got to face up to it sooner or later.'

'I have faced up to it. I'm going to keep the baby.'

'Oh, come *on*, Kate, be reasonable!'

'I am.'

'I thought it was all decided! You said yourself it was the best thing to do!'

'I changed my mind.'

They had stopped. The falling snow crystals had turned to sleet, speckling their hair with glistening beads. Lucy brushed a damp strand from her forehead.

'Look, let's get out of this muck and talk about it.'

'There's nothing to talk about. I've told you, I'm keeping it.'

'You *can't* keep it! Just think about what you're doing! The father's a raving lunatic who's on the run for murder, he's already threatened to kill you, and you're still going to have his baby?'

'It isn't the baby's fault. The doctor was right, I can't blame it for what its father's done.'

'And what if it turns out like him? And it might, I don't care what the doctor says. What will you do then?'

'I'll have to risk it. But it'll be as much me as him, and I'll do everything I can to make sure it has more chances than he did.'

'And it's that simple? You think it'll thank you when it's old enough to understand who its father was? What will you say?'

'I don't know, all right? I can't even think about what I'll be doing tomorrow, let alone God knows how many years from now! I just know that I'm not going to kill this baby!'

'For God's sake, Kate, it isn't even a baby yet! Don't be stupid!'

'I'm not being stupid.'

'No?' Lucy cast her eyes skyward. 'This is just so typical of you! You won't listen to anybody, will you?'

Kate's own anger had only been waiting for a focus. 'If I'd listened to you I'd have been married to him by now!'

'I admit he fooled me as well, but I said from the start this was a bad idea. But you wouldn't take any notice! You were hell bent on doing things your way, and look where it's got you!'

'So you think this is my fault, then?'

'Since you ask, yes! Nobody made you do it, it was what *you* wanted. God, I could shake you sometimes! I'd have thought you'd have learned your lesson by now!'

'What's that supposed to mean?'

Lucy's cheeks had flushed an angry red. 'Nothing. Forget I said it.'

'No, come on, I want to know what you mean.'

'You know what I mean. I mean Paul Sutherland. You should have walked out on him months before you did, but no, you'd got to wait until he threw you out. I swear, I don't understand you, Kate! It's like when things get bad you go out of your way to make them worse!'

'This is nothing like that!'

'Yes, it is, it's exactly the same.'

Kate's face was hot. 'Except this time only one of us has slept with him.'

She knew, as she said it, that she was moving the argument on to a different level, but by then it had developed a momentum of its own. Lucy glared at her, white-lipped.

'Oh, now we're getting to it! I wondered how long it would be before you threw that one back at me!'

'I'm not throwing anything back at you. I'm just reminding you that you're not as perfect as you think.'

'Perhaps not, but at least I'm capable of having a relationship without it turning into a disaster!'

'Oh, fuck off!'

They stared at each other, wide-eyed at the suddenness of the breach. Their breath steamed in a cloud around them. All at once neither could meet the other's eye.

Lucy spoke first. 'All right, I will. But just don't come running to me and Jack in future.'

'Don't worry, I won't.'

They began walking in opposite directions. Kate half expected to hear Lucy shout her, and half wanted to turn round and do the same herself. But Lucy didn't shout, and Kate kept on walking.

When she reached the corner and glanced back, Lucy had gone.

Morning sickness was a joy Kate hadn't counted on. She'd known, intellectually, that she could probably expect it, but she had found out that expecting it and experiencing it were two different things. She had put her attack of nausea in the library down to shock at first, until it happened again the next morning. Since then it had been a regular part of her daily routine; along with showering, getting dressed, going for the tube, she knew that at some point she would also have to incorporate vomiting into her schedule.

It wouldn't be so bad, she thought, if it came along at the same time every day. She knew that Lucy (although she tried not to think about Lucy) had been as regular as clockwork, making sure she was near a bathroom between eleven and quarter past each morning. But Kate's own attacks were sporadic. The queasiness she would wake up with could linger all day, like a low-grade hangover. Or it could send her running for the bathroom before she left her flat in the morning. It was just something else she couldn't predict.

She felt the nausea begin to build as she sat on the tube. Anxiously, she counted the stations still to go. King's Cross was still several stops away. She sat perfectly still, trying not to dwell on it. The train lurched and whined to a halt in the tunnel. The sudden jolt made Kate break out in a clammy sweat, a sign she had come to recognise as meaning that vomiting was imminent. She prayed for the train to move again, trying to think if she had anything in her bag to be sick into. There was nothing except the bag itself.

She closed her eyes, but that only made her feel worse. The train jerked forward, and with relief Kate saw the lights of a platform appear outside the windows. Without caring which station it was, she hurried off and pushed through the crowd waiting to board. Breathing as steadily as she could through her nose, she ran up the escalators, eyes scanning desperately for a toilet sign.

There was one on the upper concourse. She had a bad moment when she couldn't find a twenty-pence piece for the turnstile, but then she was inside and bolting the cubicle door behind her.

The only thing to be said for it was that it was over quickly. Feeling wretched, but less so than before, she rinsed her mouth out at a sink and dried it on a paper towel. She looked at herself in the mirror above the taps. Her face looked pale, the skin under her eyes bruised.

You wanted this, she told herself. *Too late to feel sorry for yourself now.*

The sickness left her blood sugar screaming for renewal. She debated whether to call Clive and tell him she would be late, but decided he would work that out anyway, and went into a coffee shop just outside the station. She ordered a croissant and jam, and a weak, milky tea. The coffee smelled wonderful, but she'd found that she had no stomach for it anymore. She wondered what else she would be giving up before the nine months was over.

She felt more like herself when she came out and went back down the escalator to catch a train. As if the break in her journey had set a precedent, she was in no rush now to get to work. It was almost eleven before she turned into the row of Georgian terraced houses. The light was on in the downstairs office of the agency, and through the window she saw Clive clutching a bundle of papers to his chest. She had time to notice the harried expression on his face before she opened the door and her greeting died on her lips.

The office was a shambles. The desks had been tipped over, and the filing-cabinet drawers had been pulled out and emptied onto the floor. Paper was strewn on the carpet like snow. Clive turned at the sound of the door opening, the armful of papers still held to his chest. Josefina and Caroline were both kneeling down, gathering up more sheets.

Kate found her voice. 'What's happened?'

WHERE THERE'S SMOKE

Clive set the papers down onto a chair. 'We've been burgled. Well,' he amended, 'we've been broken into. There doesn't seem to be much missing.' He looked around, wryly. 'So far as we can tell, anyway.'

She closed the door and walked inside, picking her way carefully through the turmoil. 'Have you called the police?'

'Yeah, they've been. For what it's worth. They want us to make out a list of anything that's been taken. They're sending somebody around to fingerprint, so we've got to try to avoid touching anything. But I thought we might as well start sorting out some of the mess.'

Kate just stared at it.

'Looks like they forced the toilet window at the back,' Clive went on. 'The police say there was another break-in at the newsagent's further down the road, but they don't think there's any connection. The alarm from there might have frightened off whoever did this, though, because there doesn't seem to be much missing. They just trashed down here and in your office.'

'How bad?'

'You'd better see for yourself.'

She went upstairs, Clive following her. If anything, the chaos there was even worse. She reached out for the broken fan, lying smashed on a shelf, then remembered she wasn't supposed to touch anything and let her arm drop to her side.

Clive pushed the door shut. 'Look,' he began, uneasily, 'I don't know if I've done the right thing, but . . . well, the police were asking if I knew of anyone with any grudges against us, so I told them about Paul Sutherland.'

Kate looked around at the wreckage of her office. 'I don't think he did this.'

'If he was drunk he might have. He's got a big enough chip on his shoulder.'

Kate kept her doubts to herself.

'The other thing is, did you take your Filofax home with you?' Clive asked. 'The big one you keep on your desk?'

It was an unwieldy, black-leather thing, the size of a small briefcase. Lucy and Jack had bought it for her when she had first started the agency. She took it home occasionally, when she was working from her flat, but the rest of the time it stayed in her office.

'No. It should be here.'

'Well, I suppose it might be hidden under a pile of papers somewhere, but I can't see it.'

Kate went over to where the desk lay on its side. The paraphernalia from its top was scattered on the floor in front of it, lying where it had spilled off when the desk had been tipped over. The heavy black Filofax wasn't among it.

'I thought it was the sort of thing Sutherland might have taken,' Clive went on. 'Being as it's got all the clients' addresses in it. I can't see it being much use to anyone else.'

Kate ran a hand through her hair, glad she hadn't tied it back that morning. The beginning of a headache was already nagging at her temples.

'I'd better clear up what I can, anyway,' she said.

She turned down Clive's offer of help, and looked around, wondering where to start as he went back downstairs. The violence seemed aimless and wanton. Her reference books had been swept from the shelf and she went to pick them up. As she did, something crunched under her foot.

She looked down.

It was a box of matches.

CHAPTER 17

The crematorium chapel was modern and austere. The walls were a dull, mustard yellow, with clear glass windows set high up near the ceiling. The pews were a pale oak, functional and straight-lined, like park benches. Hung on the wall at the far end, the bare wooden crucifix looked geometric and stark without the effigy of the pain-racked figure fixed to it.

Kate slipped into an empty pew at the very back. Most of those in front of her were full, lines of dark-clothed figures facing the plain pulpit that stood on a low dais. She thought of Miss Willoughby's funeral, where there had been only herself and a bored solicitor. To one side of the dais lay the coffin, surrounded on three sides by dark blue curtains. No one looked round as she quietly took her seat. A Bob Marley track was playing through the wall-mounted speakers, helping to cover the echoing rustles and coughs. It faded as the white-surpliced vicar mounted the pulpit.

He was a plump, youngish man with prematurely greying hair. He stood with his arms held loosely by his sides, waiting until the last strains of the music had died before speaking.

'We're gathered here today to celebrate the life of Alex Turner.'

His voice carried clearly in the bleak room. A choked sob came from a young woman in the front row. An older woman sat beside her, an arm around her shoulders.

'I know all of you here will have come with your grief, and your anger, at the manner of his passing. It is never easy when someone we love dies, and it is even less so when they are taken from us as Alex was, suddenly, and with violence. It is natural to feel shocked and bewildered. And it is easy to let those emotions give way to hate for the person who took Alex's life. But today, I want you to put those feelings aside. We should remember that Alex dedicated his life to helping others. For him to lose his life in doing so is a cause for sorrow, but Alex himself would have been the first to urge us not to condemn. But to try to understand.'

The young woman sat with her head bowed. Kate could see her shoulders shaking. Further along on the same pew, an elderly man blew his nose and dabbed at his eyes.

'It is not always easy. We have lost a friend. A son. A husband. And a father, because the child that Kay, Alex's wife, is carrying will now never know him.'

For an instant Kate thought he had said her own name. She looked again at the young woman in the front row.

'One of the tragedies is that neither will Alex see his child when it's born, a child that he and Kay have long wanted. For them to be finally blessed, only to have their happiness snatched away in a senseless act of violence seems especially cruel. Yet to give way to thoughts of bitterness, of anger and revenge would be an even greater waste. Because to do that is not only to dishonour Alex's memory. It is also to refute everything he lived, worked, and ultimately died for.'

A draught of cold air brushed the back of Kate's neck as

the chapel door was opened. She looked around to see a man wearing a thick waxed coat easing it shut behind him. His shoes squeaked on the floor as he went to the end of Kate's pew and sat down. A bulky camera was slung around his neck. Kate looked away as he began to fiddle with it.

'I was privileged to know Alex through the work we both did in the community, and I can truthfully say I found him to be a patient and kind man, who genuinely cared for the people who came to him for help. So, as we pray now for Alex, I would like us also to pray for the tortured young man who took him from us so suddenly. And also for each other, so we can find the strength within ourselves to forgive him.'

Abruptly, Kate's eyes filled. She hung her head, letting the tears drop directly onto her coat, where they quickly soaked into the rain-damp fabric. In the general shuffling as the congregation prepared itself to pray, she took a tissue from her pocket and quietly blew her nose.

A noise from the end of the pew distracted her. Glancing up, she saw that the photographer was also bent over, but only to change the lens on his camera. He had a bag open on the seat next to him, and as he took one from it, he knocked another onto the floor. She heard its thin rattle, and the man's muttered, 'Shit,' over the vicar's resonant voice.

The prayer ended. The vicar continued, but now Kate's attention was divided between what he was saying and the photographer's preparations.

The service was short. There was no hymn. Instead, they sat in silence as Elgar's cello concerto was played through the PA system. At the end of it Kate would have slipped out, but the photographer blocked the end of the pew.

'It is our hope and belief that Alex's spirit will not have

died, that the Alex we knew and loved still continues, apart from us, but still whole,' the vicar continued. 'But Alex remains with us in other ways. He will always be a part of our hearts, always be in our memories. And he will continue in the child that Kay gives birth to, a living reminder of the Alex Turner whom we knew and loved, and to whom we now bid goodbye.'

The curtains closed over the coffin with a jerky rustle. As they swayed to a standstill, the vicar stepped down from the pulpit without another word. Kate looked over at the photographer again. He was poised on the edge of his seat, camera at the ready. She turned away, wondering if she could squeeze out at the other end but the pew was pushed up against the wall.

She looked back in time to see the photographer bob up to take a couple of shots as the young woman rose to her feet. He slid out of the pew and went to the door. Kate stood up to leave also, but by then the people from the front were already coming down the central aisle.

She sat down again, head averted. From the corner of her eye she could see the young woman draw level with the end of the pew. An elderly couple supported her at either side, while behind her followed the man Kate had seen wiping his eyes earlier. The young woman walked slowly, like an invalid, and Kate had time to see the heavy belly under the black coat, the pale and tear-blotched face.

Then they were behind her, making their slow progress to the door. Kate kept her head down. She could hear the young woman's stifled sobs as the unsteady footsteps came closer. She ducked her head further, waiting for them to stop, tensing for the cry of recognition, of accusation.

The door creaked open. The footsteps diminished, and were drowned by the shuffling tread of the other mourners as they filed past.

Kate didn't move. She kept her eyes on her hands, clasped tightly on her lap, as the procession dragged on. Finally, she could hear that it was coming to an end. The rest of the chapel was quiet as the stragglers made their way behind her to the door, and Kate prepared to leave.

'Hello, Miss Powell.'

She jumped at the sound of the voice. She looked up at the man standing over her unable to think who he was. Then the bristly grey hair, the faintly mournful eyes under thick black brows slotted into place and she recognised the Detective Inspector.

'I wasn't expecting to see you here,' he said.

The last of the mourners had disappeared through the door. They had the chapel to themselves.

'I wanted to come.' Kate looked over to where the coffin was hidden by the closed drapes. 'I thought it was the least I could do.'

A mechanical, whirring sound came from behind the curtains. They swayed slightly.

'We'd better go,' Collins said. 'There's another funeral scheduled.'

Kate made her way along the pew. Collins waited for her. He was wearing the brown suit and tweed overcoat that he always seemed to have on. He held the door open for her, and they went along the short corridor to the main doors.

Outside, the air was cold and sharp. The mourners were clustered in loose groups on the wide tarmac drive around the young woman. The elderly couple stood near, still supporting her as people waited their turn to speak a few brief words, occasionally to embrace her. The second elderly man stood close by, but slightly to one side, not quite a part of their group.

'That's Turner's father,' Collins said. 'His mother couldn't come. She's in hospital, dying of cancer.'

The man had a slightly dazed expression as he nodded and shook hands with the people who approached him. Kate looked away.

'I'd better go.'

Collins regarded her. 'If you want to hang on a second I'll give you a lift.'

'No, it's all right. Thanks.' She was suddenly in a hurry to get away.

'I'd like a word with you anyway. I won't be a minute.'

Without waiting for her to reply, he went over to where the young woman stood, surrounded now by a group of weeping women. He waited on the edge, his bulk towering over them, then stepped forward. Kate saw him speak to Turner's widow, taking both her hands in his. The young woman nodded, and then Collins moved on to shake hands with the man and woman on either side of her, and lastly the man he had pointed out as Turner's father. He came back towards Kate.

'The car's parked at the other side.'

They moved around the mourners towards a line of parked cars. Then Collins stopped. She felt his hand on her arm, restraining her, and looked up to see him staring ahead at the photographer who had been in the chapel. The man's attention was on the central group around the widow. Kate could hear the click-whir of his camera motor as he took shots.

'Let's go this way,' Collins said, taking her arm and leading her back the way they had come.

They went around the back of the chapel, coming out behind the photographer, so he was facing away from them.

'Why didn't you want him to see you?' Kate asked.

He glanced at her, then away again.

'It was more you I didn't want him to see. We've kept you out of it so far. I don't want the press to start sniffing around now over some "mystery woman" at the funeral.'

The murder of a psychologist by one of his patients had made national news, but none of the reports had made any mention of Kate's involvement. She was surprised by the Inspector's consideration.

'Thank you.'

'No need to thank me. The press coverage was bad enough when they thought it was just another failure of Care in the Community. They've lost interest now, but if they find out why Ellis killed him we'll have every tabloid in the country breathing down our necks. It'll turn into a three-ring circus, and that sort of thing doesn't help anybody.'

They reached the line of waiting cars. Collins went to a grey Ford. The sergeant who had been with him the first time he had visited Kate's office was in the driver's seat, reading a newspaper. He quickly folded it.

'We're giving Miss Powell a lift,' Collins told him, opening the rear door for her.

The sergeant grinned at Kate, then seemed to think that might be too familiar and looked more serious. He cast a glance at the Inspector, as Collins eased his bulk onto the back seat next to her.

'Where to?'

'The nearest tube station's fine,' Kate said.

The sergeant started the car. Others from the line were already pulling onto the drive.

'I've been in touch with the Wynguard Clinic,' Collins said, as they passed through the crematorium gates. 'Not that they were able to help much.' A trace of a smile touched his lips. 'Your Dr Janson's a worried woman. It seems the clinic never chased up the check with Ellis's GP. They didn't seem to think there was any real need, because he was a "known donor". Is that the right term?'

Kate nodded.

'Anyway, that's between you and them, but I wouldn't be surprised if you'd got a case for negligence. I doubt that Ellis knew who the real Alex Turner's doctor was, so if the clinic had tried to get hold of his medical records they'd have known something was wrong straight away. I'm not sure how the law stands on that but it might be worth you taking legal advice.'

She shook her head. 'I can't blame them.'

Collins let the matter drop.

'The other thing I wanted to tell you is that Paul Sutherland's been released,' he went on. 'He still claims he can't remember where he was on the night your office was broken into, but from what the officers who arrested him said, that's pretty easy to believe. Apparently it was a while before he was sober enough to talk any sense at all. But they've managed to account for at least some of his movements, and it doesn't look as though it was him.'

The car smelt of cigarettes. Kate wound down the window a little to let some air in.

'I never thought it was.' The breeze was cold on her face.

'No luck with fingerprints, either, I'm afraid.' Collins's knees pressed into the back of the seat in front. Sitting next to him, Kate felt like a little girl. 'Looks as though whoever did it wore gloves. So they either knew what they were doing, or they'd got cold hands.'

'What about the matches?'

Collins turned down his mouth and shook his head.

'Doesn't prove it was Ellis, if that's what you mean.'

'So you don't think it was.'

'I don't think a box of matches proves anything, one way or another. It could just have been a burglar who smoked. We'll keep an eye on your office as well as your flat, but I wouldn't read too much into it.'

Kate gazed out of the window. 'Did you find out where he called from?'

She had dialled 1471 after Ellis had phoned her. His number had been logged on the caller-return system, and she had passed it to Collins. But she could see from his expression that it had been a wasted effort.

'He used a public phone box near Oxford Circus tube station. Nobody can remember seeing him.' The Inspector sounded disgruntled by the admission. 'Somebody like that's not going to be able to keep out of sight for very long, though. He'll turn up sooner or later.'

The sergeant pulled into the kerb. 'This okay? There's a tube station on the other side of the road.'

Kate said it was and got out. The tobacco smell seemed to follow her, caught on her clothes. Collins climbed out as well.

'Don't worry,' he said, his hand on the passenger door handle. 'We'll find him before much longer.'

The car sank down slightly as he eased into the front seat. As it pulled away, Kate looked to see if the road was clear to cross.

Outlined against the grey clouds, the thin column of the crematorium chimney was poised like a rebuking finger.

That night she cooked herself a cheese and ham omelette, with Brussels sprouts and two slices of wholemeal bread. Sprouts weren't her favourite vegetable, but they were rich in folic acid, which was important in pregnancy. Even though she had no appetite, there was an incentive to make an effort. Part of her noted the irony that, now she was able to eat as much as she liked without feeling guilty or running to the gym, she wasn't able to enjoy it.

Kate found that she had moved to an acceptance of being pregnant without really being aware of it. The thrill she had expected to feel seemed to have been subsumed in the larger emotional turmoil. At odd moments the knowledge would hit her, and there would be a vertiginous plunge that was almost terror. But even that was already growing rarer.

She forced herself to eat the omelette and helped down the final breadcrust with a glass of milk. Taking her plate and glass into the kitchen, she washed and dried them. When she had put them away she looked at her watch. It was eight o'clock. She went back into the lounge and stared at the television until it was ten o'clock and she felt she could reasonably go to bed.

Sleep came hard. Often it was little more than a restless, half-awake state that would last until the early hours, leaving her feeling grainy and listless when it was time to get up. It was like that now. Kate groped for the clock as the insistent beep of the alarm dragged her towards consciousness. She fumbled to turn it off before realising that the noise was coming from outside her room.

She sat up. It was still dark, without even the subtle lightening that indicates dawn. Still hazy with sleep, it took her several seconds to understand what had woken her.

It was the smoke alarm.

She threw back the covers and ran into the hall. The yammer of the alarm was immediately louder, and now she could smell the smoke that had triggered it. She switched on the hall light and blinked against the sudden brightness. There was a faint grey haze in the air, but no fire.

Kate ran to the lounge. It was as she had left it, dark and quiet. The smell of smoke was fainter. She hurried out to check the kitchen, noticing that the smoke in the hallway was already thicker. As she passed the top of the stairwell a noise made her look down.

Smoke was oozing from around the door at the bottom. The foot of the stairs was in shadow, but a bright glow came from the translucent cat flap. It was bumping inwards as though blown by a wind, nudged by the heat on the other side. The plastic was already beginning to bubble.

Kate sprinted into the kitchen. She turned on both taps full to fill the washing-up bowl and then, leaving them running, dashed to the phone. Her hands were shaking as she dialled 999.

'Emergency, which service do you require?'

'Fire. My flat's on fire.'

A second later another operator came on the line. Kate

tried to keep her voice level, but couldn't stop the tremor as she gave the details. The smoke alarm continued to shrill in the background.

'Is there anyone else in the property?' the operator, a woman, asked.

'No.' Miss Willoughby's flat had remained vainly for sale ever since the old lady had died. Kate was thankful now that it was empty.

'Can you go outside?'

'No, the exit's on fire, for God's sake!'

She heard the panic in her voice, but the operator remained calm as she told Kate to go to a room facing the street, close the door and open the window.

'Stay by the window so they can see you,' the operator said. 'And hang a towel or something out of it as a marker.'

The smoke was already thicker, given a toxic bite from the melting plastic of the cat flap. Coughing, Kate hung up and ran back to the kitchen. The washing-up bowl was overflowing and, without turning off the taps, she picked it up and staggered out with it. Water sloshed onto the T-shirt she wore to sleep in as she reached the top of the stairs and heaved the entire bowl towards the bottom. Without waiting to see what effect it had, she stumbled back down the hallway and into the lounge.

The air in there was clearer, and it wasn't until she had closed the door that it occurred to her that the room was directly above the fire. Belatedly, she wondered if the bathroom would be safer. But she balked at the thought of going back out into the smoke.

Leaving the room dark, she crossed to the window. It was a sash, and years of paint had stuck it together. Every summer since she had been in the flat Kate had meant to repair it, but never had. It slid open easily for six inches and then jammed. She struggled with it for a few seconds and then gave up. A bar of cold air breezed against her midriff. She had forgotten to grab a towel, so she stripped the cover off a cushion and draped that through the gap instead. Resting her head against the cold glass, she looked out. The street was empty, with no sign of the police patrols Collins had promised. The path in front of the front door was lit by a moving, multi-coloured light. Flickering patches of blue, red and orange danced on the garden as the flames shone through the stained-glass facets. A faint tinkling came to Kate as, one by one, they shattered, until the harlequin glow was a uniform yellow.

There was a movement in the shadows. She peered into them and saw Dougal sitting on the garden wall. The cat's eyes gleamed with reflected light as he watched the fire. Kate's breath misted the window, and when she wiped it clear Dougal had gone.

Dimly, in the distance she heard the wail of a siren.

Water dropped from the ceiling. A sooty pool of it scummed the floor, covering the cracked ceramic tiles. The walls and ceiling were blackened, the woodwork of the doors and door-frames charred and blistered. Miss Willoughby's welcome mat lay where it had been pushed into a corner by the pressure of the hose, a shrunken black square. Hanging over everything was the tickling, charcoal reek of dead fire.

The fire officer straightened. Behind him other uniformed men were coiling the hose and packing it away. Glass crunched under his feet. The bulb in the ceiling had shattered, but enough light came from the stairs to see by.

'We'll have to wait for the forensic results, but I don't think there's much doubt,' he said. He was a stocky, middle-aged man. His hair had been flattened by the yellow helmet he now held under one arm.

He nodded down at the cat flap at the base of the door. It had melted and congealed like candle-wax, a surreal twin to the one set in the inside door.

'They poured petrol through the outside flap, then stuck a piece of cloth through and set fire to it.' He nudged with his foot at a charred fragment that could have been fabric. 'Whoever did it knew enough not to get their fingers burned by sticking their hand through with a match. You're lucky it was only in the entrance area. There's nothing much in here to burn. Not until it got into one of the flats, anyway. Our friend either didn't know that, or expected it to be contained. Not that that's any excuse. It could still have been nasty if you hadn't got a smoke alarm.'

He looked at the stubs of smoky glass in the top half of the front door and shook his head. 'Any idea who might have done it?'

Kate hugged her bathrobe more tightly around her. The porch was cold from the water dripping from every surface. 'He's ... uh, the police are already looking for him.' Her teeth chattered, from reaction as much as cold.

The fire officer waited for her to say more, then looked around as a white patrol car pulled up in front of the red engine. 'I'll need to make out a report, but I'll leave you to tell them, then.'

He stepped down onto the path. His boots splashed in the grimy puddles.

'One thing, though. I wouldn't have another cat flap when you have the new door fitted. Whoever it was might make a more serious try next time. All it would take would be a length of pipe and they could pour the petrol straight into your flat.'

He stared at her, to make sure his words had registered, then winked.

'Puss'll just have to wait until you let him in.'

CHAPTER 18

Kate's birthday was on a grey, windy day, when all the lights had to be switched on to counter the unrelieved twilight, and the approaching spring seemed like another country. She hadn't given much thought to it before; too much else had been happening to dwell on such irrelevancies. But that morning she woke up with the awareness that another year had been ticked off her life's calendar.

The post arrived before she left for work. She collected it from the cage covering the letter-box on her way out. The new front door had been fitted the day after the fire, a sturdy hardwood slab with a small frosted-glass window. The door to Miss Willoughby's flat had also been replaced, at the insistence of the estate agent. Ironically, her own only needed repainting, but the coconut mat in front of the other had acted like a wick, charring the wood deeply.

She left the junk mail inside and closed the front door, glad to be in fresh air. Several days after the fire, the stink of it still permeated everything. The painters were due at the end of the week, and Kate told herself that things would seem better when the flat smelled of wet paint instead of the oily reek of petrol and smoke.

A police car cruised by. Kate wondered if it was coincidence, or evidence of Collins's assurance that they would step up patrols outside her home. The car went past without either of the occupants glancing at her, and she turned her attention to the post.

There were two birthday cards. One was from an aunt who lived in Dorset, while the other was from a girl she had been to college with, one of the few people she'd given her new address to when she'd moved, and who kept in occasional touch by letter. There was nothing from Lucy. Kate felt a skim of anger masking the hurt. They had never missed each other's birthdays before. She'd felt sure that Lucy would still send her a card, and had already anticipated using it as an excuse to phone her again. Now, though, the snub only made her more resolved not to.

No one mentioned her birthday at work. Clive had usually remembered in the past, but obviously hadn't this time. Kate knew she was feeling sorry for herself, and in danger of wallowing in it. *Pathetic cow*, she thought, angrily, and went up to her office and shut herself away.

It was almost lunch-time when Clive buzzed through on the intercom. 'There's somebody to see you,' he said. His voice sounded odd. 'Can you come down?'

'Who is it?'

'Er . . . I think you'd better see for yourself.' There was a hesitation. 'It isn't anything to worry about, though.'

He cut the line. More irritated than puzzled, Kate went downstairs. She opened the door to the office. A police constable was standing in the centre of the room.

'It's all right, there's no problem,' Clive said, quickly. Kate noticed him flash Caroline a glance, but her attention was on the policeman. He was young and good-looking. He stepped towards her.

'Kate Powell?'

Her mouth was dry. 'Yes?'

She was vaguely aware of Clive nodding reassuringly. The policeman opened a notebook.

'Is today your birthday?'

'Uh, yes. Why, what's—'

'In that case I'll have to charge you with being thirty-four in possession of an eighteen-year-old's body,' he said, and tore open his tunic.

It came apart in a rip of velcro, revealing a shirt and tie bib over a bare chest. He cast them flamboyantly to the floor with his helmet and ripped open his trousers. Underneath he wore only a black posing pouch, with a police badge pinned on the front. Kate jerked her eyes from it as the young man kicked free of his trousers and began singing.

'Happy birthday to Kate, happy birthday to Kate, happy birthday dear Ka-yate, happy birthday to you!'

He ended with a flourish and grinned. 'Now I've got a surprise for you,' he said, and Kate took an involuntary step back as he put his hand into his pouch and began to pull something out.

'No!' she exclaimed, and then he was holding up a stuffed cloth truncheon. He waggled it at her.

'The sentence is a kiss, or I'll hit you with this,' he said, but before Kate could answer Clive had stepped forward.

'I think we'll skip that bit, thanks.'

The stripper gave them a quick look, then nodded cheerfully. 'In that case, have a happy birthday,' he told

Kate, and bent and kissed her on the lips before she had time to move. Scooping up his clothes, he dressed with practised efficiency and went to the door. He gave her a wink.

'I'll let you off this time with a verbal,' he said, and went out.

There was a silence. The alcohol scent of his aftershave lingered in the office.

'It, er, it was supposed to be a vicar,' Clive said apologetically. He gave Caroline a hard look.

'They said they could only do a cop-o-gram!' the girl protested. 'It was either that or a gorilla!'

It was their anxious expressions that did it. The pressures that had been building up for days were abruptly lanced, and Kate lolled back against the edge of a desk as laughter swept over her. There was an edge of hysteria to it, but it was no less purging for that. Wiping her eyes, she looked at the other three, whose own laughter was touched with relief.

'Let's go for lunch,' she said.

They went to an Italian restaurant that wasn't too far from the office. Clive ordered a bottle of wine, most of which Caroline and Josefina drank. He raised his eyebrows when Kate asked for mineral water but said nothing. After they'd eaten and had coffee, he surprised her by telling the two girls to go back to the office alone.

'We'll be along in a while,' he said.

They watched them through the window, leaning on each other and laughing as they disappeared from view. Clive shook his head.

'Somehow I can't see them getting much work done this

afternoon.' His smile faded. He slowly stirred his coffee. 'Sorry if it was a shock, walking in and seeing a policeman. I should have known better than to leave it to Caroline to sort out.'

Kate smiled. 'Whose idea was it?'

'Hers and Josefina's. I went along with it, though. We thought it might cheer you up.'

She looked down at her glass. 'It's been that obvious, then?'

'I could tell something was wrong, let's put it that way. You've not been the same since the police came to see you.' Clive paused. 'Do you want to talk about it yet?'

Kate found she did. She glanced around. No waiters were within earshot.

'I'm pregnant.'

Clive didn't seem surprised. 'I did wonder.' He nodded at her mineral water. 'No wine or coffee. And you've started drinking herbal tea at work. Well, congratulations. Or is that the wrong thing to say?'

Kate tried to smile. 'I'm not sure myself, to be honest.' She felt her eyes filling up. She wiped them with the napkin. 'Shit. Sorry.'

'No need to be. If I hadn't wanted to know, I wouldn't have asked. So what's happened?'

She hadn't intended to tell him everything. But now that she didn't have Lucy to talk to, the need to unload on somebody was too great. He listened in silence until she'd finished, then sat back and gave a low whistle.

'Well, I was expecting boyfriend problems, but not quite like this.'

'Original, isn't it? And before you say it, if anyone else tells me I've been stupid, I'm going to scream.'

He shrugged. 'I don't think you've been stupid. You've been bloody unlucky, but that's all.'

'You don't think it's my fault, then? That I've brought it on myself?'

'Christ, Kate, how is it your fault? All you've done was try to be careful. I don't see how anyone can blame you for that.'

'Didn't get me very far, though, did it?'

'No, but how could you expect something like this?'

Kate had told herself that countless times, but a masochistic voice still whispered that she deserved it. 'So you think I'm doing the right thing, keeping the baby?'

'If that's what you want, yes.' He leaned towards her. 'Look, it's your life. You get one crack at it, so do what you want. If you felt you wanted an abortion . . .' He spread his hands. 'Fine. Your choice. But if you want to keep it, then that's your choice too. It doesn't matter what anybody else thinks.'

Kate spoke lightly, watching her hands crumble a piece of breadstick onto her plate. 'Perhaps I should have listened to Lucy, after all. She said I should have asked you to be the donor.'

Clive didn't answer. When she looked up he was gazing out of the window, an unreadable expression on his face.

'Sorry, I didn't mean to embarrass you,' she said.

'You haven't. I'm flattered.' He seemed to choose his next words carefully. 'I don't think I'd have been a good choice, though.'

'Why?' Kate hesitated. 'Because you're black?'

'Actually, I was thinking more because I'm gay.' He turned back to her with a half-smile. 'Wouldn't be fair to dump too many prejudices on the poor little devil, would it? A father who was black *and* homosexual? Try explaining that on Open Day.'

Kate could see he was waiting for her response. She shook her head.

'Have I been really dense, or is this something you keep quiet about?'

'I don't keep quiet about it. I just don't make a point of telling people, that's all. Like I say, my life, my business.' A wariness crept into his manner. 'Does it make any difference?'

'What do you think?'

He grinned. 'So,' he went on, in a brisker tone, 'what are the police doing about this character?'

Clive's revelation had made Kate temporarily forget her problems. Now the weight of them settled on her again.

'I don't know. They say they're keeping an eye on my flat and the agency, but all that amounts to is a patrol car going past every now and again. Other than that . . .' She let the sentence go unfinished.

Clive frowned down at his empty coffee cup. 'Perhaps you should keep away from your flat until this all blows over,' he said, slowly. 'All right, he probably won't do anything else, but I think you should still consider it. You're welcome to stay at my place. There's a sofa bed going empty.'

Kate had already thought about retreating to the safety of a hotel, putting a buffer of anonymity between her and an incendiary madness. But she had dismissed the temptation. She wasn't going to run away.

She reached across the table and squeezed Clive's hand. 'I appreciate the offer, but it's okay. I'll be all right.'

She stood up.

'Come on. We'd better get back.'

They had security bars fitted on all the downstairs windows at the agency. A burglar alarm was installed, and Kate had the letter-box sealed and replaced with an American-style mailbox. She also bought one of these for her flat, since the mesh cage on the new door provided only token protection at best. The filing cabinets were lined with fire-proof foam sheets, and what records they had on computer were copied and the discs kept at Clive's flat. Extra fire extinguishers were bought – powder-filled ones, this time, because they were more effective against petrol fires than water – and Kate took one home with her, as well.

Short of installing a sprinkler system at the office, which they couldn't afford, they had done as much as they could, she felt. The fact of doing *something*, other than passively sitting back and waiting, made her feel better. Even so, Kate found herself tensing for the sight of charred window-frames and scorched bricks whenever she approached the agency. Each time there wasn't, her relief was accompanied with a growing hope that the fire at her flat could be an end, not a beginning. For the first time, she began to feel, if not actual optimism, at least that one day life might return to normal.

The feeling was reinforced when she went to the office one morning and saw that demolition work had begun on the burned-out warehouse. She would be glad to see it go, she thought, as the wrecking ball crumpled another section of wall and blackened timbers into a pile of dust and rubble. She reached the agency's street, relaxing a little when there were no fire engines parked in the road. As she searched in her bag for the keys she noted distractedly that the bill posters had been active again. The abundance of boarded up buildings provided a canvas for bands, clubs and political fringe groups to advertise. The constantly changing display was so much a part of the scenery that Kate rarely noticed it, and when she pulled out the keys and looked up, her first thought was that she had stopped in front of the wrong building. Then she looked again, and shock drained the use from her limbs.

The posters completely covered the ground floor, not just of the agency but also the buildings on either side. They were pasted on haphazardly, overlapping each other and crookedly running over windows and doors. Every one was the same, so that the entire terrace front was a jumbled collage of a single repeated image.

Kate stared at it. Suddenly, she twisted away, clutching at a street lamp as she doubled up and vomited. She heard footsteps running towards her, and recognised Clive's voice.

'Kate? Kate, are you all right?'

She didn't answer. She clung to the lamp post until the spasm of retching had passed. Clive hovered beside her. She heard him say, 'Oh Christ.'

Shakily, she straightened. Clive's face was shocked as he turned to her. 'Don't,' he said, but she needed to see again. She looked past him.

The posters were A3 size and full colour. They showed a naked woman, squatting with her legs spread wide. The woman was fat, with what looked like cigarette burns on breasts that spilled loosely over her stomach, and bruises on her flabby upper thighs. Her crotch was hairless, and she was pulling apart her labia to reveal the livid wetness of her vagina. Below it, a penis was buried in her anus.

Topping the obese body was Kate's own face. Her head had been grafted on in place of the woman's, clumsily but no less effective for that. She was laughing and happy, grotesquely indifferent to both the sodomy and the message blazoned in bold red letters across the poster's base.

KATE POWELL IS A MURDERING WHORE.

Kate turned away and was sick again.

CHAPTER 19

Collins's face gave no indication of his thoughts as he studied the poster. It had ragged edges from where it had been torn from the wall, but most of it was intact. From the street came the wet hiss of the steam cleaner as it blasted the front of the terrace. Even with the windows closed, the office was humid with the smell of damp paper.

The Inspector put the poster down on the desk. 'Well, I think we can safely say he's putting his work experience at the printer's to good use.'

Kate looked away from the upside-down image in front of her. 'I'm glad you think it's funny.'

The chair protested as Collins tried to ease his bulk into a more comfortable position. He gave up and sat uncomfortably, his big hands resting slackly on his thighs.

'I don't think it's particularly funny, Miss Powell. Though I'd rather he occupied himself making posters instead of lighting fires. Upsetting, I know, but not as bad as burning the building down.'

Kate didn't answer. The fire at her flat had shaken her, but this seemed worse, somehow.

'Do you recognise the picture? The one of you, I mean?' Collins asked.

She nodded, still without looking at it. 'It looks like one

of the ones he took at Cambridge. From the same day as the one I gave you. I don't think he had any others.'

The memory seemed to belong to another person. It gave her a dull ache in her chest, like heartburn.

'Does it matter where he got it from, anyway?' she snapped, to dispel it. 'The point is that he put the bloody posters up! What happened to the patrols you said were going to keep watching for him?'

Collins rubbed the bridge of his nose with a thick forefinger. 'None of them noticed anything out of the ordinary when they were in this area.'

'They couldn't have been in the area very long, then. How could they have missed him, for God's sake? He must have been here half the night!'

'King's Cross isn't the easiest area to police, Miss Powell. Our officers do the best they can, but they can't be everywhere at once.'

'It doesn't seem like they were around here at all.'

Collins looked at her, reproachfully. He had a shaving nick on one of his jowls, she noticed.

'Actually, Miss Powell, we kept a car stationed here and near your home for several nights after the arson attempt. But we're a police force, not night-watchmen. We can't mount twenty-four-hour surveillance indefinitely, just on the off-chance. I'm very sorry this happened, and we'll step up our patrols again, but someone like Timothy Ellis isn't what you might call predictable at the best of times. And if he's stopped taking his medication to treat his schizophrenia, as we've got to assume, he's going to be even less so.'

He fixed her with a bland stare. 'Particularly now he believes you've had an abortion.'

WHERE THERE'S SMOKE

The pointed reminder brought colour to Kate's cheeks. She didn't say anything as Collins handed the poster to the sergeant, who had been keeping an even lower profile than usual.

The Inspector pushed himself heavily to his feet, wincing slightly as his knee joints cracked. 'We'll take this away and see if we can find anything out from it,' he told her.

He didn't sound hopeful.

Clive waited with her as she locked up that evening, insisting on walking her to the station. She had closed early, almost as soon as the steam cleaners had finished. The atmosphere at the office had been subdued all day. Caroline and Josefina had had to be given some explanation, and although there was a brittle attempt at normality whenever Kate went downstairs, she recognised it as a façade. No one knew quite what to say.

She set the burglar alarm and pulled the door shut, then stepped back and looked at the front of the building. The pavement was littered with scraps of paper left by the cleaners. Water dripped from the walls and pooled on the floor. The door and window had been scoured clean, but tiny flecks of white still clung to the rougher surfaces of the bricks and mortar.

'Not too bad now, is it?' Clive said.

He didn't sound convinced. Kate shook her head, not trusting her voice. She tried to imagine the figure working in the darkness with its brush and paper. She wondered what had been in Ellis's mind as he went about his business, and realised with a jolt that she was now thinking of him by that name. Ellis. Not Alex. With a subtle tug of loss, she finally understood that Alex Turner was dead.

There was only Timothy Ellis now.

Kate turned away. As she did she saw that a scrap of poster had stuck wetly to her shoe. She scraped it off with her other foot and stepped away.

'Let's go,' she said.

She left Clive at King's Cross and caught a tube to the health club. Although it wasn't far from her flat, she hadn't been since finding out she was pregnant; partly because she'd had other things on her mind, partly because she didn't want to subject the delicate foetus to her usual strenuous workout.

But the habit of regular exercise was hard to break. She had packed her swimsuit that morning, intending to start a new regime. Now, though, all she wanted to do was go home and lock herself in her flat. Which was all the more reason not to.

The health-club gymnasium was busy with the usual post-work crowd. Kate changed into her black one-piece costume and looked down at her stomach. She wasn't showing yet, and she put her bloated feeling down to lack of exercise and imagination. Eager now, she went downstairs into the low basement that housed the club's swimming pool.

Inside, the air was warm and moist, like a greenhouse. A few other swimmers were already in the pool, performing their laps with disciplined regularity. Obeying the sign not to dive, Kate lowered herself into the water. It was blood warm. She felt it wrap around her, comforting, and on impulse she closed her eyes and lowered her head below the surface.

WHERE THERE'S SMOKE

The external world ceased. She let herself sink, giving herself up to the water. There was a roaring in her ears, like listening to the seashells she had found on beaches as a little girl. Through it came the deep, steady pulse of her heart. *Womb music. This is what it's like inside me. We're hearing the same sounds.*

Lulled by the sensual, sensory deprivation, she floated, suspended, until a message of discomfort intruded. Her lungs pulled for air, and for an instant Kate felt an impulse to draw a breath and let the water engulf her inside as well as out. It was gone almost immediately. Opening her eyes, she kicked through the amniotic warmth for the surface.

She swam thirty laps before climbing out. Her body ached with the afterglow of exertion as she showered, then dressed and dried her hair. Luxuriating in the feeling, she contemplated getting a takeaway on her way home. The exercise had made her hungry, but reduced her inclination to cook. By the time she came out of the changing room she had decided to indulge herself fully and eat out. She was dimly aware that the attendant on the reception desk gave her a strange look as she left, but was too preoccupied over whether to go for Italian or Chinese to pay much attention.

The club took up most of the first two floors, and part of the basement, of a converted warehouse. Its entrance on the ground floor was a doorway set between a fruit shop and a chemist's. They had been open when she arrived, but both were closed now, with steel security shutters pulled down over their windows. As Kate came out, still considering where to eat, she realised that there was something different about them. It was a second or two before she understood that the grey metal was flecked with specks of white.

She stopped. More aware now, she noticed the scraps of paper specking the pavement in front of the shops. She looked back at the door to the club. The steel sheet that covered it had fresh scratches gouged in its surface, as though something had been scraped off.

Kate looked along the length of the other shops, but there was nothing to indicate that anything had ever been pasted onto them. She became conscious of a pain in her hands. Her nails were digging into the palms of her clenched fists. She opened them, turning away from the mottled shutters that didn't, after all, prove anything.

Her appetite had vanished. Intending to go home, she went to cross the road. A bus shelter stood on the other side, opposite the entrance to the club. She had passed it on her way in, walked right by without giving it a glance. Now, though, it was directly facing her.

The posters almost covered it.

During the next two days, it seemed that Kate saw the poster wherever she went. Her features smiled out from on top of the fat woman's body all over the city. Sometimes there would be only one, slapped in a prominent position in the middle of a wall or window. At others there would be a cluster. Coming up from Tottenham Court Road tube station she saw a line of them running parallel to the escalators, raggedly pasted between and over the everyday advertisements. Most had been partially ripped off, but on some her face or name still remained. Kate ducked her head and stared at her feet as the escalator carried her past them. At the top she stumbled when she stepped off and saw one stuck to the floor. It was dirty and scuffed from the hundreds of feet that had trampled it, but still recognisable. KATE POWELL IS A MURDER – it said, before a missing corner obliterated the rest of the message.

Buffeted by the other people coming off the escalator, Kate walked over it.

'How can he do this?' she protested to Collins. 'He's supposed to be wanted for murder! How can he just go around sticking posters wherever he likes?'

Even over the phone the Inspector sounded tired as he answered.

'Thousands of illegal posters go up in this city every night. We don't see any of those being put up, either. And as for Ellis being a murder suspect, so far no one's made the connection between Alex Turner's killing and the pornographic posters that have been popping up in odd places. Personally, unless I can see some advantage in changing that, I'd like to keep it quiet. I imagine you would too.'

'But you must be able to do something!'

'We're doing everything we can. London's a big place to find one man in, Miss Powell, and there's no way we can simply predict when or where Ellis is going to surface next. It only takes a matter of seconds to put a poster up. A quick slap of paste, and he's away.'

A headache was forming in Kate's temples. She massaged one of them. 'Where's he getting the money from? How's he paying for all this?'

'Good question. He's obviously producing the post-ers himself, putting them together on something like an Applemac and then running them off on a colour copier.

Ellis used computers at work, so that wouldn't be a problem for him. As for money, he was apparently left a bit by his grandmother. Not a fortune, though, and it looks like he's been drawing on it fairly heavily since he met you. We found his savings book at his bedsit, and the account's almost empty now. But that isn't to say he doesn't have savings we don't know about. Or he could just have stolen the money. You can buy second-hand hardware cheaply enough, and all he'd need then would be somewhere with a plug socket to hole up in. We're checking small hotels and boarding houses, but it's a long business.'

'Is that supposed to make me feel better?'

'No, Miss Powell, it's supposed to show you what the difficulty is.' There was an uncharacteristic bite to Collins's voice. 'Believe me, I don't enjoy having a murder suspect running around like this, and if I could do any more to get my hands on Timothy Ellis I would. But with the information we have at the moment, there's nothing more we *can* do, and if you can offer any constructive suggestions, I'd be very happy to hear them.'

Immediately, he seemed to regret his loss of composure. His tone became conciliatory. 'Look, I *know* it's distressing. We *will* catch him, I promise you that. But you'll have to accept that there's only so much we can do. He's obviously targeting areas where he knows you go, but that still covers most of West and Central London. It's a big city and we can't just guess where he's going to turn up.'

Afterwards, Kate berated herself that she didn't have to guess, that she should have known what Ellis was going to do next. But it wasn't until the call from the Parker Trust the following morning that she saw the inevitability of it.

'Hello, Mr Redwood,' she said, wondering what petty complaint the Trust's chairman had now. 'How are you?'

There was no reciprocal pleasantry. 'You know why I'm calling, I expect?'

Kate hastily tried to think if there was something she'd forgotten. 'No. Should I?'

'It's about the poster.'

Oh, God. 'Oh?' Kate heard herself say.

'I presume you know what I'm talking about?'

She tried to sound indifferent. 'Perhaps you should just tell me, Mr Redwood, and then we can both be certain.'

'Very well. I'm talking about a highly offensive poster concerning you that's been brought to my attention. Is that plain enough?'

The receiver felt heavy in her hand. She'd known there was a chance that some of her clients might see them, but she had told herself it was a slim one.

'I'm sorry,' she said.

'So are we, Miss Powell. This is hardly the sort of profiling we anticipated when we hired your agency.'

'I'm not happy about it myself.'

'If you don't mind my saying so, that's small consolation. I presume you knew about the poster's existence already?'

'Yes, but—'

'And yet you didn't inform us?'

'I didn't think it was any of the Trust's business.'

'I disagree. I made it clear at the outset that anything which affects the Trust is very much our business.'

'The posters are aimed at me, not the Trust. I'm sorry

that you've been involved, but I can't see that you've any cause to be concerned about them.'

'Miss Powell, your agency currently represents the Trust, and as long as it continues to do so any adverse publicity you receive reflects on us by association. As a publicist I would expect you to know that. I also would expect you to realise that we cannot continue a relationship with a company whose head is involved in some kind of sordid smear campaign. And I might add that we have no intention of doing so. Under the circumstances—'

'Under the circumstances you're not concerned that an associate of the "charitable" Parker Trust is the victim of what's obviously a sick and malicious slander, is that right?'

She had spoken heatedly, without thinking, but it gave Redwood pause.

'Obviously, we're not unsympathetic,' he said, cautiously, 'but our sympathies can only extend so far.'

'Obviously. But, equally obviously, it wouldn't enhance the Trust's reputation as a humanitarian organisation if it became known that it had treated the victim unfairly. Callously, even. Particularly not when the victim was a woman, the Trust is run by men, and the slander was largely sexual in nature.'

Redwood was silent. Kate gripped the receiver, forcing herself to wait him out.

'The Trust doesn't respond to threats, Miss Powell.'

'I wouldn't expect you to. I'm only telling you what would happen under those circumstances. As you say, I'm a publicist. I'm expected to know these things.'

She held her breath. Her knuckles on the phone were white.

'We'll let it pass this time, Miss Powell,' Redwood said, finally.

Kate breathed out, silently.

'But only this time. Any further hint of scandal or controversy concerning either you or your agency, and you can consider your relationship with the Trust terminated. I'll notify you of that fact in writing. So there's no misunderstanding of the position in future.'

'Thank you. I really am very sorry about this, and if you'd like to send us a bill for cleaning the posters off your walls—'

'That won't be necessary, since there's only one, and it arrived in the post.'

'The post?' Kate echoed.

'That's right. It came this morning. And while you, no doubt, think that your personal life is your own concern, when it comes to an issue as emotive as abortion, I might remind you that the Trust believes strongly in upholding Christian ethics, and that particularly includes the sanctity of life. Be it born or unborn.'

Kate felt control of the conversation slipping away from her. 'What are you talking about?'

'I'm talking about what the poster accuses you of. While we obviously don't accept the accusation at face value, nevertheless—'

A terrible comprehension was growing in Kate. 'What does it say?' she demanded.

'I hardly think there's any point in my repeating it—'

'I want to know what it says!'

There was a pause, in which she could sense Redwood swing from puzzlement to understanding. Something like satisfaction entered his voice.

'Perhaps you'd better check your own post, Miss Powell,' he said, and hung up.

Her head throbbed as she buzzed Clive on the intercom.

'Has the post arrived yet?'

'Yeah, I'm just sorting through it now. I'll bring it up.'

She listened to the downstairs door open and close, then the approach of his footsteps. He came in, smiling until he saw her expression.

'What's wrong?'

Kate shook her head without answering. She held out her hand for the pile of envelopes. Clive watched, worried, as she shuffled through them. She stopped when she reached the large brown envelope. Her name and the agency's address were written on the back in untidy block letters. She slit it open.

Inside was a single sheet of paper, folded in half. Kate took it out.

This time her head had been put onto the body of a woman wearing a white nightgown. The front of the gown was gory with blood, and the woman's hands, which she held stiffly by her sides, were dripping and red. Printed in the same colour across the top was a single sentence.

KATE POWELL KILLED HER UNBORN BABY.

Kate set it down on her desk. Her hands were unsteady. 'He sent one to the Parker Trust,' she said. 'He posted it.'

Clive was folding up the poster with a look of angry disgust. 'The bastard. The fucking sick bastard.'

Kate began to say something, but then an awful thought swept whatever it was away.

'Oh, shit.' She stared at Clive. 'The Filofax.'

She saw understanding spread over his face. He sat down.

'He's got a complete list of all our clients. Every one.' She fought for control as the enormity of it registered. 'He doesn't even have to bother sticking the posters up, he can just send them the bloody things! Christ, he probably already has!'

'You don't know that for sure, he might not have.' But Clive clearly didn't even believe that himself. 'Anyway, who's going to take any notice of them? Nobody's going to be taken in by that sort of garbage.'

'Aren't they? And they don't have to believe it. A lot of people aren't going to want to be associated with anything like that, whether it's true or not. God, I should have seen this coming!'

They stared at each other as the implications sank in.

'What do you think we should do?' Clive asked.

'God knows,' Kate said.

CHAPTER 20

'**H**e's getting more circumspect.'

Collins set his teacup back in the saucer with a slight rattle. The chair creaked under the big policeman as he leaned forward and placed it on the coffee table.

'I don't see what's circumspect about a bloodstained poster accusing me of having an abortion,' Kate said.

When she had answered the door to her flat that evening she had been surprised to find the Inspector standing outside. She'd spoken to him only that morning, when she'd told him about the second poster. Seeing him there had given her a start, but he'd quickly reassured her. No news, he said. Just an informal visit.

He settled back heavily in his seat, legs apart, meaty hands resting on his thighs. His brown suit looked even more rumpled than usual.

'It isn't so much the poster, as what he's doing with it.' Collins shifted on the chair, uncomfortably. 'Sorry. Got a problem with my back,' he explained.

'Would you like a straight-backed chair?'

'Oh, no, I'll be fine, thanks.' He stopped fidgeting. 'No, the thing about this second one is that he doesn't seem to be as keen to paste it everywhere for you to see. He took a lot of risks with the first poster, sticking it up in underground

305

stations and busy streets. But how many of this new one have you seen so far?'

'There were one or two near King's Cross on the way home.' She considered. 'It was dark, though. I could have missed more this morning, because I was still looking out for the first one.'

'Even so, there aren't as many. He isn't going as berserk this time.' The Inspector gave a wry smile. 'I'd like to claim credit for that and say it's because of our patrols. Which I don't doubt it partly is, but I think there's another reason as well.'

He leaned forward and reached for the cup and saucer again. They looked like a child's tea-set in his hand.

'The first poster was almost purely for your benefit. He was hitting out. Calling you . . . well, insulting you, using pornography, and putting them where he knew you'd see them. He was getting something out of his system. Now he's calmed down a bit, and instead of risking himself putting them up willy-nilly, he's latched on to the idea of sending them to your clients by post. Even the poster itself is less . . . well, less hysterical. More deliberate.'

Kate looked down at her tea. It had gone cold. 'You make it sound as if he's building up to something.'

'I don't think it's possible to say for sure what he's doing. Ellis isn't exactly a rational individual. He might be just doing whatever comes to mind.'

He flexed his shoulder and winced, careful not to upset the cup and saucer. His voice was studiedly casual. 'Still, I think it might be a good idea for you not to go anywhere on your own for a while. Either get a taxi or ask someone to walk with you. A man, preferably.'

'You think he might attack me?'

'I mean I don't think you should take any chances.'

Kate folded her arms protectively over her stomach. The gas fire hissed into the silence. Wanting to change the subject, she asked, 'Have any more of our clients been in touch so far?'

She had decided that the only chance of minimising the damage done by Ellis's poster was to confront the problem directly. She had spent the rest of that morning drafting and faxing a letter to each of her clients, explaining that the posters were part of a campaign to discredit her, and asking that anyone receiving them should contact Collins. Then she had added a footnote.

Kate Powell is also proud to announce the forthcoming birth of her first child.

It gave her an odd thrill to see the words written down, and she had handed the letter to Clive before she could change her mind.

'That's fighting fire with fire,' he grinned, then pulled a face. 'Sorry. Bad choice of words.'

The Inspector took another drink of tea. 'Quite a few. I think you were right to assume that he's sent it to all of them.'

It was no more than Kate had expected, but the bald statement still produced a hollow tightness in her chest, like brief asthma.

'So far it looks like he's stuck fairly rigidly to the same routine,' Collins continued. 'Same brown envelopes, cheap quality paper, but we haven't traced where they were bought yet. Postmarked central London, with nothing inside except the new poster. That's pretty well the same sort of job as the first, so there's nothing new there, either.'

Kate forced a smile. 'Well, we weren't really expecting a return address, I suppose.'

'No,' he agreed. He made another attempt to ease himself into a more comfortable position. 'How have your clients reacted to all this?'

'Two cancelled their accounts this afternoon.'

One was a small publishing company that specialised in children's books. The other was a fine-art dealer, who used Kate to promote occasional exhibitions at his Covent Garden gallery. Neither were big accounts, or currently active, but the dealer's was a prestigious one, and Kate had enjoyed the contact with the rarified art world. The publisher had been polite but firm when she had telephoned. The art dealer, a man called Ramsey whom Kate had always liked, refused to discuss it.

'No chance of getting them to change their minds?' Collins asked.

'No.'

The Inspector tugged thoughtfully at his earlobe. 'Ah, well. I suppose it could have been worse.'

He didn't have to say what he was thinking. Ellis had only sent her clients the poster. He hadn't set fire to anyone's premises.

So far.

Collins drained his teacup and set it down with finality on the coffee table.

'Would you like another?' Kate asked.

'No, thanks. I'd better be off. My wife's expecting me.' He made no attempt to leave. He nodded at Kate's stomach. 'How's the, er . . .'

She glanced down at herself. 'Oh, okay. Thanks. It doesn't really feel like I'm pregnant yet. Apart from the morning sickness.'

'My wife was like that. Started early, and went right on until she was eight months. Not that that means anything,' he added.

Kate smiled. 'How many kids have you got?'

'Just the one. A daughter, Elizabeth. She's a doctor.' He said it with automatic pride.

'In London?'

'Manchester. Husband's a surgeon there.'

'Any grandchildren?'

'Two grandsons. They'll be six and four now.' His smile was fond and sad. 'Don't see much of them, but it's difficult, I suppose. With both parents being so busy.'

It had the sound of an old rationalisation, used to brush over a lingering pain.

'How about you?' Collins asked. 'Have you any brothers or sisters?'

'No, there's just me.'

'What about your mum and dad?'

'They're both dead. But even if they weren't, I wouldn't go running to them for help now, if that's why you were asking.'

He didn't bother to deny it. 'Didn't you see eye to eye?'

Kate looked into the gas fire, trying to put the complex emotions into a simple sentence. She remembered a similar conversation with someone else, and the subject was suddenly uncomfortable.

'Not really,' she said. 'Anyway. Past history now.'

'But wouldn't you like them to have seen their grand-child?'

There was an intense curiosity about him, almost a bewilderment. *His daughter*, Kate realised. *He still doesn't understand what went wrong.* And all at once, as Collins sat there, she saw him as a father instead of a policeman, stranded on the wrong side of a generation, unable to fathom the hurts inflicted by his own blood.

Was I like that? She had only ever considered the pain and injustices she'd received, not any she might have caused. The thought was disturbing, and she had enough to think about with the present. She pushed the doubts away from her, uncomfortably aware now that they would never completely go.

'All things considered, it's perhaps as well they can't,' Kate said, making light of it. 'They'd share your views on how I got it.'

The Inspector looked down at his hands, smiling. 'It's probably an age thing.'

It was the closest they had come to acknowledging their differences. The concession made them awkward. Abruptly, Collins's stomach gave a rumbling growl.

He looked startled. 'Pardon,' he mumbled, patting it. Kate was amused to see him blush.

'Well,' he said, putting his hands on his knees and standing up, 'I'd better be going.'

Kate walked downstairs with him. He examined the freshly painted entrance.

'Glad you got rid of the cat flap,' he commented, tapping the new door. He went out onto the path. 'You remember what I said, now. Watch yourself.'

She was surprised to find she appreciated his concern. She wanted to tell him she'd enjoyed talking to him, but the words wouldn't come.

'Goodnight,' she said, and closed the door.

The young man was waiting on the other side of the road to the agency. Kate noticed him as she walked up the street, but after her first quick glance she paid him no further attention. Collins's visit the night before had left her in an odd mood. She had gone to bed and, unusually, fallen asleep straight away. Even rarer, she had slept right through to her alarm clock going off. But she had woken with the dispersing memory of a dream, in which her father had stood outside the ruins of a house and accused her of burning it down with her baby inside. She had tried to tell him that she couldn't have, because she was still pregnant, and she had looked down to see her naked and swollen stomach. Then, in the smouldering rubble of the house, she had seen a figure, and even though it was an adult she had known it was her baby. She had been happy, because that meant it had escaped the fire, but then she had seen it had Ellis's features, only strangely unformed. And she had been frightened, because she knew he had started the fire, and also that it hadn't happened yet. But when she tried to tell her father, she saw that he had become Collins. He stood in front of the smoking house and told her that things could be worse, they could always be worse, and then the alarm had gone off and woken her.

The dream had been disturbing, and rekindled unwelcome memories of bonfire night, when the man had thrown himself into the flames. Kate was still trying to shake off its pall when she became aware that the young man across the road was openly watching her.

She looked across at him again, expecting him to turn away. He didn't. He was leaning against a street lamp with his hands in his pockets and his collar turned up against the morning chill. As she approached he straightened, breath steaming from his mouth, not taking his eyes from her.

Kate looked away. All at once she was conscious of how empty the street was. She began walking a little faster, hoping Clive had already arrived, and pulling the keys from her bag in case he hadn't. The young man started across the road. She reached the door. It was locked. She fumbled with the keys, trying to appear calm, and as she got the door open he came up behind her.

'Kate Powell?'

She turned, hand still on the door, poised to dart in and slam it. 'Yes?'

He looked in his early twenties, with long, reddish hair and a thick leather jacket. His eyes were very pale, a non-colour. He gave her a grin.

'Glad you've turned up. I was starting to freeze over there. My name's Stu Clark. Been waiting to have a few words with you.'

'What about?'

He nodded towards the half-open door. 'Be warmer talking inside.' His grin seemed a permanent fixture.

'Talking about what?'

'I've got a proposition for you. I think you'll be interested.'

His brashness grated. 'Tell me what it is, and I'll tell you if I am or not,' she said, her arm still barring the doorway.

'It'll sound better over a cup of coffee.'

'I'm not letting you in, so either tell me what you want or go away.'

There was something about the way he looked at her that made his grin seemed mocking.

'Have it your way, love. It's about certain posters that have been popping up all over the place.'

Kate felt the shock run through her. She tried to brazen it out. 'I don't know what you're talking about.'

'I'm talking about the ones with you on them.' His gaze flicked down her body. 'Well, your face. I don't think the rest is you. Not unless you've lost weight.' He held up his hands. 'Only joking, love, no offence.'

She stared at him. 'You're a reporter, aren't you?'

'Journalist, if you don't mind.'

'Who do you work for?'

'I'm freelance. I work for whoever's paying. But I'm telling you, there'll be so much interest in a story like this that they'll be queuing up for it.'

'There isn't a story.'

'Oh, come on, Kate – can I call you Kate? A nasty poster campaign accusing a pretty young woman of all sorts of things? It's a great human-interest story.'

He cocked his head to one side. 'Specially when I've heard it's the nutter who murdered that psychologist who's doing it.'

He gave her a wink. 'Now, how about that cup of coffee?'

Kate felt her face drain of blood. Then it came rushing back. 'Who told you that?'

'Sorry, love, I can't reveal my contacts. You know how it is.'

'Was it the police?'

She knew the leak had to have come from them, but the look of triumph in his eyes told her she had made a mistake.

'So it *is* him, then?'

'I'm not saying anything.'

She made to go inside, but he put his hand on the door, holding it.

'There's no need to get upset. I'm on your side. All I want to do is give you the chance to tell your version.'

'Move your hand.'

'If it's a good enough story, there might even be a fair bit of money involved.'

'Are you going to move?'

'Look, it's going to get written, anyway. It's in your own interests to co-operate.'

She pushed on the door, barging his arm out of the way. He stood in the doorway, preventing her from closing it.

'So why's Timothy Ellis so pissed off with you, Kate? What's your relationship with him?'

The grin hadn't slipped from his face. Kate went to where the fire extinguisher was clipped to the wall.

'Did you get rid of his kid, is that it? Is that why he flipped and killed the shrink?'

Kate tugged the extinguisher free and turned with it. His grin dropped when he saw what she was holding.

'Okay, okay, I'm going.'

He stepped backwards onto the pavement as she advanced, pointing the nozzle, and almost bumped into Clive. Clive looked from him to the fire extinguisher in Kate's hands.

'What's going on?'

The journalist held up both his hands, edging away. 'Nothing, just having a chat. It's cool.'

He reached the pavement edge. 'Thanks for your help, Miss Powell.'

Grinning, he walked across the road. Clive watched him go, then turned back to Kate. He nodded at the extinguisher.

'You're getting pretty handy with that.'

'I'm getting plenty of practice.'

She moved aside to let him in.

'So what was it all about?' he asked.

Kate dumped the fire extinguisher on a desk. 'He's a journalist. He's managed to find out who the Kate Powell on the posters is.'

'Oh, shit. How much does he know?'

'I don't know. He was digging, but he already knew who was putting up the posters. Shit! I could do without this.'

'Which paper was he from?'

'He wasn't. He said he was a freelance.'

Clive took off his coat and began preparing the coffee. 'That's not so bad, then.'

She looked at him. 'Why isn't it?'

'Because freelances are ten a penny. He's still got to sell the story, and you know how hard that is.'

Kate did, from the numerous press releases she'd had

ignored by editors herself. But it was difficult to be objective when she was so intimately involved. It fogged her thinking.

The coffee filter gave a hiss as Clive poured water into it. 'Don't worry,' he told her, setting the jug to catch the drips. 'It'll probably never get into print.'

The story appeared two days later. Kate was sitting on the tube, on one of the long seats that face each other across the aisle. A man on the other side was reading a tabloid newspaper, folding its pages back on themselves, and she looked at it for a while without comprehending what she was seeing.

Then, all at once, the words stopped being abstract shapes and formed into a sentence, and Kate felt the carriage spin round her. As though he had been waiting for that moment, the man turned the page, and immediately all she could retain of what she had seen was the single word, POSTER.

Suddenly, the train was full of rustling newspapers. It slowed to a halt, and Kate stood up and got off. She was half-way up the escalators before she realised that it wasn't her stop.

She went back down to the platform and caught the next train. Outside the station at King's Cross was a newspaper stand. Kate went to it and stared down at the assembled piles of newsprint.

'What can I do you for, darlin'?' the vendor asked.

Kate couldn't remember what paper the man on the train had been reading. She knew it was a tabloid, but that was all. She shook her head and began to walk away, then abruptly went back and picked up a copy of every newspaper on the stand.

'You setting up in competition, or what?' the vendor grinned as she paid.

Kate didn't answer. She was dimly aware of his muttered, 'Yeah, and a nice fucking day to you too,' when she walked away, but her mind was already on the thick stack of paper under her arm.

Clive had already arrived at the office. His smile of greeting faded as he looked from her face to what she was carrying. Kate went straight upstairs. The newspapers made a heavy thud as she dropped them onto her desk. Separating the tabloids first, she began to go through them.

She found it in the *Mirror*. The article took up most of one page, topped by the headline she had seen on the train.

PSYCHOLOGIST'S KILLER WREAKS POSTER REVENGE ON LOVER.

The story was billed as an exclusive. It referred to Ellis as a schizophrenic wanted in connection with the 'frenzied killing' of psychologist Alex Turner. It explained how, while still on the run from the police, he was carrying out an 'obscene poster campaign against attractive PR boss Kate Powell'. The posters were described with relish, especially the first one, and the story dwelt on her refusal to comment on either her 'affair' with Ellis, or if she'd had his 'love-child' aborted. There was no mention of donor insemination. It ended with a quote from an unnamed source, speculating that Ellis could have murdered the psychologist because he was 'maddened with grief'.

Inset in the article was the police photograph of Ellis, and also one of the second poster, less lurid in black and white.

Beneath it was a photo of Kate herself. It had obviously been taken outside the agency. She was caught mid-step, and had a harried expression on her face as she walked obliquely towards the camera.

I look old, she thought, with detachment.

There was a *crack*. Kate looked with surprise at the broken pencil in her hand. She couldn't remember picking it up. She dropped the two halves into the bin, then went to the window. A little further down the street, on the opposite side of the road, was an alleyway. The photograph could have been taken from there. Or from one of the deep doorways.

She turned away as Clive knocked and entered.

'It's in, then?'

Kate nodded, waving him to the newspaper still lying open on her desk. He read the article, then closed and folded the paper.

'Well. He can't write for shit, anyway.'

She had to smile. But not for very long.

The story wasn't in any of the other newspapers, but now it had appeared in one, the rest picked up on it. The telephone rang repeatedly with requests for interviews, information. Kate didn't take any of them. Caroline, Josefina or Clive would politely say that no, she had no comment to make. Several journalists actually called at the office, where they were told the same thing. When she went to her window she could see a group of photographers idling on the other side of the road, looking cold but patient. Kate moved away before they saw her.

Collins was phlegmatic when she phoned him. He had already seen the article.

'It was bound to come out, the longer all this went on,' he said. 'We've been lucky to keep it quiet as long as we did.'

'What should I do?'

She heard him sigh. 'That's up to you. You could always go public. Tell them you're still pregnant, and hope that Ellis sees it and believes you.'

Kate thought about the mocking grin of the journalist who had started all this. 'I don't think I can.'

'There's your answer, then. Just keep your head down and keep saying, "No comment." The murder's old news, now. They'll get bored if you don't give them anything new to write.'

The Inspector was right, but sooner than he could have expected. In the afternoon Clive came up to tell her that the waiting photographers and journalists had gone. 'They just all took off at once,' he said. 'Something else must have happened.'

The incident was in the evening news, a block of flats that had collapsed, providing scenes of carnage and death for the eager press. Kate was all but forgotten. Some of the papers ran small pieces on her the following day, but they were little more than recaps of the first and completely overshadowed by coverage of the more dramatic story.

The damage had been done, though. When she arrived at work next morning, the post had already been delivered. There was no sign of Clive, and Kate huddled under her umbrella as she opened the mailbox and took out the selection of envelopes. She recognised the Parker Trust's expensive stationery straight away. Unlocking the office, she left her umbrella to drip onto the floor and sat down behind a desk without taking off her coat or switching on the lights. The other envelopes were ignored as she slit open the thick white one with a plastic paper-knife. Rain rattled against the window like hail as she withdrew the letter.

It was brief and to the point. The Trust regretted that, in view of the recent negative publicity received by herself and her agency, they were withdrawing their account. Such publicity was contrary to the Trust's interests, as had already been made clear to her. While not wanting to appear in any way judgemental, it was nevertheless felt that there was no option but to terminate the Trust's relationship with Powell PR & Marketing.

Kate could hear Redwood's desiccated voice as she read it. She reached for the phone, then stopped. Her umbrella dripped onto the floor with the slow insistence of a clock. The window rattled as a gust of wind struck it. She lowered the letter.

The door opened and Clive came in. He closed it quickly against the blast of cold air and rain. Kate drew herself up, preparing to tell him, when she saw his travel bag. Then she noticed his face.

'Clive? What's wrong?'

He had made no attempt to take off his wet coat. He stood awkwardly, not looking at her.

'I've got to go up to Newcastle.' His voice was raw. 'My mum phoned last night. My brother's been in a car crash. He's, uh . . . he's been killed.'

Kate just stared at him. The inadequate *I'm sorry* went unsaid.

His Adam's apple bobbed as he swallowed. 'The thing is, I don't know how long it'll be. The funeral's got to be fixed, and—'

He broke off, covering his eyes. Kate saw his shoulders spasm. She quickly put the letter back in the envelope before he could see it.

He wiped his eyes with the heel of his hand. 'I know it's come at a bad time. I'll get back as soon as I can.'

'Don't worry about that. Just take as long as you need.' She didn't know what to say to him. 'You didn't have to come here to tell me. You could have just phoned.'

He adjusted his grip on the travel bag. 'The train's from King's Cross, anyway. There's one in half an hour that'll get me there for dinner-time.'

'Have you got a ticket?'

'No. Not yet.'

'You'd better go. I don't want you to miss it.'

Clive nodded but didn't move. Kate came out from behind the desk, slipping the envelope into her pocket as she went over and gave him a hug. He returned it, then they broke apart.

'I'll phone you.'

He went out. The umbrella still dripped onto the carpet, but more slowly now. Kate switched on the lights and started the coffee filter, then went down to the kitchen and stood her umbrella in the sink before going back upstairs to her office.

The letter from the Parker Trust crinkled in her pocket. She took it out and looked at the envelope without removing the letter. Abruptly, she tore it in half, ripping it into smaller and smaller pieces that she flung from her. They fluttered to the floor like dead moths as she snatched up her handbag and began pawing through it.

She pulled out the old packet of Camels. Her hands were unsteady as she put a cigarette between her lips and tried to get a flame from the lighter. It clicked, drily.

'Shit! Come *on*!'

She banged it on the desk and shook it. The next flick produced a yellow smudge. She held it up to the cigarette, poised for a moment, and then with a sudden dip of her head put the tip into the flame.

It glowed brightly. A thin ring of fire chased towards her, leaving behind a fragile cylinder of pale ash as she drew the smoke down into her lungs. The cigarette was stale, but there was an instant nicotine hit. Her head swam, and for the space of a heartbeat she held her breath, letting the feeling soak through her. Then she was gagging. The smoke burned the back of her throat and nose as she choked and coughed. Eyes streaming, she stubbed out the cigarette in a half-empty teacup.

It died with a swift hiss. Kate pushed away the sludge of cold tea and ash and sank into her chair. Her mouth tasted foul. She dug in her bag until she found a screwed-up tube of mints. The peppermint sweetened her mouth, but didn't take away the lung-deep feeling of pollution, or the fear that the single drag was already poisoning the foetus she carried.

Kate stared at the phone, then picked it up and dialled a number. It rang several times at the other end before she heard Lucy answer.

'Lucy, it's Kate, look, I'm sorry—' she said in a rush, then broke off. Lucy's voice continued. Kate listened to the recorded message for a few seconds longer, then hung up.

Caroline and Josefina arrived downstairs. She heard them moving around, talking. Some time later the intercom beeped. Kate watched the light flashing on it, but didn't move. Eventually it stopped.

Later still she took the tea cup with the cigarette in it and washed it out in the kitchen.

CHAPTER 21

They lost several more clients in the wake of the newspaper story. One was a company that made maternity outfits. Kate almost smiled at the irony of that.

She was aware that the agency was approaching the stage where it was becoming more a matter of survival than of making a profit. She knew she should be taking a more aggressive approach, actively seeking out new clients as well as reassuring the remaining ones. But knowing that was one thing. Bringing herself to do it was something else.

Caroline and Josefina tiptoed around her at the office, hushed and deferent as nurses at a sick bed. They needn't have bothered. Nothing touched her. Even when one or two clients phoned to congratulate her on being pregnant, her pleasure was a surface feeling, short-lived and shallow.

It seemed barely conceivable that it was only a week since the first posters had appeared on the agency walls. Her world had contracted to the journey between her flat and the office. She no longer went to the health club. The one time she went to the supermarket, driven by an empty fridge and cupboards bare even of cat food, she had faltered outside the harsh arena of stacked shelves and fluorescent strip lights. When she had gone in, the brightness and colour was like a migraine. She pushed the trolley down the aisles, avoiding meeting anyone's eye as she worked her way through the maze. Confronted with the profusion of cans and boxes her mind went blank. She stacked the trolley without any clear notion of what she was buying, walking faster and faster away from the faces that seemed to glance at her with recognition, and whispered conversations that became innocent as soon as she was close enough to hear. Once she heard someone behind her say, 'Kate,' and she jerked the trolley into a display of tinned fruit. It teetered without falling, and she turned to see a little girl, laughing as she ran to her father with a bar of chocolate. While the child's laughter turned to protests, Kate unsteadily steered her trolley from the tins and pushed it away. The nape of her neck was clammy with sweat as she bypassed the rest of the shelves and went straight to the check-out.

She took a cab home. Sitting with the carrier bags at her feet, it occurred to her that taxis were a luxury she couldn't afford now that the prop of the Parker Trust account had gone. She stared out of the window as the taxi pulled up at traffic lights near her home. A tramp entered the illuminated aura of a street lamp. Muffled by a bulky coat and scarf, his head was buried in his turned-up collar, so that only matted tufts of hair were visible. He clutched two carrier bags, and Kate had time to think that one looked as though it had porridge in it, before he passed from under the lamp's glow.

The taxi pulled forward with a brief scrape of gears as the lights changed to green. It came to a halt again almost immediately as a lorry up ahead tried to turn, blocking both lanes. The cab driver barged his steering wheel in annoyance. Kate looked at the ticking meter, then back out of the window. They had stopped by a building site, shielded from the street by a high plywood fence. As her eyes adjusted to the darkness she saw the dark squares that ran along its length. The cab shunted forward a little, and some of the squares caught the light from the next lamppost. The words, KATE POWELL KILLED HER UNBORN CHILD seemed black in the yellow sodium glare.

Kate saw how the paper glistened, wetly, and how the wood around each poster was dark with fresh paste. She twisted to look back through the rear window, trying to catch sight of the solitary tramp with his carrier bags. But the street was empty.

'It's a threat, isn't it?'

Kate stood over her desk. The smell of petrol filled the office. She had wiped her hands, but they still felt greasy. The telephone handset was slippery in her palm.

Collins sounded unperturbed. 'Just try to calm down.'

'Calm *down*?'

'He's trying to rattle you, that's all.'

'Well, he bloody well is doing!'

She stared down at the open Jiffy-bag on her desk as though it would ignite by itself. It had arrived with the post. The effect of seeing the poster the night before had faded a little in the daylight. As soon as she arrived back at her flat Kate had phoned the police incident room to tell Collins about the tramp. But the Inspector couldn't be reached, and the policeman who had taken her message sounded uninterested and patronising. She had slammed down the phone before she shouted at him.

Trying to put the incident from her mind, she had gone

into work that morning and occupied herself with opening the post. There were no more large brown envelopes, and Kate had begun to relax.

Until she had opened the Jiffy-bag.

Collins was still unruffled. 'He wants to scare you, that's why he's doing all this. You've hurt him, and now he's trying to hurt you back by frightening you. If he was serious, he'd have done something by now.'

'He's already tried to set fire to where I live, for Christ's sake!'

'If Ellis had been serious about trying to burn down your flat, he's had enough experience to make a better job of it than that. If he'd used more petrol, perhaps pushed a few rags through as well, then waited for the fumes to build up, that little entrance hall would have gone up like a bomb. There are all sorts of different ways he could have done real damage. If he'd wanted to.'

'So you're saying I've got nothing to worry about?'

'No, what I'm saying is – sorry, just a second.'

There was a hollow whisper of a hand being put over the receiver. Kate could hear distant, muffled voices. The cloying smell of petrol oozed into her pores. She looked again down at the Jiffy-bag. Its mouth gaped, and the self-sealing polythene bag that had been inside was draped half out of it like a pale tongue. The oily black ashes that had spilled out when she had dropped it lay wetly on the desk. Kate knew she should clean them up before the surface was stained, but she couldn't bring herself to touch them.

Only one part of the poster had been left unburnt. She could imagine Ellis carefully turning the burning paper, until everything except her face had been consumed.

Then he had soaked the ashes in petrol and sent them to her.

There was a rattle as Collins took his hand away from the receiver. Then his voice was back.

'Sorry about that. Where was I?'

'You were telling me why I'd nothing to worry about.'

Collins overlooked her sarcasm, which made her feel worse. 'Try and look at things in perspective. The posters are upsetting and I know they've damaged your business. But they can't hurt you.'

Kate wanted to believe him. 'Can't they? What about *this*?' She waved her hand at the burnt remains of the poster, as though the Inspector could see it. 'It's like he's telling me what he's going to do! He's psyching himself up for it!'

'Look, Kate.' The policeman spoke with weary patience. The unexpected use of her Christian name was somehow comforting. 'I'm not trying to kid you that Ellis isn't dangerous. But you're taking every reasonable precaution that you can, and he's made himself too conspicuous to get away with what he was doing earlier. He's got to be more careful where he puts the posters because he knows we're watching for him, and he's going to find it more and more difficult to go out in public at all. He's probably getting frustrated, so he's looking for different ways to get at you.'

'But if he's frustrated mightn't that make him do something?'

Collins took a moment to answer. 'I wasn't going to tell you this. I didn't want you to get your hopes up, but we've had a sighting of Ellis. It was last night, at Piccadilly Underground. A transport police officer spotted him. He was carrying a couple of plastic bags, and when the officer went to challenge him, he dropped them and vaulted over the barriers and ran out. There was a roll of posters in one and paste in the other.'

Kate remembered the bags the tramp had been carrying. 'He got away?' She felt a strange mix of adrenaline and disappointment, as though the outcome were still in doubt.

'Unfortunately, but it proves my point. Every time he pokes his nose out now, he increases the risk of being caught, and it won't be long now before he is.'

That thought buoyed her up for the rest of the day. It was a fragile optimism, but better than the feeling of being buried alive. A uniformed police constable called around later that morning for the Jiffy-bag and burnt poster, and once that had gone Kate felt encouraged enough to venture out.

It was the first time since Clive had gone home that she had left the office without getting straight into a taxi. It had only been days, but it seemed much longer. The street seemed wider and longer than usual under the grey and agoraphobic plain of the sky. She walked out by the pavement edge, away from doorways and alleys, checking behind her every few minutes. When she reached King's Cross she felt the uneasy relief that comes with a fading of tension.

She caught the tube for the three stops to Oxford Circus. By the time she emerged from the Underground, a watery sun was shining through the cloud. Kate turned her face to it gratefully. People thronged past, intent on their own business. The rest of the world was still there, unchanged. She called in at a café and had a cup of hot chocolate. After drinking it she decided she was hungry and ordered a mozzarella and tomato sandwich. The taste of olive oil made her think of summer. It would soon be spring, she realised, with surprise. The thought gave her a further boost.

Kate left the café and browsed outside shop windows. She stared into a display of baby clothes. There were tiny sweaters and jackets, miniature jeans and boots. She caught sight of her reflection in the glass and saw that she was smiling.

Everything passes, she told herself.

She wasn't confident enough to walk to the station that evening, though, or not to take a taxi back to her flat at the other end. As the light fell, some of her earlier fears revived. Kate asked the taxi driver to wait until she had unlocked the front door. Dougal was waiting outside by the step. He yowled irritably when he saw her. Even though he had rarely used it, he seemed to have taken the disappearance of the cat flap as a personal slight.

The tom cat ran upstairs ahead of her. There was always a moment of anxiety as she went from room to room, quickly drawing the heavy curtains before turning on the lights. But, as usual, the flat was empty.

She fed Dougal, and grilled herself a piece of plaice. She baked a potato in the microwave, putting it in the oven to crisp while she chopped carrots into strips, then blanched them quickly in boiling water and drained them out onto a plate. Dougal showed more interest in her fish than his own food, and eventually she gave in and flaked a small piece into his dish so he would leave her alone.

She took her plate through into the lounge. She had developed the habit of taking the fire extinguisher with her from room to room, but tonight she resolutely left it in the kitchen. Curling her legs under her, she ate with a fork while she read the brochures she had picked up at lunch-time. They showed push-chairs and prams, cots and cradles. Kate felt almost intoxicated as she looked at them. This was the future, this was what she should be focused on, not the petrol fantasies of a disturbed mind.

When the phone rang she thought it would be Clive. He had already called once, briefly, to say he would be away longer than he expected. His brother's funeral had been the day before, and she guessed he would call again soon, if only to say he still didn't know when he'd be back.

She set her plate on a shelf, out of Dougal's reach, and went into the hall to answer the phone. 'Hello?'

'Kate?'

It was a man's voice, familiar but not Clive's, and she stiffened for the instant it took to place it.

'It's Paul.'

She put her head against the wall. Her heart thumped with anticlimax.

'Are you still there?' he asked.

Kate straightened, wearily. 'What do you want?'

'Nothing. I just thought I'd phone, see how you are—'

'I've got nothing to say to you.'

She was already lowering the phone.

'No, wait, waitwaitwait! Please!'

It was that *please* that stopped her. She hesitated, then raised the phone again.

'All right. I'm waiting.'

She heard him breathing. 'Look, I'm – I know you don't want to talk to me, and I can't blame you. I just phoned because, well, because – oh, shit, look, I'm trying to say I'm sorry.'

Kate was too surprised to answer. Paul waited a moment, obviously hoping she would.

'Kate? I said I'm sorry.'

There was none of the arrogance she'd come to expect in his voice. Even so, she half expected some catch.

'You're sorry?' It was all she could think of to say.

'Yeah, I know it's a bit late in the day, but . . . I just wanted to tell you.'

Curious, now, she tried to detect some hint that he was acting. But he spoke without any of his usual bombast.

'What's brought this on?'

'I've been doing a lot of thinking, lately, and . . .' He gave an uneasy laugh. 'All right, it was getting arrested that did it. Arrested again, I should say.'

Kate tensed for the accusation. It didn't come.

'It was . . . well, it was no joke.' He sounded sober, still shaken by it. 'The first time I got arrested, after I'd put the brick through your window, I was too pissed off to think about what was happening. I blamed you. You know what I'm like, it's always somebody else's fault, never mine.'

His tone was thinly jocular. He cleared his throat.

'I was pissed off this time as well. But I was too drunk to get any sense out of, so they put me in a holding cell to sober up. I fell asleep, and when I woke up I felt like death. It stank of piss and puke, and I could hear all these drunks in the other cells, shouting and singing. Then I heard a couple of coppers coming down the corridor, talking about this drunk they'd picked up for a burglary, but it didn't dawn on me until they started unlocking my cell that it was me. Even then, I just thought, "Fucking coppers, who do they think they are?" And then I sat up, and saw I'd pissed myself and been sick all down my front.'

He broke off. Kate heard him swallow.

'Anyway, in the end they traced the cabby who'd taken me home. He remembered me because I'd argued with him and then puked in his cab.' He gave a humourless laugh. 'Good job, as it turned out. Once they'd spoken to him, they gave me my shoes and belt back and let me go. Trouble was, when I got outside I realised I hadn't taken my wallet when they'd arrested me, and I hadn't got a cent to get home with. So I stood there, covered in puke and piss, and I thought, "What the fuck am I doing? I'm thirty-seven, I've lost my job, I've managed to piss off nearly everybody I know, and I've got to walk through the streets stinking like a wino." And I just started crying. If I'd had any money on me, I'd have probably bought something and got pissed again, but all I could do was walk home. By the time I got back I was freezing and stone cold sober, and I thought, "That's it," and binned all the bottles in the house before I'd got time to think about it. Emptied them down the sink first so I couldn't change my mind. Then I got the phone book out and phoned Alcoholics Anonymous.'

There was a dramatic pause. Kate wondered if he had rehearsed the ending, expecting a fanfare. But she was immediately ashamed of her cynicism.

'So how often have you been?' she asked, feeling obliged to say something.

'More than half a dozen times now.' If he resented the anticlimax, there was no sign of it. Kate felt churlish.

'You go as often as you need, wherever there's a meeting,' he went on. 'I still need to go pretty often. There're twelve steps they say you've got to take. The main one is accepting that you've got a problem. That's supposed to be the hardest, that and apologising to people you've been a bastard to. Like you. But I've finally managed it. And I've not had a drink since.'

There was a faint note of pleading now, of wanting his accomplishment to be recognised. Kate relented. 'It can't have been easy.'

'Hardest thing I've ever done.' He sounded proud. 'Next to this phone call, that is. But I wanted to tell you. I know I gave you a hard time. Not just recently. Before, as well.'

That wasn't just drink! You're still making excuses! She felt a flash of the old anger, but it quickly burned itself out.

'It's a long time ago. Let's just forget about it.'

'No, I mean it. I know what you think about me, and you're right. I was a bastard to you. I wish I could blame it all on the booze, but I can't.'

She tried to find a suitable response. It wasn't so much that she didn't believe him. Just that none of it seemed to matter now.

'Okay,' she said, and then, because she knew he expected more, added, 'I'm glad.'

She could almost hear him trying to gauge if she meant it. He seemed to decide that she did. 'I came to the office this afternoon to tell you, but I couldn't bring myself to go in. I didn't think I'd be welcome, anyway. Not after last time.'

Kate made no comment to that.

'I saw your friend outside,' he added.

The change of tack threw her. *Lucy?* she thought.

'You know,' Paul continued. 'The guy you were with at the restaurant.'

Understanding came in a rush.

'Outside?' she said, stupidly.

'On the other side of the road. He was in a doorway. I thought he must be waiting for you.'

'He was there this afternoon?'

'Yeah, about four o'clock, but—'

'What was he doing?'

'Nothing, he was just standing there. I couldn't place who he was at first. In fact, I thought he was a dosser to be honest. He looked like he should have been selling the *Big Issue*.'

Kate didn't laugh.

'Yeah, well, he was in a bit of a state, anyway. I wondered about going over and apologising for . . . well, you know. But then he saw me, and gave me this look, and I thought, "Perhaps not". I'd got myself into enough trouble, and if he'd had a go nobody would've believed I hadn't started it.'

A faintly aggrieved note had entered his tone, but Kate barely noticed.

'Did he do anything?'

'Not while I was there, but like I say, I didn't stay. I just got as far as your office and turned back. He was still staring at me when I left. Look, are you going to tell me what's wrong?'

The words wouldn't come. 'The uh . . . the police are looking for him.'

Distantly, she heard Paul exclaim, asking why, and her own voice answering. There was a roaring in her ears. When it passed Paul was shouting at her.

'Kate? Kate, you still there?'

'. . . Yes.'

'So this guy's stalking you, then?'

The effort to explain was too much. 'Sort of.'

'Christ! I wish I'd known!' The familiar aggression was back. 'Are you by yourself?'

'Yes, but—'

'I'll come over.'

It was a statement. Kate felt herself teeter on the edge of acceptance.

'No, I don't think . . .'

'I'll be there in about an hour,' he said.

'Paul . . .'

'Don't worry. If I see him again you won't have any more trouble. Listen, have you eaten? I can stop off for—'

'*I said no!*'

There was a silence.

'I only thought—' Paul began.

'*No!*' Kate checked herself. She tried to relax her tensed muscles. 'I know. But I don't think it's a good idea.'

Her anger was directed at herself for being tempted. She waited for him to argue.

'No, I expect you're right,' he said, after a pause. He gave a strained laugh. 'I can't really blame you, I suppose. Still, the offer stands. If you need any help, just shout.'

The *thank you* lodged unspoken in Kate's throat.

'Well, that's all, then,' Paul said. He seemed to search for something else to say. 'Look after yourself.'

She nodded, then remembered that he couldn't see her. 'I will.'

The connection remained for a few seconds, then the line went dead. Kate put down the phone, telling herself she had no cause to feel bad. In her distraction she even forgot what he'd said about Ellis.

She jumped at a sudden clatter from the lounge. She hurried through.

Dougal leapt down from the shelf where she'd left her plate. It lay on the floor with the carrots and remains of the fish scattered around it. The baked potato sat on the carpet like a dead tortoise.

Kate went to fetch a cloth.

CHAPTER 22

T he weak sun of the previous afternoon was stronger next
morning. It gave a hard, clear-edged quality to the dead
verges and the bare black branches in the gardens. The streets
had the clarity of old photographs, almost monochromatic
in their brightness.

Kate watched them pass outside the taxi window. It
dropped her outside the tube station, and the sun touched
her briefly as she stepped out of the cab. Then she was in
the shadow of the Underground, where the crispness of the
day was lost in the stale, subterranean air.

She was later than usual. The early-morning commuters
had already gone, and the station looked abandoned in
the post-rush hour quiet. The dying rumble of a recently
departed train was fading down the tunnel as Kate emerged
onto the empty platform. She sat down on one of the plastic
seats fixed to the wall.

Her eyes felt gritty with tiredness. She had hardly slept
the night before. She had tried calling Collins but he wasn't
in, so she'd left a message for him to ring her.

After that she hadn't been able to settle. She had gone
downstairs to check the locks on the door, and then turned
off the lounge light and peered through the window. The
dark street outside was empty and full of shadows. She had

waited for one of them to move until her eyes hurt. When she had gone to bed, she had lain awake and listened to every creak of the cooling house.

The electronic sign said a train was due in two minutes. Kate yawned. From the entrance to the platform came the echoing scuff of a shoe. Still yawning, she put her hand to her mouth and glanced around, expecting someone to appear.

No one did.

She was about to look away when she heard the scuff again. It was softer this time, but nearer. She waited, watching the opening in the wall.

The noise came a third time. Now it was from the other side. Kate turned. There was a second entrance on her right, this one only ten feet away. A faint squeak, like a rubber sole on concrete, came from it. But still no one appeared.

Kate looked quickly around. The platform was silent and deserted. She stood up, gripping her bag in front of her. Slowly, she began to edge as quietly as she could away from the second entrance. She tried to visualise the layout on the other side, how far away the steps were. The scuff sounded again. She stopped.

She didn't know which of the openings it had come from.

Kate didn't move. There was no further sound. She waited, then began to creep along the platform once more. The first entrance was twenty feet away, then fifteen, then five. She halted at the corner, listening.

A faint, rustling whisper from the other side, like blown litter. Or breathing.

I'm imagining it. There's nothing there.

WHERE THERE'S SMOKE

The opening in the wall lay in front of her. Through it she could glimpse the bottom of the steps, disappearing upwards. *Just run.* She tensed for the effort, and then there was a noise behind her, and she remembered the other entrance.

She spun around, the scream choking off as the windows of the train flashed past, elongated squares of light framing faces and bodies. Kate sank back against the wall as it slowed and stopped. She looked back down the platform. It was empty.

The train doors hissed open, and people were stepping off. Clutching her bag, Kate ran to the nearest carriage and jumped in.

She watched, but no one else got on.

By the time she reached the agency, Kate had almost convinced herself that it had been nothing. A wind from the tunnel, a piece of paper, and her imagination. She actually smiled at the thought of leaping out to confront an empty crisp packet. Then she remembered Ellis standing in the doorway the day before, and her smile faded.

Even so, it was a good day. An importer of South American artefacts phoned out of the blue and commissioned her to handle the publicity for an exhibition of Mexican jewellery. She had been recommended by a friend, the man told her with a faint American accent. He had been out of the country for the past month and would be out again the following week, so he didn't have time to waste sifting through PR agencies. Was she interested?

She was.

The acquisition of a new client lifted her some way back towards the optimism she had begun to feel the previous day. It felt good to speak to someone without worrying about what they had seen or heard. She was eagerly reading the material the importer had faxed her when Caroline buzzed through and said that Detective Inspector Collins was downstairs.

Kate told her to send him up. She wondered why he was calling in person. *They've caught him*, flashed through her mind. She felt a spark of hope.

But when Collins walked in she could see that they hadn't. The policeman looked tired. His face was seamed and grey. The chair creaked as he lowered himself into it. The sergeant gave her a smile as he took the other chair, but his heart didn't seem in it. A smell of cigarette smoke came into the room with them.

'Did you get my messages?' Kate asked.

Collins nodded. He was about to say something, but Kate couldn't wait any longer to tell him her news.

'He was here,' she exclaimed. 'Yesterday afternoon.'

Collins came alert. 'Ellis? You've seen him?'

'No, but someone else did. I only found out last night, that's why I called you.'

'What time was this?'

'I think it was about four o'clock. Ellis was standing in a doorway across the road.'

'Who saw him?'

'Paul Sutherland. He's the one who was picked up for the break-in. He phoned last night and . . . What's the matter?'

They were both staring at her. The sergeant had frozen in the act of writing his notes. Kate saw him glance at the Inspector.

'What is it?' she asked. 'What's wrong?'

The sergeant dropped his gaze back to his notebook. Collins spoke gently.

'Paul Sutherland was killed last night.'

Kate felt herself blown back to another time, being told by the same two men of another death.

'Someone set fire to his house,' the Inspector said. 'They poured petrol through the letter-box and then lobbed petrol bombs through the upstairs and downstairs windows.'

'Someone,' she echoed. She could hear Paul's voice, quite clearly. *He saw me and gave me this look . . . He was still staring at me when I left.*

Collins rubbed his eyes. His skin wrinkled up like old leather where his fingers pushed it. 'We haven't got a definite ID. But some neighbours heard the glass going and saw a man standing in the street outside the house. They called the fire brigade and then went out, and the man was still standing there. They say he was just watching. He only ran off when they shouted. They didn't give a very good description but . . .'

Kate closed her eyes. She saw flames, smelt petrol.

'You say you spoke to Paul Sutherland,' Collins said. 'Can you remember what time?'

'I don't know . . . not late. Eight o'clock, perhaps.'

'This was just after three. But I only found out an hour ago myself. Otherwise I'd have let you know sooner. There's supposed to be communication but you wouldn't know it, half the time.' He sounded apologetic.

Her stomach lurched as a thought struck her. 'Oh, God, you want me to identify him, don't you?'

Collins was startled. 'Good God, no! No, that's already

been done. I just came to tell you, that's all.' He shifted uncomfortably in his seat. 'I don't want to upset you needlessly but ... well, it might not be a bad thing if there's someone you can stay with. Just for a few days.'

He seemed to find it difficult to look at her.

'You think he was planning to do something to me, don't you?' she said. 'Then he saw Paul and followed him home and set fire to his house instead.'

'Not necessarily. I just think you might be better off somewhere else, that's all. But we'll still keep a close watch on your flat and here, regardless.'

He gave an unconvincing smile as he stood up.

'Don't worry. We won't let him get to you.'

Caroline and Josefina were clearly surprised when she closed the agency soon after the two policemen had left, but Kate didn't offer any explanation. She took a taxi home rather than face the Underground. The streets that had been sunny that morning were now grey with the coming dusk. They hit a traffic jam, and Kate watched the meter ticking away as they sat among the fumes and car horns, and wondered if she had enough cash for the fare. Part of her hoped she hadn't.

Her conversation with Paul played in a loop in her head. Every nuance, every inflection sounded with a new and callous finality. She thought about the last thing he had said to her. *Look after yourself.* She hadn't bothered to tell him to do the same. *Be careful*, she could have said. *He's dangerous. He burns people. Look after yourself.*

But she hadn't.

It was growing dark when the taxi turned onto her road.

She paid the driver, almost disappointed to find she had enough money to spare herself that humiliation. The cab pulled away, leaving her alone on the pavement.

Kate glanced up and down the street. It was empty. She went up her path and had almost reached the door when something about the scene belatedly registered. She went back to the gate again. There was still no one in sight, but further along on the pavement, indistinct in the fading light, was the object that had struck a jarring note.

She began to walk towards it. It had too many angles and edges to make sense, but as she drew nearer they began to resolve into distinct shapes. A square of cardboard on the kerb edge. Under it, a still, furry heap.

Kate reached it and stopped. Four paws and a thick brush of tail stuck out from beneath the cardboard. On it, in what looked like lipstick, someone had written, SORRY.

She bent down and lifted off the cardboard.

Dougal lay on his side. He was unmarked, but his eyes were half open, and the tip of his tongue was sticking out between his teeth. His fur looked dusty. Pieces of grit were caught in it. His legs were crossed, as though he were running.

'Is it your cat?'

A little girl of about six or seven was standing nearby, watching with solemn interest. Kate nodded, looking down at Dougal.

'A woman in a car did it this afternoon,' the little girl said. 'She ran over him and put him there. She was crying. Are you going to cry?'

Kate didn't answer. Taking the piece of cardboard, she gently slid it under the cat's body. He began to roll off, moving with it. She tentatively steadied him with one hand while she pushed it the rest of the way underneath. The cat felt cold and heavy.

The cardboard sagged in the middle when she stood up. She had to support it with both arms.

'Are you going to bury it?' the girl asked. Kate didn't look at her.

'Yes.'

She left the little girl on the pavement and carried Dougal back towards her flat. Her bag slipped off her shoulder and swung from her elbow, bumping against her legs, but she ignored it. She went through the gate and took a few more steps before coming to a standstill. The tiny garden confronted her with its covering of paving stones. Only the small hole where the rose bushes were choked in the centre had been left free. Kate looked at the slabbed ground as she stood holding her dead cat, and the first sob tore loose from her throat. She stumbled forward, chest heaving as she laid Dougal by the wall and blundered for the front door. Tears blinded her. She put the wrong key in the lock and struggled to pull it out before finding the right one. She clutched at the banister as she ran upstairs, not bothering to turn on any lights. In darkness, she groped for the phone and dialled by the glow from the answer machine.

It rang four times before it was interrupted. When she recognised Lucy's recorded message Kate sagged with despair. Her stomach hurt with the force of her sobs, and she could barely wait until the recording finished.

'Lucy, it's Kate, I'm sorry, please—'

The phone was picked up at the other end.

'Yes?'

Lucy's voice was inflectionless. Kate struggled for composure. 'I . . . it's me. Look, I . . . I know I shouldn't just call you but . . . oh, God, look, please, can I come over?'

There was no answer.

'Please!'

Another hesitation. 'Okay.'

Kate managed a choked thanks and fumbled the phone down. She stood for a moment, head bowed, and then dialled the number of a taxi firm from memory.

She waited in the dark until the cab honked outside. The street lights had come on, throwing the area in front of the garden wall into deep shadow. The cat's body was invisible as Kate slammed the front door and ran down the path. It felt like someone else she had let down. She was about to get into the taxi when she remembered all her change had gone on the other cab. She dashed back inside and searched in drawers until she had scraped together enough money for the fare. The driver tutted, irritably, when she returned.

Kate huddled in the back seat and watched a normal world go by.

The nervousness didn't start until the cab had dropped her outside Lucy and Jack's. It seemed an age since she had been to the big house. She hesitated with her hand on the gate. *I'm doing exactly what Lucy accused me of. Running to them now I'm in trouble.* She didn't care how much contempt and blame Lucy heaped on her, though. Just so long as there was no rejection. She couldn't stand the thought of losing anyone else.

Kate went up the path. She wiped her eyes as she rang the bell, knowing that she must look a mess. She heard someone approaching, and then Lucy opened the door.

They looked at each other without speaking. In the background Kate could hear the chatter of the TV, see the cheerful spill of light from the lounge and kitchen. It silhouetted Lucy in the unlit hall. Kate couldn't make out her expression.

Wordlessly, Lucy stood back so that she could enter. Kate couldn't look at her as she crossed the doorway. She retreated from her silence and made her way uncertainly towards the lounge. Lucy closed the door and followed her as Kate stepped around Jack's heap of boxes in the hall. The house smelt of food and dirty nappies. She went into the brightly lit room.

The TV was blaring out some frantic children's programme. Jack and Emily were engrossed in watching it, their backs to Kate as they sat side by side on the settee. They didn't notice her go in. Angus was in his playpen next to them, which surprised her since he had outgrown it long since. He began to cry when he saw her, holding out his arms to be picked up, and Kate instinctively went towards him. The forced, bright greeting was already on her lips when she reached the settee and the words died.

Jack and Emily's mouths were covered with brown parcel tape.

The image registered, but Kate's mind refused to make sense of it. There was a sound from behind her. She turned.

Lucy stood in the doorway. Her head was tilted up by the blade of the long kitchen knife held to her throat. Ellis stood close behind her. The hand not holding the knife was gripping Lucy's bare arm, fingers digging into the flesh above the elbow.

'*I'm sorry.*' Lucy's voice was a whisper. Her face was puffy and tear-streaked, Her eyes, as she looked at Kate, were terrified. '*I'm sorry.*'

No one moved. The moment stretched out, suspended, then burst with a silent pop of pressure.

Kate stepped backwards.

Ellis herded Lucy further into the room. He didn't take his eyes from Kate. They were bright and feverish, purple smears discolouring the pale flesh underneath. His face was gaunt, and his hair stuck up in matted tufts. There was a straggly growth of beard on his cheeks.

He looked like someone Kate had never known.

Lucy's chest was heaving. 'I'm sorry,' she whispered again, and now Kate took in her stained clothes and unwashed hair. She looked thinner. 'He threatened the *children*, Kate! He said if we didn't do what he wanted, he'd – he'd—' Her gaze flicked to Emily and Angus, agonised. 'He'd got a *knife*! We didn't have any *choice*! We tried, Jack—'

'Shut up!'

Lucy fell silent. Her mouth was trembling. Her chin was still held high away from the knife, giving her a model's self-conscious posture. There was a muffled noise from Jack. Kate glanced at him and saw now that his hands and feet were also bound. There was a yellowing bruise on one temple, and the look he gave Ellis was full of violence. Kate saw him straining against the tape, but it was wrapped around him too many times.

Beside him, Emily was similarly fastened. Tears were rolling down the little girl's face, and the sight of them filled Kate with outrage.

'You bastard!' she cried, turning back to face Ellis. 'What have they done to you?'

He blinked at her outburst, but didn't take the knife from Lucy's throat.

'They kn-know you,' he said. His mouth twisted. 'They're your friends!'

He stressed 'your'. His hand tightened on Lucy's arm, and she lifted her chin away from the pressure of the knife.

Kate forced herself to stare back at him. She pointed at Emily. 'She's a little girl, for God's sake!'

She strode over to the settee.

'Hold tight,' she said, trying to smile as she took hold of the tape covering the girl's mouth.

'D-don't!' Ellis said, as Kate pulled it off.

The tape came free with a tearing sound, leaving the skin red underneath. Emily began to cry.

'Happy now?' Kate demanded, glaring at Ellis. He looked confused, almost defensive. She went over to the playpen where Angus was also crying.

'L-leave him!'

She took no notice. Augus's feet were taped together so that he couldn't climb out of the pen. She bent to pick him up.

'*I said f-fucking leave him!*'

Kate froze. Ellis's eyes were wild, his knuckles white knobs of bone on the knife handle. Its point made a taut depression in Lucy's skin. Lucy had closed her eyes.

Kate straightened, slowly. 'All right. I'm sorry.'

'G-get away from them!'

She moved back into the centre of the lounge.

'Look, I know you're angry with me, but don't take it out on them. They haven't hurt you.'

'Shut up!'

'At least let the kids go.'

'I s-said shut up!'

'Look at them, they're scared to death! They're only children, for God's sake! How can you do this to them?'

'*Because my child's dead!*'

Kate flinched back from the shout. Ellis's face was contorted. But he didn't do anything else. She waited for her breathing to steady.

'I lied to you,' she said, as calmly as she could. 'I didn't have an abortion. I only said it because—'

'You're lying n-now!'

'No—'

'Fucking *liar*!'

'Listen to me! I haven't had an abortion—'

'Liar! Lying *b-bitch*!'

His face was twisted. Kate recoiled, silenced by the hate in it.

'He won't believe you.' Lucy's voice was quavering.

'Shut up,' Ellis said, flatly.

Tears rolled down Lucy's cheeks as she stared across at Kate. 'I said – I told him you hadn't, but he wouldn't believe—'

'*Don't talk about me as if I'm not here!*' Ellis screamed, and Kate saw his arm tense. *No!* she thought as he pulled back the knife, but the blade was unbloodied as he shoved Lucy towards her.

Lucy stumbled forward and almost fell. Kate went to help her, but stopped when Ellis pointed with the kitchen knife.

'Leave her!'

Lucy wiped her eyes with the palm of her hand. Her head was nodding, like a palsied old woman's. She was no longer looking at Kate.

'Sit over there,' Ellis told her. 'In the chair.'

Lucy did as he said. He turned to Kate.

'Get the t-tape.' He gestured to a roll of parcel tape on the coffee table.

'Listen to me—'

'Get the *fucking t-tape*!'

She went and picked it up.

'Wrap it round her ankles first, then her wrists.'

'Please, you can't—'

'*Do it!*'

Kate looked at where Jack was sitting bound on the settee. His eyes stared at her over the brown strip, trying to communicate some message, but Kate didn't know what. Beside him, Emily's bottom lip was quivering. Only Angus was making a noise as he sobbed. Standing this close, Kate could smell the sour, unwashed odour of their bodies. On the floor around them were opened and empty tins of food, some furred with several days' worth of mould. Wadded up pieces of parcel tape lay among them, too many to count. Kate tasted bile in the back of her throat as she grasped the significance of what she was seeing.

How long has he been here?

'Ankles first,' Ellis said.

Kate knelt down in front of Lucy. It wasn't her moving. She was watching this happen to someone else. She pulled the end of the tape free with numb fingers, but stopped as Jack gave a muffled grunt. She looked up at him. He was staring at her with a desperate intensity. He shook his head, violently.

'Now!' shouted Ellis, and took a step towards where Angus was snivelling in the playpen. She saw him shift his grip on the knife. With a last glance at Jack, Kate wrapped the tape once around Lucy's ankles. The red marks from earlier strips formed bands on her flesh.

'Do it again. T-tight.'

She hesitated, then did as he said. The roll of tape dangled, still attached. Kate felt a weak hope. 'I've nothing to cut it with.'

'B-bite it.'

The hope went out. She tore the tape with her teeth.

'Now her wrists.'

She could feel the tremor in Lucy's hands as she bound them. There was no accusation in Lucy's eyes when they looked at each other, only fear.

'Put a strip over her m-mouth.'

'What good—?'

'Just do it!'

Lucy shut her eyes, compressing her lips as Kate stuck a piece of tape across them. Kate straightened and threw the tape down.

'Feel safe now, do you?'

Ellis stared at her, then pointed to a corner of the room.

'P-pick that up.'

Kate looked to where he was pointing, and felt as though she had been punched on the heart. Against the wall were materials for Jack's desktop publishing, a sprawling pile of cardboard boxes and containers. On top was a stack of posters. Seeing them, Kate felt events nudge into a final focus. She wondered, almost absently, whether Ellis had gone there with the intention already in mind, remembering all the conversations he'd had with Jack about printing and publishing. Or if the idea for the posters had only come later, with Lucy and Jack bound and impotent under the threat of his knife, and all the equipment he needed lying idle in the cellar.

But it wasn't the posters that Ellis was pointing to now. Standing near them was a red plastic petrol can.

She looked at Ellis, understanding now what Jack had been trying to tell her. 'Oh, no.' She shook her head. 'No, you can't . . .'

'P-pick it up.'

'Please—' She tripped over what to call him. 'Please, just think what you're doing.'

'Pick it up.'

'At least let them go! You've got me here now, you don't need them!'

He advanced towards her. She backed away, but he stopped when he reached Jack. He put the knife against his neck.

'Pick it up.'

Kate slowly walked across the room towards where the petrol can waited. The sheaf of posters drew her eye. They were new ones. This time her smiling face had been planted on a journalistic photograph of a woman holding a dead child. It was black and white, obviously taken from some war zone, and flames had been clumsily superimposed to make it look as if mother and baby were on fire. KATE POWELL BURN IN HELL BITCH was printed across the bottom.

She looked away. The petrol can was at her feet. Next to it was a shallow cardboard box filled with the small yellow tins of lighter fluid that Jack used as a cleaning agent. Beside that was a cluster of aerosol cans of spray adhesive. The 'flammable' sign was printed on all of them. Kate reached down and took hold of the red container. It was heavy. A faint sloshing came from inside when she lifted it.

'T-take the lid off.'

Kate did as she was told. It felt greasy. It dangled from a plastic strip when it was unscrewed. The smell of the petrol was a sickly, sweet taste at the back of her nose and throat.

'P-pour it out.'

'Please, don't do this.'

Ellis took hold of Jack's hair, pulling his head back to expose his throat to the blade.

Slowly, Kate tilted the can. Petrol glugged out of the wide spout. It splashed over the boxes and containers of ink, ran down into the carpet. It ran across the image of her face that smiled up from the posters, pooling over the cold likeness of the flames.

'P-put some on the curtains.'

The heavy drapes were drawn across the french windows. Kate made throwing motions at them with the petrol can. The fabric stained dark where the fluid soaked into it.

'Now the carpet,' Ellis told her. His voice sounded thick and drugged. The stammer had almost gone. 'Work your way over here.'

He stood back as she walked towards the settee and chairs,

sloshing liquid from the can as she went. It was more than half empty now. The room reeked with petrol.

'Now pour it over them.'

Kate shook her head, mutely. Ellis put the blade back to Jack's neck. His eyes were bright. Kate could see that his pupils were black and dilated.

'Do it.'

Emily began to cry in lost little sobs, a counterpoint to Angus's huskier wails. The can felt slick in Kate's hands.

'I can't!'

Ellis's breathing was heavy. He held out his hand. 'Give it to me.'

Kate didn't move.

'I said f-fucking give it to me!' There was urgency in his voice now. 'P-please!'

She backed away from him.

He blinked, rapidly.

'Remember what you said?' He was reaching into his pocket, moving away from Jack now. 'They threw it in the incinerator, you t-told me. Remember?'

He pulled out a box of matches.

'I'll show you what suffering is,' he said, and as he opened the matches Kate flung the petrol can at his face.

It struck his upraised arms, a swirl of liquid hanging in the air behind it like a tail, and then Kate was running past him. She felt a tug on her arm, but didn't stop. She ran down the darkened hallway, careening into Jack's boxes and pushing them over behind her. She slammed into the front door. It was locked. Kate wrenched at it until she heard a noise from the lounge doorway, and turned to see Ellis emerging.

She ran upstairs. The landing at the top was in darkness.

WHERE THERE'S SMOKE

There was a banister railing edging the open side where it overlooked the downstairs hall, and from it Kate could hear him blundering over the boxes. She pushed herself away, into the deeper darkness of the upstairs corridor. A pale square at the far end showed where the window was, and by its faint light Kate began to make out textures in the shadow that were the doors. They were all closed. Lungs burning, she ran past them, one by one. She reached the end of the corridor. Footsteps pounded up the stairs. Kate opened the nearest door and went in.

The room was even darker. She stood with her back against the door and faced the blackness. It was unrelieved by even a glimmer of light, but a sweetness of talcum powder and crayons told her she was in Emily and Angus's bedroom.

A door was opened further along the corridor.

Kate felt for a lock or bolt. There was nothing. She moved blindly into the room, hands outstretched in front of her. She tried to remember if there was anything she could use. Anywhere to hide. She jumped as she walked into a bed. Feeling her way along it, she came to the bookshelf.

And the wall.

She groped across its unyielding hardness. Her heart thudded when she barked her shins on the small table. She reached out to steady it and her hand hit a lamp, almost knocking it over. She grabbed at it, heart thudding.

A second door was opened.

She gently set the lamp upright and shrank back against the wall. She pressed herself into the cranny between the bookshelf and table, knowing the shelter was illusory. Her breath came in rasps. She tried to quiet it, listening for the sounds from the corridor. Another door opened, nearer.

357

There was a dull ache in her arm. She reached up to touch it, and almost cried out at the sudden slash of pain. Biting her lip, she touched her arm again. This time she was more prepared when the petrol on her fingers stung the long cut above her elbow. She remembered the tug on her arm as she ran past Ellis, thought about the sharp length of the knife.

She felt sick.

The door of the next room along was opened. Kate squeezed her eyes shut. Bright flashes of light danced in front of her. The cloying stink of petrol was nauseating. She heard the scuff of a footstep from outside and folded her arms over her stomach. She could feel her heart beating, banging against her ribs, and thought of the smaller one keeping time with it, a tiny pulse of innocence.

The door opened. It made a whispering sound of wood on carpet. Kate opened her eyes. She saw nothing, only blackness and fading sparkles of phosphene after-images.

'Kate.'

The word was like a shout in the silence. Kate pressed back against the wall. A dull glow came from beside her. She turned towards it and found herself looking at the lamp on the table. The room came into being around her as it grew brighter, small beds and cuddly toys. Mickey Mouse capered on the lampshade.

Ellis stood in the doorway with his hand on the dimmer switch. His eyes were red from the petrol. She could see the dark splashes of it on his clothes. He stepped into the room, bringing a stronger reek of it with him. Kate stepped to one side, hoping to dart around him to the door, but he moved to block her. The knife was still gripped in his hand. Kate saw the dark smear on its blade.

She backed between the bookshelves and the table again.

Ellis stopped in the middle of the room.

'You shouldn't have d-done it.' He sounded calmer. Kate wasn't sure whether he meant run, or have an abortion. She couldn't speak.

'You'd n-no right,' he said. 'It was my b-baby. You'd no right.'

She shook her head, but he wasn't looking. He was staring at her arm.

'You're bleeding.'

He sounded surprised. Kate looked down. There was a gaping slice in the left sleeve of her coat. Her arm was soaked in blood. She had forgotten about it, but now it began to throb again. The pain goaded her.

'What are you looking so upset about?' she demanded. She wiped her hand on her bloody sleeve and held it up to show him. 'This is what you wanted, isn't it?'

A stricken expression crossed his face. 'I – I didn't mean to.'

'You didn't *mean* to? What the fuck *did* you mean, then?' Suddenly the weeks of fear boiled over. The sight of him infuriated her. 'Is *this* my fault?' She thrust out her injured arm. 'Is it? Did I make you cut me?'

'N-no, I—'

'So who made you? Who made you do any of this? Who made you kill Alex Turner?'

He tore his eyes from her arm. 'I t-told you! I d-didn't want that!'

'He's still dead, though, isn't he? You didn't want to, but you still did! And his wife was pregnant, did you know that?'

Kate could tell that he hadn't. He looked stricken.

'N-no!'

'She was eight months pregnant! She might even have had the baby by now, and Alex Turner's never going to see it because you killed him!'

'N-no!' He shook his head, violently. 'I-I didn't . . .'

'You killed him, and now you want to kill an innocent family as well!'

'Shut up!'

He took a step towards her, but she was reckless now. 'Why? You're going to burn me anyway! You've already cut me! What else are you going to do?'

'*I don't know!*' he shouted. 'Leave me alone!'

'Leave *you* alone?' Kate stared at him. 'For God's sake, just listen to yourself! Think what you're *doing*!'

His features were contorted with pain. Seeing him, the anger drained out of her.

'Put the knife down.' She almost called him Alex, and in her haste to cover the slip she spoke without thinking. 'You need help.'

His head jerked up.

'What f-fucking help? People asking stupid qu-questions, telling me what my fucking p-*problem* is? They don't want to *help*! They just want me to *behave*! So long as I don't b-bother anybody else, they don't care! But nobody cares whether I'm bothered! Nobody c-cares about *me*!'

I cared. The thought went unspoken.

'Lucy and Jack did,' she said instead.

'No, they d-didn't! I thought they did, but they didn't! That's why I c-came here, but they're like all the rest!'

'What about Angus and Emily?'

'I don't want to t-talk about it!'

'So you're just going to kill them, too? Burn them, like you did your own family?'

Shock bleached his face. 'Who t-told you that?'

'Never mind who told me, it's true, isn't it?'

'N-no!'

'Yes, it is! You set fire to the house while your mother and father and your brothers were asleep, and then you stood and watched them burn!'

'I d-didn't! It wasn't like that, it was an accident!'

'An accident that you set fire to the house?'

'Yes! No! I d-don't—' His voice was anguished. 'I didn't mean to *hurt* them! I just wanted them to take *n-notice* of me! They were always fighting, and leaving me with M-Michael and Andrew and – and they'd d-*do* things to me, and then I'd try to tell my m-mum and dad and they wouldn't *believe* me! Even though I kept *telling* them, they wouldn't. And then my g-gran tried to help, she tried to t-tell them, and they started shouting, and – and then Gran was on the floor, all *blue*, her f-face was *blue*. And they said she was – she was *dead*, and nobody – nobody c-cared except me. So I lit the fire, and I thought, *N-now* they'll listen, *now* they'll know, they'll be sorry . . .'

His eyes were focused on something Kate couldn't see. 'And it started b-burning, and I could see right into the flames, like it was another world, all clean and pure. I watched them, and . . . and nothing worried me any more. They got bigger and bigger, until there wasn't anything else, and they were . . . they were beautiful.'

'But it isn't beautiful afterwards, is it?' Kate said.

His face clouded, losing its transcendent quality.

'No.'

For a moment he looked like a young boy, lost and scared.

'You didn't mean to hurt them,' Kate said.

'N-no.'

'Do you want to hurt Angus and Emily?'

He shook his head.

'Let them go, then! Please!'

'I c-can't.'

'Why?'

'It's too l-late.' It was a whisper.

'It isn't!' Kate shouted. 'It isn't too late! Think about it! Think about how you'll feel afterwards!'

He looked at her. 'There won't be any after.'

She had seen the same expression on his face when the man had thrown himself onto the bonfire. *Perhaps it didn't seem horrible to him*. She hadn't understood it then.

'This is what you want, isn't it?' She couldn't keep from saying it. 'This is what you've always wanted.'

His gaze was still on faraway flames. She noticed his grip shift on the kitchen knife.

'It's g-got to be done.'

She could feel him slipping into the fatalism of earlier. She tried to cut through it.

'Got to be *done*? Like Paul Sutherland? Did killing him "have to be *done*" as well?'

362

His eyes snapped back to her. 'He was a d-drunk. He deserved it. Drunks are b-burning themselves up already.'

'So you thought you'd save him the job?' she mocked. 'Come on, what's your excuse? You've always got one! Let's hear it? Was it because he hit you?'

'No.' He had a sullen expression.

'Why, then? You didn't even know him?'

'I knew what he'd d-done!'

His sudden heat surprised her. It took Kate a moment to realise what he meant.

'Oh, my God. You killed him because of what he did to *me*?'

Ellis wouldn't look at her.

'What about what *you*'ve done?' she demanded.

'That's d-different!'

'How? How is it?'

'Because you k-killed our b-baby!'

'*I haven't killed our baby!*' she screamed back at him. 'I haven't killed *anything*! I'm still *pregnant*, for God's sake! I've been sick every fucking morning and . . . oh, Christ!'

She broke off, putting her head in her hands. When she looked up, Ellis was still watching her. But now he had a strange, almost frightened expression.

'I lied about the abortion,' Kate said, quietly. 'I wanted to hurt you. I'd been told you were dead, and gone to identify you and seen it was somebody else, and found out you weren't Alex Turner, and . . . And I wanted to hurt you *back*!'

She felt tears closing in. 'Jesus Christ, what did you *expect*? I *loved* you!'

He was looking at her like a man woken from one bad dream, only to find himself in another.

'You're still p-pregnant?'

Kate closed her eyes, nodded wearily.

There was an almost inaudible moan. She opened her eyes. Ellis was hugging himself, gently rocking backwards and forwards. Tears were trickling down his face.

'Oh, G-God.' He closed his eyes in anguish. 'Oh, God. Everything's gone wrong.'

Kate moved fractionally away from the wall. 'Just let us go. You can do that now, can't you? There's no need to hurt anybody.'

He didn't say anything. Just rocked himself, crying quietly.

'You don't want to hurt the baby, do you?' Kate urged. 'Not after all this?'

Ellis shook his head.

'Let us go, then. Give me the knife and let us go.'

He didn't seem to have heard. He was still shaking his head.

'I'm sorry,' he said. 'I've made such a m-mess of things. I'm sorry.'

He was crying as he came towards her, and Kate was never sure if he was apologising for what he had done, or for what he was about to do. She saw the knife in his hand and instinctively swept the lamp off the table at him.

There was a *bang* as the bulb exploded. She cringed back, dazzled by the flash, waiting for the cut of the knife. But none came. And then the darkness was broken by a new, unsteady illumination.

The igniting petrol on Ellis's clothes filled the room with a sick light. As Kate's eyes adjusted she saw him beating at the flames on his arm and chest. The next moment they had spread like a floodtide to his shoulders and head.

There was a clatter as he dropped the knife. He cried out, taking wild swipes at himself as his hair caught fire. The light in the room was brighter now, more yellow, and the stink of burning hair and petrol made Kate gag. She stood, too stunned to act, and then ran forward and began to slap at the fire leaping from Ellis's head. Her hands came away covered in blue gloves of flame as the petrol on them caught. Panicking, she beat them out against her coat, feeling the first sting of it, and then grabbed a quilt from the nearest bed.

She tried to throw it over Ellis but he reeled away, lurching first into the wall and then from the room. Hindered by the bulk of the quilt, Kate chased after him. The flames threw a crazy light on the walls as he staggered blindly down the corridor, flailing at himself, and she knew what was going to happen an instant before it did. She shouted as he hit the railing at the end of the corridor, too far away to grab him, and in a swift, choreographed motion he toppled over.

There was a thud as he hit the floor below. Everything was suddenly dark again. Kate rushed down the stairs, not pausing to search for a light switch, and ran to the figure lying in the hall. Ellis had landed on the boxes by the cellar door, splitting them open and scattering paper over the carpet. Some of the flames had been snuffed by the impact, but he was still burning. Fire was already beginning to lick at the surrounding paper and boxes, less dramatic in the light from the open lounge doorway. Kate flung the quilt over him and beat at the motionless body, but a sudden pain in her leg made her cry out and jerk back. One corner of the quilt had been trailing in a cluster of burning papers, and had caught fire. She snatched it away, trying to stifle the flames, before she saw it was starting to burn in other places as well.

Kate flung it against the floor, stamping and kicking at it, cursing Lucy for buying a cheap, non-retardant quilt. Something stung her cheek. She brushed off a glowing piece of ash. Looking up, she saw the hall was full of them. The stink of petrol from the lounge returned like a forgotten threat, and she turned in time to see burning scraps of paper drift like black leaves through the open doorway.

The light from it suddenly changed.

Angus screamed.

'Oh, Jesus, no,' Kate breathed.

She dropped the smouldering quilt and ran past Ellis to the lounge. The heat struck her before she reached it. The room was full of fire. Flames clamoured from everything the petrol had touched. The carpet was awash with them. The curtains were blazing rags, while the stack of posters was a torch that sent waves of smoke and ash across the Victorian mouldings. Kate recoiled, but the children's screams were a stronger spur. She could see beyond the flames that the area around the leather settee and chair was still clear, and without waiting she pulled her coat around her head and darted through the doorway.

Hot hands patted her back and nipped her legs, and then she was through. She kept to the side of the room away from the windows, where the fire had yet to reach, and ran to the settee. Jack was ducking forward, thrashing his head around, and she could see how the back of his hair was singed and smouldering. A yard or two behind him the remains of the petrol can was a roaring yellow beacon that flared to the ceiling. He had managed to pull Emily so she lay across his lap, shielded from the worst of it, and Kate slapped at his hair, feeling the bite of the sparks on her already burned hands. Across from her Lucy's eyes were frantic as she sat bound and gagged in the leather armchair, protected so far by its high, winged back.

Jack pulled his head away, lifting his chin for Kate to remove the tape from his mouth.

'Get the kids out!' he gasped, when she yanked it off.

'What about you?'

'No time! For Christ's sake, do it!'

Kate wavered, knowing she would never get back in for Lucy and Jack. It was already like trying to breathe in the open door of a furnace. The room was filling with smoke as the flames spread, crowding the enclosure formed by the chairs and settee. Kate looked across at Lucy. Her blue eyes were wide and tearful over the tape as she nodded.

Kate snatched Angus from the playpen and grabbed up Emily from Jack's lap. Emily began screaming, 'Mummy! Mummy!' as she carried them away. Kate saw Jack gnawing at the tape around his wrists, and suddenly she went back. Still holding the children, she awkwardly knelt in front of him.

'What the fuck are you doing? Get out!' Jack shouted, but she had already bent to take the tape binding his ankles between her teeth. She tugged and worried at it, then it ripped and with a jerk he pulled his legs free.

'Right, now go!' he shouted.

She stood up, hoisting Angus and Emily into better positions, her wounded arm throbbing under their weight. Jack was on his hands and knees, biting at the tape binding Lucy's feet, pulling at it with his still fastened hands as Kate struggled with the two children to the wall furthest from the flames. She flinched at a pop from overhead as the light-bulb burst, but its light was hardly needed now. Squinting against the heat, she pressed their faces into her coat as she edged passed the blazing petrol can, and then stopped.

Through the smoke, she saw that the door-frame and the carpet in front of it was engulfed.

'Jack!' she shouted.

She heard him swear, and then there was a sudden clatter. She turned and saw him dragging the rug from the floor, his wrists free and bleeding now, tipping the coffee table from it. He lurched towards her, wincing and clumsy with the pain of returning circulation, while behind him Lucy hobbled and almost fell. Kate started forward to help, but hot smoke suddenly took the air from her lungs. Coughing and fighting for breath, she turned her face and buried her mouth and nose in her coat as Jack pushed past and began to lash with the heavy rug at the flames around the door. Lucy made it to her and half collapsed on Kate's shoulder, chest heaving as she struggled to draw in air and cough with her mouth still covered by tape. She tried to peel it off, but her wrists were also bound, and another choking spasm doubled her up. Kate supported her as best she could, unable to do anything more with the children clinging to her. The skin of her face felt tight as they staggered after Jack. She could smell her hair beginning to burn. It was becoming difficult to see through the heat and smoke. She ducked as a sudden *bang* from the far side of the room threw a punch of white-hot flame at them. It was followed straight away by two more as the aerosol cans exploded. Cowering against the wall, Kate could hear a metallic pinging even above the roar of the fire and remembered the tins of lighter fluid. So did Jack, because she saw him dart a glance towards that corner before turning to where she and Lucy were huddled.

'Come on!' he shouted, and swept the thick rug over them like a man sheltering under a jacket. 'Move!'

They stumbled towards the door. The carpet in front of it was still on fire, but Jack had beaten it down enough to pass, and the tented rug shielded them from the burning doorframe. Kate felt the hot lash of flames on her legs, and then they were out in the relative cool of the hall.

Ellis still lay face down. His clothes had largely burned away, and most of the papers and boxes around him had now caught. Kate faltered, but Jack draped the rug between them and Ellis's pyre, blocking it from view as he herded them past.

Further along the quilt was blazing where Kate had left it, lying across the width of the hall. Jack stepped forward and flung the rug over it. It landed with a heavy *whumhf*, snuffing the quilt's flames like a candle. They went over it to the front door. The smoke was suffocating as Jack struggled with the lock. Then it clacked free, and he pulled open the door and ushered them out into the night's sweet, cold air.

They staggered down the path in a cluster, supporting each other, not halting until they reached the gate. Kate looked back. Smoke was billowing out through the open door, and without thinking what she was doing she set down the children and ran back to the house.

She heard Jack shout, then she was in the hallway and the thick heat and smoke closed around her again. Holding her breath, she ran to where Ellis lay, barely able to see as she kicked aside the flaming papers and took hold of his feet.

His raw ankles looked bony and pathetic above the scorched training shoes as she dragged him backwards. After a few steps she stopped, pulled her coat over her mouth and nose and took several quick breaths. She was reaching down for his feet again when the tins of lighter fluid exploded.

There was a noiseless flash, and a hot pressure knocked her sideways. The hall was instantly an oven. She felt the skin of her face flayed and knew her hair was on fire. She drew breath to scream but choked it off as the overheated air scorched her throat and lungs. Blind and burning now, she floundered, and then something banged into her.

She was enveloped in darkness as the rug smothered the flames. She felt Jack pull her towards the front door, but broke away, emerging from the rug to seize one of Ellis's ankles again.

She saw Jack mouth curses at her, but her head was full of ringing from the explosion, and she couldn't hear. She shook her head anyway and carried on pulling, and a moment later he threw the rug over them both and took hold of Ellis's other ankle.

Together they dragged him towards the front door, stumbling backwards over the smoking quilt as fast as they could. She nearly fell down the step, and then Ellis bumped down over it onto the path. Kate felt a dim nudge of memory, but it was gone before she was really aware of it.

They pulled him to the gate before they stopped and shucked off the smouldering rug. The cold air was like a balm on Kate's skin. She sucked it down into her lungs, wincing with the pain of it. Through streaming eyes, she could see that Lucy was sobbing as she tried to hug Jack with her still-bound hands.

Kate turned back to Ellis. He lay half on his side, almost in the recovery position. Kate had avoided looking at his face, but she did so now. His hair had gone, and the skin was cracked like overdone meat. She nearly gagged on the smell. She felt sure he was dead. She didn't know herself why she had gone back for him. Then his eyes flickered. Most of his eyelids had been burned away, and Kate knew he must be blind. But his eyes moved, as though he were searching for something. His hands weren't too badly burned, and Kate gently took hold of one.

Her throat felt as though there was broken glass in it when she tried to speak. She tried again.

'I'm here.'

The grating voice wasn't hers. It echoed, hollow and distant, through the ringing in her ears. His eyes fixed on the sound of it. She could feel quivers running through him. His mouth opened slightly, and with a sure intuition Kate knew what he wanted.

'I've still got the baby,' she croaked in a whisper.

He continued to stare towards her, his sightless eyes looking slightly to one side. But he didn't move again. After a while she knew he was dead.

She set his hand down and stood up. The house was blazing fiercely now. Smoke gouted through the doorway and windows. She became aware that the pain from her burns was growing. She went over to where Lucy and Jack were standing with the children.

Lucy's hands and mouth were free from the tape now. She was still crying. She and Kate looked at each other, then stumbled into a hug. Kate felt her own tears begin to rack her, and the two of them clung to each other and sobbed as the house burned, and sirens began to sound in the distance.

EPILOGUE

The hospital smell is hot radiators and antiseptic. She cries out as the pain clubs at her. It seems as if it will never stop. Then, at last, it does. She sinks back.

Her short hair, still growing back, is plastered to her head. Below one sleeve of the white cotton gown, the pink line of a newly healed scar shows. As the pain ebbs, she raises her head as a white-smocked woman approaches, holding something wriggling feebly in her arms.

The woman smiles.

'It's a boy.'